Books in the series 'The Colonial Economy of NSW 1788-1835'

REFLECTIONS

of

TIME

GORDON BECKETT

For book orders, email orders@traffordpublishing.com.sg

Most Trafford Singapore titles are also available at major online book retailers.

Printed in Singapore.

ISBN: 978-1-4907-0006-9 (sc)
ISBN: 978-1-4907-0007-6 (hc)
ISBN: 978-1-4907-0008-3 (e)

Trafford rev. 07/05/2013

 www.traffordpublishing.com.sg

Singapore
toll-free: 800 101 2656 (Singapore)
Fax: 800 101 2656 (Singapore)

CONTENTS

CHAPTER 1

FOREWORD

It is suitable to finish a series of twelve volumes about economic aspects of the colonial era of NSW with a collection of essays relating to the years of the close of the colonial period, that is the years from about 1890 to 1901; the period of federation debates, creation of statehood from coast to coast and planning for the new 20th century.

These studies cover much of the history of Australia since early colonisation in 1788

The subject matter of the essays is diverse and ranges from the early development of colonial political parties (in particular the Free Trade Parties), and from a study of the Financial aspects of the Federation debates to a review of Australian High Court decisions which have followed Federation and have affected Commonwealth-State relations. One other essay of economic substance is an analysis of, and justification for, regional development in Australia together with a model for regional growth. A biography of a\n eminent colonial free trader and federation senator and an 'uncle' of the writer is included as an indication of the lives of those passionate about politics in the closing days o the colonial period and their contribution to the big debates about white Australia, free trade and protection and the establishment of a national public service framework.

The twelve volume series commenced with an economic analysis of the founding of the colonies in Australia and an overview of the events that contributed so \much to the sound economic foundation of the colony

1

and then the federation and the dramatic growth of both population numbers and GDP from all sectors of the economy.

As has been discussed in the earlier part of this introduction to this collection of essays, there are seven topics, all of which loosely inter-relate to each other. For instance the essay on the History of Public Accounts, out of necessity includes a reference to the financial negotiations and debates leading to Federation, but this is followed by an analysis of the financial aspects of the Federation debates and then the post-Federation handling of the Financial clauses of the new Constitution and the handling of the surplus revenue as set down in the Braddon clause. The McMahon Biography includes references to his understanding of Federalism and whilst Treasurer, his handling of the Commonwealth-State Financial relations in particular, the Commonwealth Grants Commission and the Uniform Taxation Legislation—both topics which caused a divide on the interpretation of Federalism and a rift in Commonwealth state Relations. McMahon had exposed a philosophy on Federalism which cannot be supported in practice, especially whilst he was Treasurer. Another link is the reminder that McMahon was a prominent member of the Liberal Party of Australia, which was a successor (by name change) to the original Free trade Party in NSW (the Party of Edward Pulsford and Sir Henry Parkes, Sir George Dibbs and Sir George Reid), the Nationalist Party of Joe Lyons and the 'All for Australia' Party of McMahon's uncle, Sir Samuel Walder. The second essay in this collection relates to the History of the Free Trade Party in NSW, which was influenced greatly by Henry Parkes and Sir George Dibbs. This movement was epitomised in NSW by The Free Trade Association, of which Edward Pulsford was the Secretary and the Editor of its publication, the Free Trade Journal—'*Our Country*' (1900-1901). So there is an interesting link between all of the essays—McMahon, Free Trade, Federation and the resulting Commonwealth-State Financial relations, and the History of Public Accounts, and, of course, the Beckett Family History which includes great uncle Edward Pulsford. A topical study of Regional Development for Australia is included as a non-historical economic contribution.

The purpose of this collection is to set out the details of seven interesting studies which are of topical interest and which complement each other in both substance and conclusion. The catalyst is obviously the great relevance of the disclosure of a past family member having such close ties to matters financial and economic, the subject of which is of great interest to the present author. The tie that binds them all together is the story of men, events and philosophy of the economic and financial history of the Colony

CHAPTER 2

BUILDING A FUTURE FOR REGIONAL AUSTRALIA

(Together with a model for action)

It is a fundamental principle of underwriting and sustaining rural economic identity that regional Australia attracts labour-related industry to country areas. This can be done in a number of ways—in most ideologies, forced relocation is not feasible, but new industry can be attracted to regional centres by offering a variety of cash and non-cash economic incentives. The extent of the incentive should revolve around a 'pay-back' of any financial consideration made available to a new industry.

Two philosophical questions should be asked.

Should regional governing bodies 'pay' for jobs, or should the free market forces create the attraction?

Should new industry be offered incentives to come in from outside the region rather than existing industry be offered an incentive to grow?

It has been shown in the USA that outside jobs are costing over $5,000 to attract, but existing businesses can grow new jobs at less than $2,000 (per job). An important factor in this equation is the financial capacity of regional government to raise funding to attract new industry. It would probably require changes in current law to enable local/regional government to make payments to new industry, and modifications to existing capital raising mechanisms to provide capital pools for this purpose.

A further question to be asked is, do we consider Australia as a whole in trying to attract new industry or should competing states be allowed or encouraged to create a 'dutch' auction in transferring industry from State to State without there being a net gain to the country as a whole?

Whatever view is reached in conclusion, it appears that regional development is an Australian Government initiative rather than a State initiative, and the proposed new tax policies should reflect the need for change in revenue sharing.

The purpose of this paper is not to discuss whether or not regional Australia is in need of growth. It is axiomatic that if new industry is not attracted to regional areas then growth will not take place and population numbers will continue to decline. The attractions of job creating industry are numerous, not least of which keeps farm family young people in or near their home towns, and as the farming community follows the city trend to more part-time work, then two job families, one working in the town and one working the farm, can be maintained. There needs to be technical training in regional areas for young people and new or expanding industry can be the 'beneficiary' of such training.

Regional development must include as a major part, job creating incentives. That is, small communities, even those of the 25—30,000 size, can easily disappear unless their growth rate can be maintained at least at 1, that is, just sustaining itself. The impact on retaining young people in the community is paramount; the ability of the education system to survive troughs of new youth intakes; the sustaining of retail services; the preservation of the social infrastructure services eg. Doctors, hospitals, road maintenance; even the Telstra servicemen being withdrawn from low need towns—all these matters require careful assessment as to their cost and impact. The social impact of any loss of these services to most regional towns would be the death knoll to its future.

So how could a regional area honourably attract industry to its regional and benefit from this attraction.

a. Can industry be attracted rather than being paid?
b. Can new industry be attracted at no cost rather than existing industry being encouraged to grow?
c. Can a region afford to act unilaterally and independently of the Federal Government?
d. Can States successfully compete against each other to entice existing industry without net cost to the Australian economy?
e. How can a region be attractive to new industry or to growing existing industry rather than have local taxpayers underwriting the event?
f. How can a region measure the need for additional growth; identify the areas of most important growth; compute a pay-back for any social cost to local taxpayers, and thereafter measure the success or otherwise of the measures taken?
g. What types of government incentive schemes could be offered, keeping in mind that not all incentives are to be cash based?

Let's analyse some of these questions and concerns and try to put this total question of financial incentives into perspective. If the answer to any of these questions is, financial incentives can be justified, then we will ask and answer the question, how can regions legitimately raise funds for local industrial development.

Industrial development assistance can take many forms.

a. tied land grants;
b. low interest loans for capital works;
c. grants for job development;
d. √ selection of suitable new employees from the unemployment rolls;
e. training of selected employees on employer equipment at regional expense;
f. start-up wage payments for new employees until they reach normal and acceptable productivity levels;
g. raising the payroll tax thresh-hold or waiving payroll taxes for a period;
h. waiving or lowering of local government rates and taxes;
i. √ creation of trade zones and duty free zones;

j. peppercorn rents on land and buildings;
k. community purchase of vacant industrial property and lease-back to new industry;
l. assistance with relocation of industry to the region;
m. assisting employee transfers;
n. √ creation of a 'sphere of influence' zone, offering special consideration to new industry for tendering to existing focus industry;
o. √ co-ordination of education services to meet training needs of new or existing industry to ensure future labour availability; and
p. Special local government assistance with relocation, expansion or establishment of business activity.

- Many of these items are non-cash items, with no net cost to the community or region, but are, in fact, business facilitation initiatives. Those thus marked (√) are worthy of special attention, since they assist both new and existing industry at no definitive cost to the taxpayer.
- Such non-cash items are a major attraction to industrial development, preferably as part of an overall package of options to industry.

In the event of cash incentive payments being required, then a special governmental fund should be accessed, on the basis that there is a net gain both to the local community as well as the state or country as a whole. The extent of any payment should be commensurate with the needs of the community, be it local, state or federal benefit. A measure of the payment should be equated to the gain in the community, the overall package of benefits, and a computation of pay-back, with special emphasis on long-term gains.

An example of this assessment could be made, based on a recent State of Alabama (USA) experience. The specific circumstances were a high state-wide unemployment rate especially in the largely black areas of the state. The state government had enacted 'right to work' legislation as a means of combating union domination in certain industries and making it a more attractive state for industry, and giving northern 'rust belt' state based industries a clear choice, other than a weather decision, for relocating to the 'deep' south.

Most Southern States were competing for new industry, and fighting to be the biggest provider of cash for each new job attracted. Payments ranged from $5,000 to $10,000, with the average being closer to the top figure. An international industry was being actively sought by most southern states—Mercedes Benz of Germany was being wooed at the highest levels when it became known that the USA was being selected as the location for a light all-terrain sports vehicle. After months of discussion, the State of Alabama offered $300,000,000 plus land, low interest loans, and employee selection and training as well as special University of Alabama research and courses. The State was thereupon selected as the winner of 1,500 direct jobs. But add to that number the jobs created from the 50 mile sphere of influence wherein engineering and other suppliers were given preference in tendering for Mercedes work, and another 4,500 jobs were created. The flow-on effect of all this new industry and employment was tremendous and research showed a multiplier effect of 5 times. So , in effect, for an infrastructure and cash cost of about $350,000,000, over 30,000 direct and indirect jobs were created and the State growth rate was lifted from less than 1% to over 3%. In a state where local sales taxes were averaging over 9%, the pay-back period was computed to be about 10 years. In real terms, when all beneficiaries were taken into account, especially the real estate industry, education, hospitals, universities etc, where there were enormous economic benefits, the pay-back time would have been much shorter. Success breeds success, so when northern industry saw that Mercedes chose Alabama, they assumed it was worthy of their taking a second look, and so there started a stream of new arrivals with little or no cash incentive payments.

Perhaps, an example of what evaluations an industry considering relocating has to make, will assist in this process.

Company X is a small, medium size manufacturer, typically under capitalised, but can see the opportunity of moving to a regional location, for some of the following reasons:

a.   more stable work-force;

b. lower overheads;
c. opportunity of owning a factory at a much lower cost than in their existing location;
d. better lifestyle for managers;
e. strategic transport corridor could be created; and
f. More community involvement for the business.

Steps which require careful assessment before the industry can make a final decision include:

1. number of key people to relocate;
2. their housing, education, and social needs;
3. housing and education availability in the new town;
4. costs of relocating key personnel, and special allowances, housing loans etc;
5. design of factory/offices required;
6. analysis of customer location for transport arrangements;
7. analysis of supplier locations and delivery arrangements;
8. New equipment required for new plant. If a new factory is to be built and new personnel hired, it would be suitable to re-arrange productivity plans;
9. equipment and layout to start the new location off right;
10. availability of labour, and level of skills;
11. hiring practices;
12. Does the new region have an economic development officer, and what assistance in site selection, assistance with placement of infrastructure services (eg? Electricity, water, sewerage); assistance with hiring and selection and training of new workers;
13. does the local technical school have access to trainees, training and initial supervision for training workers on new machinery in conjunction with the factory management;
14. Does the local economic development office have access to land in the industrial park;
15. Can the economic development office offer assistance with:

a. providing land;
b. arranging mortgage loans to build factory;
c. can the interest rate be subsidised;

d. removal expenses of the factory equipment;

e. removal expenses of the personnel transferring in; and

f. Setting up a 'welcoming' committee for new transferees to explain schools, housing, community services, connecting electricity, water etc.

These are a few of the considerations to be dealt with before this business can decide to relocate. The main business consideration is relocating to a business friendly town, where business needs and worker welcome needs are recognised, and assistance can be provided to make the transition as smooth as possible. Businesses need capital raising assistance, especially in a new community, and so the land grant and the factory construction loan are important.

The alternative is for the town or EDC to build and own the factory, lease it to the new industry 'tenant' at a peppercorn rent with the option to buy in so many years.

There are probably ways in which the EDC can provide direct financing or make incentive payments to industry. If under current state law, local shires are able to operate EDCs, and offer the full, faith and credit to the AEDC, then the EDC could participate in a derivatives leveraging and sell the forward income stream from the leased building into the market, and raise capital in that way. This could easily be structured to make a spread so that 'seed' money was available for future growth activities.

Economic development in regional Australia is paramount to sustain the rural infrastructure. The existing regional economic structure is a study on its own but many regions are moving to reconstruct their industrial focus by recognising 'cluster;' industries, whereby industries of a common nature who have a local advantage, 'cluster' in that area and feed off one another. The recognition of cluster industries is not official government policy but the Australian Business and Industry Councils have urged regional development based on government assistance and a policy of developing 'cluster' industry.

In summary, there are a variety of needs that industry has in expectation of relocating to a rural regional economy. These needs must be recognised and cross-matched with local economic development councils so that there is a clear meeting of the minds on what is required and what is available. It is to be understood that EDC s have limitations and these limitations need to be clearly spelt out for industry reviewing that particular region.

It is likewise important that the EDC be headed by individuals cognisant of industrial development and what it takes to be attractive to industry.

Any contribution to rural and regional development must achieve measurable results. Taxpayer funds are to be invested with a return in mind. Future gains should be discounted so that any analysis of returns reflects a discounted position in today's terms.

The model set out below is a definitive statement of specific action which can be undertaken by a central government but more importantly by a regional association, in the form of self-help. Such self-help is the best form of commitment by the community or region, which, if solid and well-placed is self-renewing and can take on a life of its own. It is more long-term in nature than Governmental grants. The central concept of the model has commentary which can be used to guide an implementation program.

'A MODEL' FOR INDUSTRY GROWTH USING INCENTIVES

(The model is based on experience gathered by the author during 20 years of association with Regional Development in the USA (1978-1996 and includes three ingredients for dealing with sustainable regional development in Australia)

- **A PROGRAM OF ENCOURAGEMENT FOR SUSTAINABLE REGIONAL ECONOMIC DEVELOPMENT**
- **TARGETING SPECIFIC COMMUNITY GAINS**
- **ESTABLISHING A REGIONAL FINANCE & INVESTMENT CORPORATION FOR FUNDING BUSINESS GROWTH**

THE MODEL

RESEARCHING *and* DEVELOPING A 'CLUSTER' INDUSTRY CONCEPT

Commonality of Regional Industry encourages more product research
'Like' industries become more competitive
The resulting skilled work-force is more mobile
A greater competitive spirit is generated amongst cluster-type businesses
There are many benefits to business of market specialisation

THE INCENTIVE PARAMETERS

Tied Land Grants
Low and subsidised interest loans
Delayed settlements for land/building acquisitions
Creating special trade zones
Establishing sponsored duty free zones
Coordinating education services to meet future industry needs
Local Government sponsored paper reduction and 'red tape' reduction program
Industry networking
Full-time Business Encouragement & Planning Officers available to assist
Business Enterprise Centres assist in business failure minimisation
'Links to Business' Program minimises Government Red Tape Problems

INFORMATION KITS FOR PROSPECTIVE BUSINESS AND ENQUIRIES

Videos
Prospectus
Promotional material
Business & Resources—regional database
Web Page
Information 800 phone line
Questionnaire covering help and support

COMMUNITY BENEFITS FROM ATTRACTING NEW INDUSTRY

Increase in Jobs
Local industry/business diversification
Improved local services and products
Enhanced community services
Injection of Investment funds
Life Style Improvements for the local population
Improved Local Community and regional economy
Increased local confidence and retention of existing business
Improvement of local Job Skills, Opportunities and Technologies

LOCAL and REGIONAL SUPPORT OPERATIONS AVAILABLE TO UNDERPIN THIS PROGRAM for A REGIONAL INDUSTRIAL DEVELOPMENT PROGRAM

Regional Chambers of Commerce
Local Business Advisory Councils and Enterprise Centres
Linking the Councils within the Region.
Government as Regional Coordinator
S R A D
A state Government coordinator—'Department of Regional Development'
The Federal Government coordinator—Department of Regional Development
Regional Economic Development Councils
Local and Regional Tourism Organisations.
Proposed Regional Development Funding Corporation.

ROLE OF REGIONAL DEVELOPMENT FUNDING COMMISSION

Support Services to Local Councils for Bridge Funding
Support for Local Councils to finance Industrial Land and installation
    of services
Regional Development Committees can request special financing for
    new industries for Buildings & Infrastructure, services, roads and

utilities, and relocation costs not covered by the State Government programs

Top-up assistance for new

Industries over and above the State Government Program funding

Special Funding for Councils to build factories for lease to new or growing industries

Advancing funds for incentive payments for existing industry to take on additional employees

Funding for securitised working capital for growth industries—funds can be lent on flexible basis and higher risk

Funding can come from bond sales and venture capital groups

Use of Funds localised to Capital Region and balanced by Council area

MEASUREMENT OF OUTCOMES

Increase in local employment & decrease in local unemployment

Greater local job opportunities

Greater local pools of skilled tradespeople

Increase in number of successful businesses

Improvement in local business confidence

Less close-down

Fewer vacancies in commercial property

Increased enrolments in tertiary and trade students

If GST provides local councils with growth revenue, then more business increases local revenue share

Increased number and quality of Community Service

CHAPTER 3

THE FINANCIAL ASPECTS OF THE FEDERATION DEBATES

- Setting the Stage for Federation
- The need for National Unity
- The economic climate leading towards Federalism
- Quick & Garran—concepts for federation
- Inauguration
- Pacific Islanders Labourers Act 1901
- Henry Higgins—War and support for Britain
- Establishing the High Court & Industrial Conciliation Court
- 'I love a sunburnt country'
- The march toward Federation

Introduction

Australia's first one hundred years—from the founding of the Colony to 1888, was a mixture of poverty, crude wealth and great milestones. The people grew in stature, and had great pride in their new homeland, and as well, the economy grew. The cities grew as well as the bread basket of the rural areas. Australia rode on the sheep's back, then on the back of gold and other minerals, but successive styles and colour of Governments rose to serve the needs of the people well. Government sponsored and funded the social infrastructure and enabled the Colony of New South Wales, and then of Tasmania, Victoria, Western Australia, Queensland and finally South Australia to grow and prosper. The Government led the way with the development of water, sewerage, roads, telegraph, postal services, hospitals, education and land clearing and subdivision. It was an interesting mix—a free enterprise economy with that essential government support and encouragement underpinning the provision of 'essential' community services.

It is interesting to observe that even after one hundred years, the respective colonies were still very much in line in terms of individual revenues. Assuming the fiscal policy concept was for balanced budgets, then the revenues in 1889 (**Table 1**) very much reflected the overall state expenditures, and likewise the expenditure per head on Government services was pretty much in line from Colony to Colony. The figures reflect the different attitudes towards overseas borrowing, public debt and the debt service, the population levels and the extent of growth. South Australia was content to keep population growth to a bare minimum, whilst Western Australia used the discovery of gold to expand its population base, with immigration from the remote eastern states.

Table 1

Revenue per head of Population 1889

Colony	Taxation	Land	Public Services	Other	TOTAL
NSW	2.8.6	1.18.9	3.2.11	0.14.0	8.4.2
Vic	3.7.11	0.11.2	3.10.9	0.7.3	7.17.1
Qld	4.7.4	1.13.1	2.11.10	0.9.9	9.2.0
SA	2.4.3	0.10.10	3.9.7	0.16.7	7.1.3
WA	4.10.6	2.0.7	1.11.3	2.4.0	10.6.4
TAS	2.16.10	0.9.6	0.17.9	0.7.2	4.11.2
Ave	**3.2.0**	**1.1.9**	**2.19.4**	**0.10.11**	**7.13.11**

(Source: Wealth & Progress of NSW—1886-87)

Table 2

Growth of Capital in Australia 1788-1888

	Amount of Wealth	Increase in 25 years
1788	0	Colonisation
1813	1000000	1000000
1838	26000000	25000000
1863	181000000	155000000
1888	1015000000	834000000

(Source: Wealth & Progress of NSW—1886-87)

Table 3

Public Revenue 1889 ('000)

Colony	Taxation	Land	Public Services	Other	TOTAL
NSW	2677	2137	3347	775	9063
Vic	3749	616	3909	400	8675
Qld	1734	656	1029	194	3614
SA	711	174	1118	266	2270
WA	194	87	67	94	442
Tas	422	71	132	54	679

Table 4

Taxation Per Head in the Colonies—1881 and 1889

	1881	1889
NSW	2.6.7	2.8.9
Vic	2.6.1	3.7.11
Qld	2.19.2	4.7.4
SA	1.19.2	2.4.3
WA	3.13.1	4.10.6
Tas	2.6.1	2.16.10
Ave	**2.9.4**	**3.2.0**

(Source: Wealth & Progress of NSW—1886-87)

GORDON W BECKETT

'Taxation' grew marginally in the period from 1881 to 1889 (less than 1 percent), and was lowest in the Colony of New South Wales. This low tax was another mechanism to attract immigrants, foreign investment, and domestic growth.

Table 5

Australia : Population of Capital Cities 1861-1951

	Total Metropolitan Popln	Propn to Total
1861	282008	24.14
1871	426665	24.74
1881	669799	29.04
1891	1142985	35.27
1901	1352384	35.38
1921	2400030	43.55

Table 6

Population Gains in the Colony 1788-1910

	Total Population	Ave Annual Growth Rate
1788-1790	2056	
1791-1800	5217	9.76
1801-1810	11566	8.29
1811-1820	33543	11.24
1821-1830	70039	7.64
1831-1840	190408	10.52
1841-1850	405356	7.85
1851-1860	1145585	10.95
1861-1870	1647756	3.7
1871-1880	2231531	3.08
1881-1890	3151355	3.51
1891-1910	4425083	1.80

(Source: Demography, 1949 ex Government Statistician, ACT)

The domestic population had grown rapidly until, after the first hundred years, it had reached two and a quarter million, but still had one of the lowest population densities in the world and was the envy of many an Asian region country.

By the mid-1880s the convict transfers had been stopped for 30 years and every one in the various Colonies was 'free' or, at least, not tainted with that 'convict' brush. Assisted immigration had provided almost 100,000 new Australians, but unassisted migrants still arrived, escaping the variety of skirmishes, oppression and wars going on around Europe, whilst the English arrived looking for that new opportunity in an English Colony—a 'better' way of life without changing the underlying way of life. A virtual paradise—home away from home. The British source would continue dominant for almost another hundred years.

When, in the mid-1850s the British Government had accepted the push by the colonies for self-government and authorised the various State Constitution acts, the mind of the Colonial leaders only then actively turned to Federalism, but in the interim, the States each went on their own way. The Colonies almost defeated the eventual effectiveness of Federalism by instigating Inter-State Tariffs and duties. In 1852, upon the separation of Victoria into an independent State, the State of New South Wales imposed limited tariffs on certain goods, mainly narcotics, tea, coffee, and sugar moving between the States. Being the most populated and the most advanced economically, NSW could raise significant revenues from imposing tariffs on goods leaving NSW for Victoria, South Australia, Tasmania or Queensland. Most imports at this time arrived from overseas into the Port of Sydney before being distributed to the other States, thus offering the dutiable arrangements. NSW was able to raise foreign goods import duties as well as inter-Colonial tariffs.

Customs revenues were critical to the financial well-being of the Colony, and their imposition and collection became a fine balancing act between good politics and sound economic management.

Customs Revenues between 1825 and 1850 consistently made up over half of the Colony's revenues. Customs revenues peaked in 1842 at 182 thousand pound, at a time when, for the first time, the Colony's total revenue leapt to 700 million pound. These spikes were on account of the gold discovery and the importation of goods and the inflow of people to the gold fields.

The Australian Colonies Government Act of 1825 (British Parliament) had given the Colonial parliaments the initial right to impose customs duties provided they did not discriminate between the goods of each other and the goods of other countries. In exercising the right to impose customs duties on the goods of other colonies, the parliaments raised the issues of a uniform tariff, a custom's union, and the use of the Darling and Murray Rivers for inter-colonial trade. The controversies were sharpened by the discrepancy between the political and economic frontiers (especially in the Riverina and the northern rivers districts of New South Wales, and the frontier districts between Victoria and South Australia).

John Dunmore Lang explores these challenges in his 1870 book ('the coming event of freedom or independence for the seven united colonies'). There were major doctrinaire differences over the tariff as well as the general inter-colonial rivalry.

Quick & Garran in their 'Annotated Constitution of the Australian Commonwealth' (1901) set out a detailed analysis and history of these inter-colonial tariffs. They recorded *inter alia* that Mr E.C. Weekes MLA spoke in the Legislative Assembly of New South Wales on September 10, 1862 about these matters and suggested:

"It has been long known that Melbourne has secured a large part of the trade of the southern portion of New South Wales, and that we have no right to complain of their having done so, provided that the Colony obtained the revenue of the dutiable goods which Victoria sent to this Colony. This evil, of remote colonialists paying extra duties, in order to survive, which other residents would not have to incur, has occurred from the very commencement of the separation of the two colonies, and concerns mainly the border towns on the Murray River who depend for their trading on Melbourne because of its proximity and access".

The government of the day from about 1851 thus had their attention drawn to the large amount of dutiable goods that were being brought from

Victoria into New South Wales, and on which was paid no duty in the NSW Colony. The consequence was that in 1855 Border Custom-houses were established, respectively, on the River Murray, in the Colony of Victoria as well as in New South Wales, but these continued in operation for only a short time, before the two governments agreed on their abolition.

The advent of steam navigation on the rivers system in 1856 then caused the duty question to be raised in the context of goods coming into Victoria and New South Wales via the river system from the Colony of South Australia, and a three party treaty was made through which there was only one duty paid and the revenue split three ways. There were further haggles between the three states of the fairness of the respective tariffs and their systematic application and collection. Each thought they were out of pocket. Each felt the evil of the present system so acutely that they would only go into the early Federation Conferences with a determination to arrive at a resolution to accomplish what all must desire, "a uniform tariff".

In 1885, the move toward Federation had been blocked by the 'lion in the path' (Garran's words, referring to the tariffs)— whereby neither free-trade New South Wales nor protectionist Victoria will entrust the customs tariff to the Federal Parliament. In 1891 at the First Convention it was hoped that 'when trade barriers between the States were down, both the Commonwealth and the States would guarantee that they could never put them up again'. But New South Wales, who had the most to lose, might try for risky protection barriers against the outside world, first by resolution and then in the draft Constitution. Again a reason of fear for deferral of Federation. Trade barriers, tariffs and duties were to become the bane of Federalists for a further 9 years until that the Convention in 1897 finally broke the mould and the federal movement turned into the final straight.

The tariff and duty question survived the various Federation conferences and for many became the central issue in working towards Federation.

The British Government's attempt to progress self-government in the Colony entitled the 'Australian Colonies Government Bill' was passed into law on the 24th May, 1849, but became known, commonly, as the "Bill for the better government of the Australian colonies". The Bill firstly, enabled the separation of Victoria from New South Wales but also recommended that Victoria adopt the same tariffs as those in force in NSW.

New South Wales had first imposed duties (following the separation of Van Dieman's Land from NSW) on goods coming from Tasmania into NSW. In 1842, after the separation of New Zealand from NSW, the Legislative Council of NSW passed an Act to permit goods the produce or manufacture of New Zealand and Tasmania to be imported free of duty into NSW. During the debate, the collector of Customs suggested that the exemption be extended to South Australia, 'although trade with that Colony was, as yet, inconsiderable'. This was an interesting step, since South Australia was obviously the pet colony of the British Colonial Office, but not regarded with high favour in or by NSW.

This attempt to encourage 'free trade' was frustrated by disallowance of the Act. Lord Stanley, the Secretary of the Colonial Office took the position that discrimination of tariffs between States was bad and was contrary to Britain's commercial treaties and foreign relations. Tasmania abolished the reciprocal exemptions from duty on NSW goods in 1846, and imposed the general rate of ad valorem duty (15%) on all imports. Tasmania had previously caused a level of fury in the NSW Legislative Assembly by imposing a special duty on tobacco and coal coming into the state from NSW in 1843.

As Quick & Garran point out (P80 Chapter IV—*The Federal Movement in Australia*—*'The Annoted Constitution of Australia'*—*1901*)

"Inter-colonial barriers were thus allowed to grow up, and the fiscal policies of the colonies gradually drifted apart".

Earl Grey had presented a select committee report of the Privy Council in 1949 which had enquired into the constitutional changes it might be wise to make in the Australian Colonies. The committee report recommended the separation of Victoria from New South Wales, and that each of the four Colonies should have a unicameral legislature, partly nominated by the Crown, and two-thirds elected; and each legislature would be empowered to alter its own Constitution. The report was communicated to the Colonies in 1850 but was not received well, as the impetuous Earl Grey was not the favourite son of any of the Colonies.

The Committee reported that "there remains a question of considerable difficulty. By far the larger part of the revenues of the Australian Colonies is derived from duties on customs. But if each province is authorised to impose duties according to its own wants, it is scarcely possible but that in process of time, differences should arise between the Colonies on the rate of duty".

In September 1846, the NSW Governor, Fitzroy, had communicated a resolution of the Legislative Assembly to the Colonial Office, and thus made the first recorded suggestion that there was a need for common tariffs and a central inter-colonial authority. The stage had been set, and the Privy Council acted promptly to issue its comprehensive report on constitutional needs of the Colonies in 1849. Federalism was on the move.

South Australia reacted negatively to Earl Grey's report and the resulting enabling Act, and passed a resolution stating that:

a. 'there is a great dissimilarity in the pursuits and interests of the several provinces,
b. the larger states would act in a way injurious to the lesser states, and
c. there is no need for such a central inter-colonial assembly'

From Tasmania, Governor Denison, wrote to Earl Grey, with a fear 'that the proposed uniform tariff would operate injuriously on the revenue of that Colony'.

Thus two of the aims of this Paper are to

• record and examine the various negotiations between the States, leading up to Federation,
• and how the delegates balanced the various effects of tariffs, and
• Review the financial aspects of the final Constitution.

The author is aware that very little writing has been produced on the economic considerations facing the federationists, although the author considers this must have been of major concern to the participating states and the participants at the various Federation conferences and negotiations. Although the political negotiations were paramount, the economic considerations must have been a close second in importance to the states and their various representatives, resulting in the South Australian and Tasmanian Governments submitted cautionary messages to the Colonial Office in 1849 objecting to the 'equality' of tariffs between the 'large' states and the 'lesser' states. In reality what was needed was recognition by the larger states that there was an imbalance of population size and public revenue, without there necessarily being the requisite reduction in public expenditure to complete social infrastructure. A hospital, rail service or an education for a resident of South Australia would cost the same as for a resident of NSW, and so there was the need to be a balancing of revenues per head of population between the larger and smaller states. On-going revenue out of proportion was one thing but public works expenditures and overseas borrowing needed support by the larger states to ensure equality. Thus **Table 1** would have been used by the stronger states to say to the smaller states, 'we will agree to underwrite some of your activities but tax imposition must be the same per head of population in all our states as must land tax. In this way, they would suggest, your revenue per head of population will become over 8 pound and we can agree to a cross-border subsidy or guarantee in order to help you'.

Part of this paper will be set aside to examining the nature of such discussions, the economic justification based on figures produced a hundred years after the event, but with the benefit of hindsight, we will review the results of these discussions. Surely an exciting exercise in reviewing the short history of Australia, in light of the previous study of the economic impacts from the first one hundred years of the Colony. Readers may wish to first review the author's paper which sets out the early economic circumstances of the Colony and a related study of the Colonial Financial Accounts during those years.

This continuing research continues that first study and story and links the events of the first hundred years with the important events of the next 50 years.

There are a number of purposes for this paper

1. To continue the story from the founding of the Colony of New South Wales in 1788 and account for the push towards a federation of the several states
2. To reflect on the challenges confronting the Federalists, and see how the various economies, at their various stages of development and self-sufficiency were able to compromise on eliminating the inter-Colonial tariffs and duties
3. To examine the financial aspects of the Constitution.
4. To trace the post-constitution economic balancing act that must have arisen both federally and within the states.

Setting the Stage for Federation.

The advent of 'party' politics had helped shape much of the last two decades of the first centenary. This thrust was from a variety of participants, from welfare pushers, to equality between men and women, full franchise voting for women, and then the free-traders and protectionists. The new society was full of insular interests, each trying to push their philosophies and policies. These various interests, as they generally do, shaped the pace and conditions under which the various colonies grew, prospered and coloured themselves. There was continual movements towards the dismantling of the former settlement pattens, and the substitution and development towards policies to achieve a more mature and competitive nation.

However, the generation after Federation was to finally turn an emerging national consensus into new laws and institutions. But the last 10 years of the first centenary of the Colony showed a new fervour for cohesion and opportunism in economic and social developments previously unfulfilled by state governments. The growth and success of the major cities required continuing innovation, ideas and progress on many fronts to keep the population supportive of the many parties and programs. Education, health, telecommunications, international trading and economic management were all high on the national agenda, led by the general enthusiasm for federation.

This coming national consensus for new laws, institutions and national cohesion was led by Alfred Deakin and was to become known as the 'new Australian Settlement'. The decade was putting paid to the 'old settlement' with its racial overtones, its struggles, and the hardships. There were no longer any original convicts remaining in the Colony and these shackles of disrepute were able to be buried, with only the future to be worried about.

This new movement was like a new start or beginning. The overall wealth of the Colonists, the expenditure on railways and communications, the advent of self government, the release of the British overlording gave the psychological base to the thought of Federation and a real Australia.

The key feature of this new movement to 'Australianise' the Settlement was its bipartisan approach, and was accepted by free-traders, protectionists, liberals, labour and conservative politicians. Its universality provided the bonds for eight decades of national units, federation and continued growth—both population and economic—despite the defects of this 'settlement' approach. The defects were few but important. The country lacked cohesion as yet. In reality and in its thinking it was a loose conglomeration of 6 states that had little in common, little linkage, tariffs between the States, and 6 different standards of just about every aspect of life. Even the rail gauges were different, thus making transportation between the colonies quite onerous. The mail service was essentially local to each self-governed area, rather than 'inter-state'. Federation was being looked towards as the solution to these few but important defects in the current settlement.

In the late 1870s (in the last decade prior to the centenary), the driving nationalist force did not think in terms of a Bill of Rights, or Declaration of Independence as a focus of national identity.

Unlike the American States who fought fiercely to unite under the one flag, the nationalists in the Australian Colony were united in Federation in order to benefit from the break-through of the tariffs, to be united in voice against prurient British policies, and thoughtful to develop a common shipping, rail, highway system to decentralise the population and have common interests. This nation was not going to be founded in war, revolution, or national assertion, but by practical men striving for income, justice, employment and security. This Australian settlement was their creation.

It was to be an achievement second only to the creation of a Colonial democracy, but in trying to meet the challenge of nationhood, the nationalist movement turned the last two decades of the centenary into a nation in transition, a foretaste of the continuous process of creative destruction of the old ways and the old days, from which there was no turning back.

The ideas backing this Australianising of national interests, were devoid of formal definition, but may be summarised under five headings—White Australia, Industry Protection, Wage Arbitration, State Paternalism and Imperial Benevolence. Both Gerard Henderson and Paul Kelly refer to the 'new settlement' approach. In *Menzies Child* (1994), Henderson prefers the first three icons of White Australia, Industry Protection and Wage Arbitration. Kelly in *The End of Certainty (1993)* adds the last two—State Paternalism and Imperial Benevolence. Kelly's concept is more relevant as an approach to Federation. It embraces the basic ideals that were fermenting in the collective mind of a society struggling to extricate itself from a very bad depression in the 1880; with rapid technological progress that was undoing many of the entrenched ways of life; a new found State power which believed in fundamental freedoms including freedom of the press; the cry of the political parties was being heard around the land and they were consolidating policies unheard of two decades previously. The world was being stood on its head. It was a mixture of excitement and challenge.

The national interests were being founded on a variety of pillars setting the stage for a Federation and a stepping stone for robust economic growth, faith in government authority, belief in egalitarianism, the judicial and centralised determination of wage fixation, protection of its industry and its workforce; continued dependence upon a great power (Britain) for its security and its finance. The national interest also became a focus to protect the people from the possibility of hostilities and any internal contamination from the peoples of the Asia/Pacific arena. The base ideology was protection, whilst its implementation was to be for a

Fortress Australia, part of an impregnable Empire spanning the globe. This framework would undergo many changes over the next century. It was fully expected that 1978 would be very different to 1878—as different to what 1878 was to 1778. As political parties grew and organised, their differences were sometimes bitter, but the real divide was underpinned by common underlying policy initiatives and goals.

The real division was between the international traditionalists and the sentimentalist traditionalists—the fight is over the nationalising settlement and between those who think it is unsustainable and those who want to keep the traditions. The old order would be challenged time and again. Could growth of economic and population be achieved with a White Australia policy?

The white Australia policy was not just a policy, it was a creed. It saw its origins in the closing of doors to the Chinese gold seekers. It was used to limit the coloured Pacific Islands labour brought to Queensland to develop the sugar and pineapple industries. The first Australian Prime Minister, Edmund Barton, predicted the demise in 1901 of western colonialism and the rise of new states in Africa and Asia, but his false conclusion was that the White Australia policy would act as a bulwark against any shifting tide from these near neighbours. It would be another 70 years before this myth would be fully dispelled and the policy abandoned, and even then, it took a longer time still to keep older Australians from thinking of the Asian menace especially after the land grabbing and expansionist role of the Japanese in 1945.

White Australia was the first and greatest ingredient in Australian nationalism; it was the chief motive driving nationalism and local imperialism. This was the primary plank in the first Labour Party caucus in 1901, and remained in the policy until Arthur Calwell, a staunch champion of that plank, was succeeded by Gough Whitlam in 1965. This primary and extensively supported pillar of the nationalising process was innate to the post colonising peoples who were looking for federation, unity and a national pride in those last days of the first centenary.

The second pillar of the nationalising process was Protectionism. Its appeal transcended that of an economic policy, and became both a creed and a dogma. It was considered philosophy that would make the Colony and the federation powerful, secure in prosperity and assuage its insecurity. For its followers, protectionism was a policy for both peace and war.

Kelly writes: 'White Australia and protectionism grew into an emotional national bond. These two pillars were at the core of Australia's consciousness'.

Part of the conflicting issue was resolved within the new federation tribunals by broad ranging debate and consensus between the free-traders and the protectionists. The two respective leaders, Alfred Deakin and George Reid (an American ex-patriot), fought a strong battle until the protectionists won the day. From the 1860s the Colony of New South Wales had supported Free-trade whilst the challenging and highly competitive (for population and economic supremacy) Colony of Victoria supported protectionism. This 'conflict' bred state and subsequently national leaders enthroned on these pillars. Tow sides of federation were to emerge and hold the line for the other 'lesser' states to follow. Only John Forrest in Western Australia was to offer a significant contribution to the debate outside the defined thinking of the two largest States.

The third and fourth pillars were underwritten by the first major depression in the 1860s. This period of uncontrolled depression became the dominant economic influence on the nationalising process, out of which grew a coalition between unions and employers in support of a judicial and centralised wage fixing program accompanied by State Paternalism or a state sponsored welfare system and 'the creation of human happiness through government' .

The nation was moving inevitably toward a new destiny. The time had come for the populace to reach out and re-align itself with a populist, insular and protectionist set of policies. The first centenary of the arrival of the First Fleet saw a nation transformed with a new set of goals and challenges. Away with the apron strings of Britain. Away with the cloak of being convicts. That era was put behind the people who looked forward to Federation, pride in its leaders and an international recognition.

The position of women was also beginning to change. After almost 100 years of being second class citizens, their role was growing. Individuals and small groups were active in the arts, the labour movement, and were becoming loud in their demands for improvement women's electoral rights and their legal rights. They called also for improvements in the women's cause generally. A few women were entering the professional ranks but many more were becoming associated with the Women's Christian Temperance League with its hundreds of branches throughout the Colonies.

Its aim was to curb demon drink for the sake of women, homes and children. The coalition of women sent deputations to call on Ministers and Parliamentarians. Theirs was a voice beginning to be heard, after 100 years of subservience.

The gold rushes had brought many things to the Colonies. Economic success, wealth, opportunities to diversify interests, better housing, and better working conditions in order to retain workers, shorter working hours, more imported products, all of which concerned the domestic economy in the main. Population growth fell sharply from around 9% per annum in 1800-60 to 3.4% between 1860 and 1890, by which time the population had grown to 3.5 million. Immigration was now less important than natural increase as a source of population growth.

Export growth slowed even more dramatically. Exports had risen fast during the golden days of wool and gold dominance, but in value terms began to lag during the 1880s. Growth of exports had slowed from 2.6% to less than .6% and fell from 15 pound per head of population to under 9 pounds in this period. This meant the ability to finance imports from proceeds of exports (and thus keep a positive current account balance) was seriously reduced. The simple explanation for this decline is that export growth came from exploitation of a non-renewable resource—gold—and once gold was no longer the get rich quick attraction, and production dropped away, exports fell and required growth in non-gold exporting to keep the per head export figure in balance. Wool had stagnated in the 1850s and the Colony's share of the British market declined. However after 1860, high export wool prices, growing demand for meat, and easier labour supply brought a period of rapid growth in wool output. This phase was also associated with high investment in the primary industry area. Sheep numbers rose from 20 million in 1860 to over 50 million in

1875, representing annual growth of 6%. Wool exports were growing at over 10% per annum.

After 1875, for a period of about 10 years, wool output declined due to productivity declines.

Agriculturalists had moved out into the arid areas and were cutting less wool per head than previously. Growth in physical output fell to only 2% during this period. After the 1860 depression, the next 30 years were remarkable for the absence of further severe depressions and the advent of economic stability. Overseas funds were readily available in the Colony, attracted by the steady growth and stable conditions.

However, the heavy increase in interest payments overseas seemed to create a potential instability to the domestic economy, especially since the 1880s did not produce much increase in export growth.

Capital growth (especially imported capital) was used in the pastoral industry and railway expansion as well as for purchasing imported consumer goods which in turn released local labour for use in the burgeoning construction industry.

By 1890 only 25% of the domestic workforce was employed in the agricultural sector, compared with 40% in the USA at the same time. This was accounted for by the high productivity levels found in farming and agricultural operations due to mechanisation and new rural practices of pasture management. After the introduction of self-government, the Colonial states became entrepreneurs and investors. Government was responsible for 30% of domestic investment and raised 58% of overseas loan funds in 1861-90. It would be easy to criticise the overall quality of government investment. There was much wastage and unnecessary expenditure.

National Unity

The history of the Colonies to this point had been boom, depression, drought, and bonanzas. These had been the mainstay of the chequered history of events, but when on January 25, 1885, the six Colonial premiers

31

sat down, in Hobart, for a conference on a diverse range of topics from defence to trade, it was widely assumed that Federation would be the main topic.

It was the first important gathering to discuss Federation since the National Australasian Convention.

Many of those attending were cynical of any real or positive outcome, since federation had been a topic for 40 years with very little result. But now, it was felt that there was a new spirit in the land, since the latest conference had been suggested by Sir George Reid, Premier of New South Wales and a declared opponent of Federation. If the procedural legislation foreshadowed in Hobart had been adopted by each Colonial Parliament, Federation would have been assured, but in fact the legislation was shelved and it took an economic and industrial crisis to demonstrate the dangers of continued disunity.

Sir Henry Parkes had fostered two political 'heirs'—Edmund Barton and George Reid, who were to be crucial, each in his own way, to the success of the renewed movement for Federation. Both were able lawyers, persuasive, sociable and with good reputations. But from there they differed. Reid was grotesquely stout with a high pitched voice, whilst Barton had an upright carriage and a dignified appearance.

Through a series of conferences, and long periods of wrangling, the concept of the new Constitution for a unified nation was worked out and a Constitution Bill was approved at a convention on April 22, 1891. Although each Colonial Parliament was to ratify the Bill, the reception around the country was mixed. In NSW, the lower house approved it but the upper house opposed the Bill. Most States felt uncomfortable with the original proposal and at a further convention in Sydney, 286 amendments were moved in debate. Little resulted from the Sydney meeting and delegates agreed to meet again in Melbourne on January 20, 1898 for what was to be the longest and most crucial session. The Constitution Bill was taken apart, analysed, and debated clause by clause, and after many amendments, the Bill was put together again and by early March the final passage had been agreed. Thus the embryo Commonwealth had a practicable, working constitution, and it remained now only for the people of Australia to accept it by referendum. The last step on the road to Federation was to be the formal ratification by the British Government, and as events proved, it was to be one of the hardest steps of all.

Although in 1855 Federation appeared unattainable for some time, a resolution had to be reached to mitigate the evils arising from conflicting tariffs and inter-colonial duties. Such items constituted the chief practical inconvenience of disunion; and there were too many attempts to establish border treaties, commercial; reciprocity, inter-colonial free-trade, or customs union. Quick & Garran report it this way "In August 1852, shortly after the separation of Victoria, the Government of New South Wales succeeded in greatly simplifying the tariff for its state by restricting it to a few items—chiefly stimulants, narcotics, tea, coffee, and sugar. In the same month an almost identical tariff was established in Victoria. South Australia and Tasmania retained a much longer list of dutiable items, and in 1854, Victoria decided to increase its duties. In March 1862, a conference on uniform tariffs was set up in response to South Australian legislation that imported goods tariff free from other colonies be reciprocated. The Conference resolved that 'it was highly desirable to settle the basis of a uniform tariff for the Australian Colonies including Tasmania'. On the point of inter-colonial duties the Conference resolved ' customs duties ought to be paid to the revenues of those colonies by whose population the dutiable article was consumed' However, New South Wales and Victoria failed to agree on any 'equitable' mode of distributing revenue. Three alternatives were discussed but failed to attract support:

a. division according to population
b. offsetting revenue accounted for at border points
c. annual payment to New South Wales reflecting the amount of revenue lost by that Colony

None of these propositions satisfied the Victorian Premier. The 'existing arrangements' did not suit New South Wales, which wanted ' the freedom of the border without any adjustment to accounts'. The balance of trade was in Victoria's favour, and so Victoria rejected all the proposals and New South Wales Government put an end to 'existing arrangements', and began to collect duties on the Murray.

During 1863-80 numerous inter-colonial conferences were held as the tariff question began to drive home the damage to all Colonies suffering from tariffs and duty impositions. One such conference in Melbourne 1867 saw the advent of a strong Federation supporter in Sir Henry Parkes, the Colonial Secretary of New South Wales.

Parkes addressed the Conference "I think the time has arrived when these Colonies should be united by some federal bond of connection. There are questions projecting themselves upon our attention, which cannot be satisfactorily dealt with by any of the individual Governments. I regard this occasion with great interest, because it will inevitably lead to a more permanent federal understanding". Parkes was to shortly sponsor the Bill to establish a Federal Council. The Queen refused to give Royal assent to the ensuing Act, and Parkes retired temporarily until a better time.

Parkes had become the voice of Federalism in New South Wales.

Parkes resubmitted the Bill in 1880-81, and added a codicil which stated

"1. That the time has come for the construction of a Federal Constitution, with an Australian Federal Parliament.
2. That it is time for matters of common concern to the Colonies, be dealt with by some Federal Authority
3. Than an organisation be formed in support of a Federal Movement to accustom the Public mind to federal ideas"

The March towards Federation.

1893—The Corowa Conference

After a slow start and many false steps the Federation movement, although much talked about since 1857, did not finally move in the right direction at any pace until the Corowa Conference in 1893. Sponsored by the AFL, and the ANU, 43 delegates of the AFL and 31 others (by invitation) met in Corowa on the NSW side of the Murray River, west of Albury—the 'Crossing Place'. The Murray towns were all actively and personally interested in Federation because of the high tariffs attached to all purchase made by them from their nearest 'big City' eg Melbourne

(Victoria). Edmond Barton was well aware of the general feeling to the Federal movement in these port towns, and in December 1892, while the Attorney—General of NSW was frustrated by his endeavours to pilot the Commonwealth Bill unsuccessfully through the NSW Parliament, turned to the public arena and during a visit to Albury, Howlong, Rutherglen and Corowa, prompted the formation of country branches of the Australian Federation League (the first to be established outside Sydney). In 1893, a central body called AFL had been founded in Sydney. Barton's pitch to these country people on both sides of the Murray was that the League would be strictly non-political and 'would be of great assistance to the Federation movement'. In June 1893, the Berrigan branch of the AFL decided to organise a Conference of AFL delegates to assemble their views and wishes on the Federation movement and decided to hold the meeting in the central location of Corowa. Barton (as Attorney—General) gave permission for the Corowa Court-house to be used for the assembly, without cost to the AFL. The Conference took place on Monday, the 31st of July and Tuesday the 1st August, 1893.

Although Barton's visit had promoted over 15 new branches (between January and May 1893) in the Murray Valley area, and these became active in the push for Federation, the main thrust continued to come from the ANA—the Australian Native's Association. Robert Garran was one of the AFL's 43 delegates and represented the Sydney branch of the AFL at this Corowa Conference; a further 31 delegates represented other associations and interests.

The main collated reference source for the background to the March towards Federation is to be found in the Quick & Garran text—'The *Annotated Constitution of the Australian Commonwealth*' dedicated in 1900 and printed in 1901.

It is obvious from the writing that the authors were close to the scene, and their chapter on 'The Federal Movement in Australia' is detailed and thorough and reflects a close association and understanding of the subject, but nowhere in the text do they disclose their involvement. A newspaper report of the Corowa Conference held in Corowa (on the Murray River—border between Victoria and NSW) reports the submissions of both Dr. Quick & Robert Garran to the Conference.

As reported in the Melbourne Argus of Thursday August 3, 1893 (annexed to this Paper), Mr Robert Garran, of Sydney, moved—" That in the opinion of the conference the best interests and the present and future prosperity of the Australian Colonies would be promoted by their early union under the Crown, and that such colonies have now increased in population, wealth, the discovery of resources and in self-governing capacity to an extent which justifies their union under one legislature and executive Government on principles just to the several colonies".

At the same Corowa Conference, "Dr. Quick (Bendigo) proposed a lengthy resolution, defining the objects and aims of the league to be to advance the cause of Federation by an organisation of citizens owning no class distinction or party purposes, which should cooperate with kindred organisations and unite them into one body, with one plan for operations, and pledging members at the next elections in Victoria and NSW" At the end of the *Argus* report, it states ' on the suggestion of Dr. Quick, the resolution was struck out in order not to offend NSW.'

This researcher's point is that the close involvement of Quick & Garran, colours and flavours their observations in their text, and may not give the full and objective story of the events unfolding before us, on the March to Federation. This is surely a questionable approach, since as occurs many times, the experienced and interested participants in many events make them the events best and most appropriate recorder for posterity, as no doubt happened with this event. The author's point here is that a personal disclosure of the close association would have left the reader better informed, and better able to place a reasonable interpretation on the recordings.

For instance, there is no recording in the text that the key NSW player, Sir George Gibbs, was not at the Corowa Conference. Another text 'A *Note on the Corowa Conference of 1893* (Royal Australian Historical Society—*1963)* reports Gibbs had not been invited to the Conference. However, the Melbourne Argus Newspaper of August 4, 1893 contains a Letter from the Berrigan (NSW) Branch of the Australian Federation Movement (Mr Ernest Lapthorne) denying the earlier newspaper report of July 29 containing the report that Gibbs had not been invited, and stating he had in fact been invited on two occasions, and had quoted a previous engagement, which just happened to be the opening of a new school building in northern NSW. This snub by Gibbs (now described as being opposed to Federation) of the Conference was compared with the attendance on relatively short notice of the Premiers of Tasmania, South Australia and Victoria and was to be indicative of Gibb's reluctance to embrace the Federation movement and rather to become a strong and active supporter of unification—a not dissimilar appeal to a federation unifying of the 6 colonies). Gibb's Colonial Secretary , Henry Parkes, saw himself as the 'Father of Federation' and actively pursued the goals of federation by his writings, promoting motions in the Legislative Council of NSW and by attending every available Conference or committee and travelling widely.

It seems that being silent on such important revelations, Quick & Garran leave themselves open to the charge of prejudice in favour of their support of Federation,

Robert Garran joined Dr. John Quick of Bendigo as a leading player in the Federation stakes and became his co-author of 'The Annotated Constitution' in 1901, the individual author of 'The Coming Commonwealth (1897), and of 'Prosper the Commonwealth' in 1958.

The author of the Royal Historical Society Paper referred to above 'The Corowa Conference (1963), a Mr L.E. Freedman is also the editor and annotator of the Sir John Quick's 'Notebook'.

History records that one of the most significant events in the Federation Movement came in 1893 at the Corowa Conference. Dr. Quick, representing the AFL from Bendigo attended the Conference as a delegate and was elected as a Vice-President of the Conference. As referred to above, Robert Garran moved the first important motion on the scene being ripe for a Federation movement and the resulting unity of the colonies. Dr Quick then , on the next day, moved the quintessential motivational motion, by suggesting to the Conference that the gathering advocate Enabling Acts in each Colony, and promote a meeting shortly of the Premiers at which a draft Bill setting out the necessary steps could be discussed and accepted. The Conference gave this resolution unanimous support, and Dr. Quick, after reading the Argus's article about 'who will prepare the draft outline of a common bill?' sat down and wrote the draft of the bill which was discussed at the Premier's Conference in Hobart in January, 1895. George Reid (NSW), Edmond Barton's successor as Premier sponsored the meeting and pushed for the acceptance of the Quick—drafted—Bill's principles. From this point, the Federation movement progressed much more smoothly, and John Quick can take much credit for the success of the movement from this point. The Quick Bill gave the insight of the first step of electing convention delegates and all the way to the last steps of having a national referendum. Based on press reports of the day, the Quick proposal struck the popular imagination. The electors were able to choose their representatives to frame a federal constitution **and** they were to be involved through the referendum in accepting or rejecting the constitution.

A final word, possibly, on Quick by Garran. In 'Prosper the Commonwealth (P138), Garran writes " Quick, in his early teens, was without prospects or influence, and as a boy he was employed as a puddler at one of the Bendigo gold mines. He made up his mind to rise in the world. He was a young man of tremendous energy and industry. He taught himself shorthand and qualified as a reporter at a local paper. He read and studied assiduously, gained employment at the Melbourne *Age,* and in his spare time picked up degrees of Bachelor of Arts, Bachelor of Laws and finally a Doctorate of Laws at the University of Melbourne . . . .

I had a great esteem for the man personally and for his ability, and we were always on first-rate terms as collaborators, and the only fault I had to find with him was his excessive thoroughness.

In all events, *the Annotated Constitution* did cover the subject, and became the standard work on the Constitution. For many years it was indispensable to the practicing constitutional lawyer. But one result of its size (983 pages) was that I always shied off from the idea of a second edition to bring it up to date."

Back in NSW, George Reid's primary policy was the repeal of the Barton's tariff system of semi-protection. Instead he wanted to introduce his re-orientation of the NSW Colony's fiscal—a policy intended **not** to increase the traditional government's fiscal dependence on high tariffs but to move to higher indirect taxes and introduce a direct taxation system (for the first time in Australia). The Reid declared concept of direct taxes was land and income taxes. This policy became viable after the Corowa Conference in August 1893 which had, by motion, supported the concept of the 'free interchange of colonial products.

Another political viewpoint, expressed at the Corowa Conference and gaining favour amongst the delegates was put by Mr A. J. Peacock MLA (Mildura), who stated that the fundamental move to Federation is to be set in the context that ' there is now a population of 4 million in these Colonies, and an import-export trade of over 106 million pounds sterling. There is owing to the Mother-country the sum of 159 million pounds for which we pay over 5,250,000 pound interest per annum. If Australia was federated, she would be in a far better position financially.

The Parliamentarian was obviously over stretching the point, in order to make a point. He (Peacock) was trying to suggest that the Colony owed a debt of gratitude to Britain after 100 years of sponsoring a strong, healthy economy and a healthy population of about 3 and a half-million instead of the 4 million suggested. The debt 'to the Mother country' was in the form of loans made from British Institutions to the Australian Colonies. The City of London had priced these loans well, had given the Colonies a good credit rating and earned for its investors an attractive interest—an average of 3.5%. Mr Peacock overstated, by implication, the role of Britain. He made it sound as if Britain had invested in or granted to the Colonies this sum, but it was a repayable loan, and repaid it was.

A penal Colony had gradually changed into a free, powerful and independent settlement—a substantial economic persona, full of vigorous growth and life, well founded and constantly seeking fresh opportunities.

The rest of the world watched change take place over centuries whilst Australia abbreviated all those same changes into less than 100 years, and during that time witnessed growth in monetary, population and self reliant terms such that change in Australia was compressed into a shorter period but driven by the need to catch the rest of the world and make a mark.

However, this combination of Agrarian and Industrial reform came at a price. By the end of the first 100 years, Australia's overseas debt stood at less than One hundred million pounds; while its population was little more than 5 million in a territory the size of America, which was carrying a population of over 100 million. Even if the national colonial debt had increased due to railway construction and posts and telegraphs—by 1880 there were over 2000 miles of track laid in the Colony. But more surprising still was the fact that the Colony of New South Wales operated with a budgetary surplus, such that in 1882 the state surplus was four million pounds. So sound fiscal policies were underpinning the economic growth of the Colony. The contribution of the discovery of gold was multi-fold. It increased the population substantially; it developed the cities in regional areas eg Ballarat, Bendigo and Broken Hill, but gave an enormous boost to the major city of Melbourne, which for the first time surpassed the population of Sydney. Gold became a bigger export earner than wool for many years, and underpinned the ability for the Australian Colonies to borrow large amounts overseas to complete the development of rail and telegraph services. Britain welcomed the strong economy in the great south land and provided substantial loan funds.

Just where could Federation be heading? W.G. McMinn in his learned work 'A Constitutional History of Australia' writes (Introduction P 9)

"Australian government, federal and State, is 'Westminster government'. It is based, in its essentials, on the system of government which had developed over a period of a thousand years in England, and by the time the first European settlement was made in this country, had come to be understood as 'King, Lords and Commons'—a system under which a bicameral parliament, meeting in Westminster, made the laws while the King's ministers controlled the day-to-day administration of those laws and an independent judiciary enforced them. This Westminster system continued to evolve in Australia from 1788".

It is little wonder that the ordinary people in the street were not getting too excited about the prospect of Federation. Few understood it. The model was hazy. People thought in terms of 'more of the same'. Each colony presently had two elected houses, although two states had a nominated Upper House until 1900. Each colony had one man one vote except for

Victoria where plurality remained until Federation. The Federalists were asking for unity between the States, a strengthening of those important inter-colonial items, and additional Federal powers to be transferred from Britain. The elimination of inter—colonial tariffs had been forecast with or without the Federation. The States were to have continuing constitutional self-government whilst the Federal Constitution would have specific powers and responsibility for matters such as defence, lighthouses, postal services, customs and communications. These were expensive items to establish and maintain, and the Federal sphere would have to determine revenue raising method and base, keeping in mind that international duties and tariffs were a good revenue source for the colonies. It was Barton who thought it should be a populist federation movement and took the matter to the southern areas and established outlying branches of the Australian Federation League, which led to the Corowa Conference, shortly thereafter. Garran claims 'Prosper the Commonwealth' (P101 that Barton addressed over three hundred meetings in NSW in the four years before 1893.

We will review many of these items and see the practical thinking on Federal revenues.

Sir Robert Garran in 'Prosper the Commonwealth' (1987) on Page 113 gave a vivid outline of the Deakin eloquence.

"The brilliant eloquence of Alfred Deakin more than once surprised and charmed those who were strangers to it. His facility and felicity of expression, especially when speaking on the great political principles that were dear to his heart, made a deep impression. I wish I could have heard that triumphant speech of his at an A.N.A. meeting in Ballarat, after the convention was over, when the acceptance of the Constitution by Victorian Ministers and by the Melbourne *Age* was in the balance, and when in an inspired hour, soaring from peroration to peroration, he roused the delighted audience to tumultuous applause that rocked the building and placed Victoria's acceptance beyond the shadow of a doubt." History does not record exactly what Deakin said but what it must have been like to be in the audience on such an occasion! He must have sounded the call to arms in favour of supporting Federation, and listed the many benefits that would flow. He obviously preferred Federation to unification by any other means, and threw his whole being behind it.

Key Steps in the Path to Federation:

- 1855 NSW constitution bill
- Federal Council
- Corowa Conference
- British Colonial Act
- Premiers Conference (Hobart)
- The Convention of 1897
- The Referendum of June 3, 1898

Key Players

- Barton
- Deakin
- Parkes
- Quick

Some musings and observations from Robert Garran's Prosper the Commonwealth:

There is an alternative to a formal written constitution, which is found in the United Kingdom—consisting of Acts of Parliament which together with customs and traditions having behind them nothing but use and wont and the weight of public opinion. For instance Magna Carta, often described as the charter of English liberty, is nothing but an act of parliament which can be repealed the same as a Dog Act. In fact the greater part of it, being quite out of date, has been quietly repealed by Statute Law revision Acts, without any fuss at all, leaving only a few fundamental declarations of right. The machinery of responsible government mostly consists of tradition with no statutory backing—the rules which govern the formation and resignation of ministries, the dissolution of parliament, are purely traditional. And the A House of Lords sitting as the highest Court of Appeal is really nothing but a sitting of the House, at which it is understood that no noble lord who has not held high judicial office will take part. But the rigidity of a written constitution can, in practice, never be absolute. The constitution must be able to develop to meet the changing needs of the community; otherwise it will cramp the growth of the community until breaking point is reached.

There are many illustrations of the difficulty of defining the distribution of power. There is a general principle on which the method of definition in the Australian Constitution works. The method is the same as that in the United States: to specify particular matters of federal power and leave the whole unspecified and undivided residue to the States. Thus the Commonwealth Parliament is given power to make laws with respect to defence, duties of customs and excise, bankruptcy, immigration, and so forth. As to any matter not falling within any of the specified matters, the States have, in most cases, what is called concurrent power to make laws, subject to any such law being displaced by a federal law inconsistent with it, whenever the federal Parliament chooses to legislate on the subject.

The history of Section 92 is very simple." The lion in the path" of federation had long been the unwillingness of New South Wales and Victoria to entrust to a federal Parliament the vital question of free trade or protection. This feeling was strong in New South Wales, and especially strong in the city of Sydney; but in the late 1880s it began to be seen, first that there was no certainty that an unfederated New South Wales would be able to keep its free-trade policy, and second that whatever risks federation might bring to the free trade of Australia with the outside world, it could be made certain in the Constitution that, from one of the Commonwealth to the other, there should be complete absence of trade barriers among the States.

People who write constitutions often go to great pains in inserting a Bill of Rights. I sometimes think it is a pity that they do not add an equally precise chapter on the opposite page—a Bill of Obligations. In the whole history of democracy there is much more discussion of rights than of obligations, and perhaps this is one of the reasons why we all of us think and talk more of our rights than of the obligations which are a necessary counterpart.

Heading for Disaster

Three sections of the economy faced a boom condition in the 1880s. Building houses, building railways and development of the pastoral industry. Growth of the economy was very rapid but related principally to long-term considerations rather than immediate profitability. Thus there were social gains from new rail links but initial economic losses. This problem was accentuated by certain Victorian politicians influencing the location of rail lines in order to raising the value of their land.

Similarly in the pastoral industry, the price of wool declined but pastoralists invested heavily in flock improvement and greater carrying capacity by increasing flocks numbers as well as investing heavily in fencing, water points and other improvements. A lot of this development took place in western NSW and central Queensland where overstocking and rabbits soon became serious problems. Heavy mortgages on these pastoral properties meant high debt service and many owners were unable to meet their mortgage commitments. The building boom was initially based on the real need for housing but the speculators came into the picture and their optimism took the boom to new heights. So in NSW between 1881 and 1890 the population rose by 50% but the number of houses rose by 68% In Victoria the gap was even worse.

In 1891 several Colonial Governments were unsuccessful in raising loans in the London money market. The major finance house Baring brothers failed in 1891 following investment failures in the Argentine, rather than Australia. It would not be for another 100 houses that the reborn Baring's Bank would fail again. This failure to raise fresh funds in London meant a major curtailing of public works in Australia., which in turn affected the building industry, and led to many collapses. From that point there was a general slide into depression.

In 1843 a new insolvency law had made it easier for insolvents to settle their affairs with their creditors, and exempted them from the immediate prospect of imprisonment except for fraud. By the end of December 1842 600 people had been confirmed as bankrupts by the Supreme Court and few ever repaid much money to their creditors. Men who had begun wholesale and retail businesses with little or no capital became unemployed, and often also unemployable. This table shows the

PRINCIPAL OCCUPATIONS OF THE INSOLVENTS-1842:

Settlers, farmers & graziers	78
Clerks and shopmen	44
Publicans , brewers	42
Gentlemen & Yeomen	31
Merchants	29
General Dealers	27
Mariners etc	17
Storekeepers	16
Butchers	16

Manning Clark points out—Vol 2 Select Documents in Australian History 1851-1900 (P295)that:

'It would be difficult to exaggerate the importance of the financial depression of 1890—93. The record of events which bear its scar or imprint is very impressive:-

i. The contribution of federation (the depression spread Australia wide, and encouraged the unification of the Colonies into a Federation—the interstate duties were an uneven imposition on border settlements eg Corowa NSW, whose main market and business centre was Melbourne)
ii. The aggravation of material distress which bad seasons and strikes had begun
iii. The contribution of the origins of a political labour movement
iv. The undermining of 'Victorian' optimism, and renewed faith in a capitalistic society

Clark points out as well that the material generally relevant to this event is 'flat', and an event with such results deserves the most diligent attention of the searcher for documents.

Clark writes that:

"Other than the wealth of the material on the event, the acrimonious discussion of causes, the plans for reconstruction, and the caustic comments of the self-appointed guardians of public morals, there is minimal material".

Clark records an article on the Australian Financial Crisis from the Victorian Year Book of 1893, and a speech by the then Victorian Premier printed in the Australasian Insurance and Banking Record, 1893 devoted to the Reconstruction of the Commercial Bank of Australia Ltd. This latter article records the detailed analysis of the causes of this depression.

"The affairs of the Bank have been temporally suspended in lieu of being forced to shut its doors, as a result of the events of the last few years. All monetary institutions in the Colony have more or less been affected. There is not a man or woman in the Colony who did not go in head over heels to make a fortune during the land boom in some shape or form and it was hardly possible that the reaction from such a condition of things could result in other than what must be described as a 'bust' ".

Failures (Australian Illustrated History) were spread widely from land companies and building societies—22 such failures in Sydney involving deposits of over 3.6 million pound. The Victorian law allowed for a 'composition by arrangement' with their creditors, offering a way for debtors to be discharged from insolvency without a public investigation of their affairs.

Most of the causes of trouble lay within the Australian economy except for two external factors—the precipitous drop in wool, wheat and silver prices. The biggest damage was to the pastures as a result of overstocking and holding sheep from the market. prices. Thousands of rural workers came to the Cities looking for work but the Government gave them a free ticket back because the city unemployment level was already too high. The second external cause was the cessation of the export of capital from Britain, because of doubts about the Australian economy and the fall out from the British Depression of 1890. The depression caused a world wide decline including the United States, and not for the first time was Australia involved in the World economic fall-out—as she was by dependence on exports and continued inflow of capital. The failure of banks started in January 1893 with the Federal Bank but out of the 28 banks in business only 9 kept their doors open during the depression. Thus in this year the failure of banks was a result of the depression rather than the cause of it. Some reopened their doors after a reconstruction.

Manning Clark (Select Documents in Australian History)records an article on the Australian Financial Crisis from the Victorian Year Book of 1893, and a speech by the then Victorian Premier printed in the Australasian Insurance and Banking Record, 1893 devoted to the Reconstruction of the Commercial Bank of Australia Ltd. This latter article records the detailed analysis of the causes of this depression.

"The affairs of the Bank have been temporally suspended in lieu of being forced to shut its doors, as a result of the events of the last few years. All monetary institutions in the Colony have more or less been affected. There is not a man or woman in the Colony who did not go in head over heels to make a fortune during the land boom in some shape or form and it was hardly possible that the reaction from such a condition of things could result in other than what must be described as a 'bust' ".

The depression saw the price of land and stock drop to zero. A great many business failures followed, the most important being the Commercial Bank of Australia Ltd, whose shareholder liability was unlimited, and as a result, many influential people sought bankruptcy protection.

By 1895 when recovery should have been under-way, a protracted drought kept recovery stagnant., but one good thing finally emerged from the debacle. Victoria and NSW both passed the Old Age Pensions Acts.

1891 National Australasian Convention

1891 Commonwealth Bill referred to Colonial Parliaments but delayed

1892 Barton tours Riverina area

1893 Federation Conference in Corowa

Quick drafts Australian Federal Congress Bill, as a model

1895—6 Australian Premiers meet in Hobart

The six Premiers who met in Hobart were a mixed lot. George Turner from Victoria; Sir Hugh Nelson from Queensland; George Reid from NSW; Sir John

Forrest from WA, and Sir Edward Braddon from Tasmania.

1897 Election of delegates in NSW, Victoria, SA and Tasmania to the Convention

1897 Federation Convention of 1897

1898 Constitution Bill approved by the Convention

1898 Referendum in NSW, Victoria, Tasmania and SA

Two principle anti—Billites included H.H. Higgins (later Mr Justice Higgins of Commonwealth Arbitration Commission fame) and the NSW Labor Party. But the Referendum (after a second try in NSW) was passed in all Colonies.

The post-referendum election in NSW proved to be one of the most remarkable in Australian History. The normal issues of free trade versus protection, and capital versus labour were forced into the background and Federation became the policy debate of choice. There were the free-traders led by George Reid the then Premier) who were in fact integrationists rather than Federalists; but on the other side was the new Liberal Federal Party and the National Federal Party. Reid managed to only just defeat Edmond Barton. At a following Premier's meeting, deliberations of 5 days led to 6 new amendments, one of which related to the location of a national capital. Intense lobbying from NSW gained its location in NSW but not closer than 100 miles to Sydney.

Another amendment related to financial matters between the Common-wealth and the States. 'Not more than a quarter of the net revenue raised by the Commonwealth from custom and excise duties should be used as annual expenditure by the Commonwealth. The balance was to be spread between the various Colonies'. The round of second referendums all passed and the Bill was ready for passage through the

British Parliament. The initial reluctance of WA to join the movement was based on economics. The colony was sparse, separated from the eastern colonies by a vast desert so that all travel was by sea and the Colony was completely dependent on Customs revenues which federation would remove. The threat of the WA goldfields to Federate separately led to the referendum being approved handsomely. Now with all Colonies in agreement, Barton's prophetic phrase 'a nation for a continent, and a continent for a nation' would finally become a truism.

The Financial Clauses

It is the intention behind this Paper, having set the scene for Federation and examined some of the hurdles along the way to the successful conclusion, to examine in detail the financial considerations behind the reluctance of the 'lesser' Colonies to join the Federation Bandwagon. These financial discussions were fully inclusive of the concurrent mainstream political discussions, and finally led to Section 96 (Finance and Trade), Clause 406 of the Constitution—"Grant Financial Assistance to any State"

The Convention of 1891

The first question which gave the Committee much trouble was that of the basis for apportionment of surplus revenue among the States. It was recognised that the customs revenue must be collected by the Commonwealth which was not, at the outset, to be saddled with the public debts of the States. However it was soon seen that only a fraction of the revenue would be needed for federal expenditure, whilst the States would require much of it to meet their own expenditure.

The Convention Debates—Adelaide Session—1897

It was generally agreed that the customs revenue of the colonies, in all cases, forms a very large share of the means of meeting the expenses of government; and as the Commonwealth would take over only a small part of the expenditure, the Commonwealth would start with an enormous annual surplus of many millions which it could not retain or expend, but must return to the different states. (Convention Debates 1891., Sydney., P528).

The next question was—should the revenue be credited to the several states in proportion to their populations or in proportion to their contributions? Should expenditures be charged on a population basis or on the basis of services rendered? So far as revenue was concerned, the population basis of adjustment seemed the most Federal but not the most fair. The contribution basis seemed less federal but more fair, and it was questionable as to whether the amount of dutiable goods coming into each State could be properly accounted for. It would be an accounting nightmare.

This was the basis of financial difficulty which was going to cause so much trouble. There was no consensus on these questions in the opening round of debates so the compromise was reached that the question would be left for the first Federal Parliament to deal with, and it would be based on the experience of the actual working of the federal tariff.

The next question was on what form of a 'guarantee' from the Commonwealth that this surplus would not be wasted but would be applied to the necessary purposes of the State Governments. Any such 'guarantee' would be based on one of two principles—either an obligation on the Commonwealth to return some part of its revenue to the states, or an obligation for the Commonwealth to take over some of the liabilities of the states. One proposal was that the Commonwealth could take over the public debt of the states with any amount over a set per head limit to remain with that state. The unspoken opposition to this idea was that 'to saddle the Commonwealth with the interest on the public debts would mean imposing on the Federal Parliament the duty of raising a large amount through Customs duty and thus place the free-trade party at a disadvantage'.

1897

During the Adelaide session of the debates in 1897, the financial clauses were considerably altered. The first step planned, was to enforce uniform duties within the first two years. The distribution base was then to be altered from that of existing duties (ie actually collected—and distributed—during the first two years) to the next five years which would be based on uniform duties and then after that five year period. Each period had its own basis of calculating the amounts returned to the states. This system differed to that proposed in 1891. In 1891 surplus was to be returned in proportion to population. In 1897 the return was to be based on set sums, rather than at the option of the Commonwealth.

The guarantee from the Commonwealth to the States was also varied to now became an aggregate for all states rather than for each state individually. (Convention Debates., Adelaide P1053-56)

Before the Adelaide Session concluded the debates saw a further change with the proposal coming from Sir Edward Braddon that " the Commonwealth should return to the States a fixed percentage of say 70%, of the customs revenue collected."(Convention Debates P1197-98).

The only other important financial discussion was in relation to the taking over the public debts of the states. The clause submitted was that the Commonwealth, with the consent of the State, would take on whole or a part of the public debt of the state. This was not acceptable to either New South Wales or Victoria because (1) it would amount to a permanent endowment of the States and would dictate a high tariff policy; and (2) that it would make a present of the federal credit to the bond-holders, and prevent the Federal Treasurer being able to bargain for a profitable conversion before maturity.

The clause that finally passed did not compel the taking over of the debts but empowered the federal Parliament, at its own discretion, to take over the debts of all the States as existing at the establishment of the Commonwealth, or a rateable proportion thereof.

Consideration by the Legislatures—NSW

The financial clauses drew much discussion in the Legislative Assembly of New South Wales when debate began in May 1898. The general argument was that Federation under the Bill would add many burdens but no savings; that to meet the new expenditure and the remission of inter-colonial duties there would have to be a great increase of duties on overseas imports; that in Victoria, SA and Tasmania there was virtually no reserve power of taxation, and consequently NSW would have to pay the

whole cost of Federation, as well as adopt a fiscal policy of which NSW
disapproved, submit to additional taxation of 1.5 million pound, of which
she would be lucky to receive 1.0 million in return. This argument was
largely based on an analysis showing the imports of the various colonies
under their existing and widely-differing tariffs, and deduced the amounts
of revenues that would be contributed by each colony, assuming the
imports remained the same. This model was hopelessly floored especially
in the assumption imports would remain the same. Each state's fiscal
policy would be different and trimmed to meet the on-going needs of
the population. It had already been accepted by the Convention that
the larger states would be contributing more than they drew from the
commonwealth, and the 'lesser' states' would be the beneficiaries. But
that was one of the 'costs' of Federation, and the biggest benefit of all,
that Australia would be one nation, with some degree of equality between
peoples in every state. Even today, some 100 years after Federation and the
argument supposedly settled the Labor Party in NSW raises the question
that that state is subsidising the states of Tasmania and Western Australia.
Some things never change!

The upshot of the debate in NSW was that the Bill was essentially left
blank by the omission of the Financial clauses, the removal of the senate,
the removal of the deadlock clause, and the requirement that the Federal
Capital be in Sydney. Mr Barton left the Chamber in disgust! There were
many unanswered questions still—the rivers, railways, as well as tariffs.
The NSW Legislature had not grasped the nettle as the Convention
delegates had. The debate in the other colonies was much more moderate
and productive.

The next session of the Convention met in Sydney in September 1897 to
consider the draft constitution along with the many amendments arising
from the Legislative debates.

The Convention Debates—Sydney Session—1898

The Finance Committee brought up their report and it contained
a complete reconstruction of the financial scheme of the Bill. They
recommended that the Adelaide 'guarantees' of a limited expenditure
and a minimum aggregate return of surplus eg the 70% be omitted. The

new clause was to provide against the loss of revenue which it feared might result during the first year of the tariff if merchants 'loaded up' dutiable goods in NSW in anticipation of the tariff. The new clause provided that such goods, on transportation into another state within a certain time after a uniform tariff , should pay the difference between the duty chargeable on importation under the uniform tariff and the duty already paid. The committee also preferred a return to the earlier concept of bookkeeping and accounting for all goods received into each state so the surplus could be returned based on actual consumption and therefore contribution rather than population or a fixed percentage. This recommendation was a return to the 1891 plan. The special needs of WA were to be met by a clause underwriting any deficiency or reduction of revenues by the Commonwealth. (Con Deb P774-895). The proposals were to be cautiously accepted as the best of poor choices. The Adelaide 'guarantees' had been struck out without any consensual alternative being found, except, by way of limited compromise, the words" During a period of ten years, and thereafter until the Parliament otherwise provides " were inserted

The Constitution as Passed

Clause 87. During a period of ten years after the establishment of the Commonwealth and thereafter until the Parliament otherwise provides, of the net revenue of the Commonwealth from duties of customs and of excise not more than one-fourth shall be applied annually by the Commonwealth towards its expenditure.

The balance shall, in accordance with this Constitution, be paid to the several States, or applied towards the payment of interest on debts of the several States taken over by the Commonwealth.

Notes to Clause 87:

The words 'during a period of ten years . . . . until the Parliament otherwise provides' are a constitutional provision, which only a referendum can change. This was the protection or 'guarantee' for the states. At the expiration of that time, the words would revert to the level of an Act of the Federal Parliament, **ie** by provision of 'until the Parliament otherwise provides'. Should it be desired to increase the proportion of customs and excise revenues paid to the States, the section would not stand in the way. However there would be a barrier if the Commonwealth wanted to increase the proportion which may be spent by the Commonwealth.

The words " of the net revenue" refers to the total receipts from the sources of customs and excise less the costs of collection. No attempt was made in the Constitution to define what could be construed as 'collection' costs. The Parliament under Section 51 would have power to regulate the book-keeping arrangements. It was considered that even the judiciary (in the event of a challenge) would have no power to interfere. This 'guarantee' that three-quarters of the revenue collected would be returned to the States follows transfer of these duties to the Commonwealth. The effect on Commonwealth finances was that for every 1 pound the Federal Treasurer required, he would have to raise 4 pounds. The brilliance, if that is the right word, of this clause is that it ignores the financial requirements of the states, whilst imposing on the Commonwealth this 4:1 requirement.. The net customs and excise revenue raised in the six federating colonies for 1899 was 7,402,333 pound (Coglan's Statistics of the Colonies—1900—P.23). It must be assumed that the federal tariff would be framed to not bring in less than this amount of revenue, and so the Commonwealth would keep 25% or 1.8 million pound—more than sufficient to meet its needs , according to the Convention. Obviously the federal tariff was going to be framed to meet the wants of the Australian people, and thus the interests of each state will be considered; the different financial requirements of six states cannot be met solely by uniform taxation; and it can hardly be doubted that one result of federation will be that provisional taxation will be increasingly resorted to for provincial purposes.

The words " not more than 25% . . . ." mean that the Commonwealth can spend in total, its costs of collection plus one-quarter of the net revenue collected.

The words " the balance shall be paid to the several states" allows the Commonwealth, on the basis of Sections 89 and 93 to distribute the remaining 75%, or to meet the interest on the debts of the states under Section 105. This latter section only refers to interest on debts which the

Commonwealth may take over from the states, but in any event will be construed as part of any payment to a state.

Clause 88: Uniform duties of customs shall be imposed within two years after the establishment of the Commonwealth.

Clause 89: Until the imposition of uniform duties of customs—

I. *The Commonwealth shall credit to each state the revenues collected therein by the Commonwealth.*
II. *The commonwealth shall debit to each State-*

    a. *The expenditure therein of the Commonwealth incurred solely for the maintenance or continuance, as at the time of transfer of any department transferred from the State to the Commonwealth;*
    b. *The proportion of the State, according to the number of its people, in the other expenditure of the Commonwealth*

III. *The Commonwealth shall pay to each State month by month the balance (if any) in favour of the State*

Clause 93: During the first five years after the imposition of uniform duties of customs, and thereafter until the Parliament otherwise provides—

I. *The duties of customs chargeable on goods imported into a State and afterwards passing into another State for consumption, and the duties of excise paid on goods produced or manufactured in a State and afterwards passing onto another State for consumption, shall be taken to have been collected not in the former but in the latter State:*
II. *Subject to the last sub-section, the Commonwealth shall credit revenue, debit expenditure, and pay balances to the several states as prescribed for the period preceding thew imposition of uniform duties of customs.*

Clause 94: After five years from the imposition of uniform duties of customs the Parliament may provide on such basis as it deems fair, for the monthly payment to the several States of all surplus revenue of the Commonwealth.

Clause 96: During a period of ten years after the establishment of the Commonwealth and thereafter until the Parliament otherwise provides, the Parliament may grant financial assistance to any State, on such terms and conditions as the Parliament thinks fit.

Conclusion:

a. Many conclusions can be drawn from this exercise, but the first conclusion must be that the exercise of trying to understand the financial concerns of the Colonies leading up to Federation was a worthwhile one. The message must therefore be, that as important as the political considerations were of unification, that the financial aspects of unity may have brought unification asunder unless they were handled with care, understanding and compromise. The result, as can be seen from the clauses listed above, were sensible, appropriate and meaningful. Their understanding in the context of the Constitutional construction is also worthwhile. Each clause in the Finance & Trade section of the Constitution was carefully considered by the Finance Committee of the Conventions in 1891 and 1897/8, and equal consideration given to the 'lesser' states as well as the 'larger' states. Balance was given to the free-traders as well as the protectionists, but most consideration was given to meeting the continuing needs of the states. The interim debates in the legislatures allowed members ,other than the delegates to the Convention, to consider their position and express reservations or support for each clause. Subsequent amendments were taken to the next Convention for reconsideration by the delegates. It was all very fair, equal and observant of even handedness between the States.

b. The states were being asked to release their key revenue base in exchange for the advantages of unification, and the ultimate the national advantages of a uniform tariff. This was achieved and compromise allowed the States to be assured their revue base would not unreasonably crumble. There had to be, and was, great consensus and consideration for the smaller states, essentially by the provision that their debts could be transferred to the Commonwealth and the debt service met first from their share of the customs revenues, which were undertaken not to be less than in 1899, the year proceeding federation. The fail safe provision became Section 96, which allowed special consideration by the Commonwealth of any state falling behind. This clause became to basis of establishing the future Commonwealth Grants Commission, which it would be of interest to review briefly.

c. The Colonies' collective financial goals had been met during the Conventions, and from those early days leading up to self-government in the 1850s, the every nature of fiscal policy and management was to change. From the demands of the legislatures to transfer back to Colonial discretion the revenues from Crown land and minerals in exchange for a full obligation to meet every Colonial expense including salaries of British appointments, the Colony of NSW, the first and still the biggest Colony, was to grow and prosper under its own financial management rather than the split responsibility of sharing with the British Treasury. The fall back was removed to make sure the Colony stood on its own feet, and paid its own way. The ground was a little shaky because the Colony had grown quite dependant on world trade and world commodity prices, and the big bust of 1893 reminded the Colonial Treasurers of that fact very clearly. But the Colony survived and grew, and so led the way in the financial committee deliberations of the National Federation Debate. It knew its role and the leadership by Barton, Parkes, Reid and even Pulsford reminded the other Colonies of the experience gained in New South Wales. Pulsford, it turns out, was a relation of the writer's Mother and represented New South Wales in the various Conventions, sat on the Finance Committee and made a significant contribution to the settlement of the discussions on Clause 89, relating to uniform tariffs, the Commonwealth guarantee, and the distribution of surplus revenue back to the States. He subsequently became a member of the first Senate. His role in the Federation movement was not fully known to or understood by the writer until researching the 5 volumes of Hansard records of the debates.

d. The conclusion that the States' interests were collectively met is clear, and that the final Constitution Bill achieve that fine and desirable balance between protecting the States fiscal base and the national good.

e. By the end of the National Federation Convention and the final draft of the Constitution Bill submitted to London to the British Parliament, the financial aspects of the unification were determined. There would be (within two years) a uniform tariff for goods coming into the country. There would be no duties on goods passing between the States; Western Australia would receive some special if not preferential treatment by way of retaining for up to five years differential rates of duty, place be underwritten as far as annual revenue was concerned, and have access to the special loans Council for interim funding, in the event of a shortfall circumstance. The States could have their public debts assumed by the Commonwealth and any interest thereon would be taken from the surplus revenue distribution back to the states. The surplus revenue distribution was to be based on the Commonwealth taking one-quarter of the net revenues and the collection costs of that revenue. The states were guaranteed the other three-quarters payable monthly.

f. In all a solid outcome for the people, the politicians, the Crown and ultimately the Constitution.

CHAPTER 4

HIGH COURT REVIEWS
OF FEDERALISM AND
FEDERAL-STATE RELATIONS

"I want to assure you that I do believe in a true Federal System. I believe in it for a number of reasons. The first one is that Constitutionally, they (the States) have a wide variety of powers; they are close to the people; and ought to be able to exercise those powers at least as well as us. Health, education, and transport, to mention just three. But there is one other factor, and I have lived in politics long enough to know that it can happen here. I don't believe in placing too much power in the hands of any one group for any great period of time".

William McMahon (Prime Minister) addressing the Liberal Party Federal Council on 31/5/71 on the subject of 'Federalism':

The High Court of Australia has always played a key role in determining the path of post-Federation relations between the Commonwealth and the States. From the Harvester case in 1917 to the Garnishee Case in 1932 to the Whitlam sponsored off-shore boundary Challenge in 1974 to the Keating Mabo & Aboriginal Land Rights, the High Court has provided the right of passage for the states in their challenge of key questions in internal relations. This essay traces the various judgements and the ground-breaking decisions of the High Court since Federation and how the states responded.

Federation created the various matters that would come up for challenge. The specific responsibilities of the Commonwealth must change from time to time along with progress and technology, especially since the key state revenue stream had been removed and handed to the Commonwealth along with all rights to direct taxation, so there would always be room for a challenge on revenue sharing, grants and loans; it was not until after the 1928 High Court challenge, by NSW and Victoria, that the Commonwealth Loans Council took front position in gathering the requests of the states for loans, reviewing them and then raising them centrally overseas. It was NSW and Jack Lang that thought they could (and were) doing better than the Commonwealth in seeking direct loans overseas, but he rebelled against the Niemyer report on the Australian economy in 1932 (Niemyer had been brought to Australia from the Bank of England Governors in London by James Scullin (Labor Prime Minister) and when Lang suggested he may default, on behalf of NSW, on interest to English Bond Holders it was then that Sir Phillip Game, the NSW Governor of that time, took advice and dismissed Lang and his government from office. So these were but a few of the grounds created by Federation that were possible grounds for future challenge by the states to the High Court against the Commonwealth.

All Prime Ministers and Treasurers from 1945 onwards made public declarations in support of 'federalism'. In one such, and to the Liberal Party Federal Council on the 31st May, 1971, McMahon stated " I want to assure you that I do believe in a true Federal spirit . . . . I don't believe in placing too much power in the hands of any one group for any great period of time".

We will follow McMahon and look at some of the Federal—state matters that he contended with, both as Federal Treasurer and Prime Minister, and we may be forgiven for thinking that his is the 'convenient' concept of federalism, and to be used only for declaring one's support at a convenient time and in front of the right audience. It is not a statement one would make as a 'co-operative' federalist. Before the Loan Council, McMahon's arguments were incompatible with the Financial Agreement between the Commonwealth and the States reached under the first amendment to the Commonwealth constitution (S105A) in 1928. The essence of federalism , contrary to the concept developed by S105A, is the complete independence of each government in its own sphere; S105A was also incompatible with the strict theory of responsible government. The first amendment gave exclusive control over all future loan raising, except for defence purposes, to the Loan Council (which is, in effect, a Premier's Conference attended by the Prime Minister). This revision to S105 of the Constitution is an amendment also to true state's rights and in this way responsible government is reduced to being 'co-operative federalism' through the influence of the Loan Council, (W. G. McMinn—A Constitutional History of Australia-1979 P175).

McMahon quickly embraced this new convenient concept whilst pretending to be a fervent states righter and a Liberal Party traditionalist. This new approach appeared to transfer to a quasi-government institution an important part of that financial control which a Westminster-type Parliament is supposed to exercise over the executive. It was a convenient concept and makes it easier for a Federal Leader to concede a pragmatic approach rather than confront the Henry Boltes and Robin Askins of State politics.

Practical federalism became apparent when the High Court in 1932 upheld (*in the Garnishee Case*) the right of the Commonwealth to seize the revenue of the State of New South Wales, after that Government threatened to default on interest payments which it was obliged to make under the Financial Agreement of 1927 (as ratified by S105A of the Commonwealth Constitution).

This idea of practical federalism as supported by McMahon, and his Treasurer predecessor, Harold Holt, has other examples. Whilst Treasurer, McMahon pushed hard for more tied grants under S96 of the Commonwealth Constitution. This section gave the Commonwealth power to make grants to individual states without limit and subject to any conditions. The Federal Roads Act was the start of a run of legislation imposing onerous and anti-state rights conditions on the States in exchange for commonwealth gratuities. Any State accepting funds under the Federal Roads Act had to match the funds being made available, accept full responsibility for supervision of the project and agree to locate the roads under Commonwealth direction. Similar legislation was proscribed providing money for the states to assist farmers in the purchase of rabbit-proof fencing. McMahon took this type of 'corrosion' to State powers to a high art form during his Treasury years and set the scene for full federal control of borrowing. So much for ' I do believe in a true federal system'.

The two smaller states (Western Australia and Tasmania) continued to be disadvantaged under Treasurer McMahon, whilst he gave demonstrable preferential treatment to New South Wales (Robin Askin—Liberal Coalition) and Victoria (Henry Bolte—Liberal Coalition). It was a negative reaction to this same disadvantage that led to Western Australia petitioning Westminster in 1933 for permission to withdraw from the Commonwealth.

Reaction from the Commonwealth to this endeavour by Western Australia came in the creation of the Commonwealth Grants Commission, a quasi-judicial body with power to investigate the financial problems of the three 'claimant States' and to recommend what special grants they needed. The main basis for claims to special assistance had been the contention (contained in the Constitution) that the smaller states were adversely affected by federal tariff policy and were therefore entitled to 'compensation'. But from its first report in 1934 the Commission, having found it impossible to assess the grants that were needed to 'compensate' the three States, adopted as the criterion their 'fiscal need'. McMahon saw nothing wrong in this 'cap-in-hand' ritual of the Premiers trooping to Canberra every year and returning home usually disappointed (except for the two most powerful states which held the most electors, the most federal electorates, and contributed the most revenues to the Commonwealth). A Premier who has to justify to a Commonwealth officer the need for some particular expenditure must have his tongue very tightly in his cheek when he describes his State as 'sovereign'. McMahon's position regularly earned him negative reactions from the States for his approach to Federalism that was 'convenient ' , 'pragmatic' , 'co-operative' and 'corrosive' of State powers.

The State of New South Wales always regretted participating in the Loan Council, because the State considered it has lost its independence. From the days of the Bavin Nationalist Government, there was concern expressed by each State Treasurer. Bavin's successor as Premier in 1932, J. T. Lang claimed (in 'The Great Bust—The Depression of the Thirties'—P262) that "the Bavin Government had 'tied up' this state in matters of Federal Finance.

"We had become (Lang claimed)involved in such questions as tariffs and trade balances. Previously we had raised money on the basis that it would be invested in works that would be productive—would return their capital and interest. The Harbour Bridge and the city railways were already more than paying their interest in direct return through savings effected on both (investments). Every penny of money invested in NSW could return the interest on borrowed money. My Policy (wrote Lang) was to get rid of the shackles of the Loan Council and recover the state's independence. State Governments could not be servile to Federal Governments and remain sovereign states."

This opposition to the Loan Council was based (according to Lang) on 'depriving the states of their sovereignty; shackling the states to the Commonwealth and involving them in their loss of freedom to act on behalf of their citizens and it would eventually destroy the principles of Federation, leaving the states with all their obligations but without the means of honouring them'. This over simplistic opinion by Lang in 1932 was self-serving in view of later events but it did have a ring of truth to it. But the more important question was, could Australia do without a Loan Council ? The Loan Council was constructed to have exclusive control over all future borrowing (all the states and the commonwealth agreed to stop competing between themselves in the international loan markets and in future, through the Loan Council, to raise loans at market competitive rates and on the best terms and conditions) raising except loans for defence purposes. The Financial Agreement had benefits for both the Commonwealth and the states. Although the states resented having been coerced into the Financial Agreement of 1928, it seemed to lay the foundations for an improvement in their relations with the Federal Government. It was the more successful as a means of resolving the economic complexities of the federal system because of an informal understanding that went with it: the states included the needs of local government and of 'semi-government instrumentalities'.

So, the McMahon concept of Federalism was this pragmatic attempt to show support for the states but place the Loan Council, each year ' in the front line of negotiations with the states, and make them justify to the Commonwealth every dollar raised and expended, and of giving away a basic tenant of responsible government, and resort to the Loan Council antics as being incompatible with traditional views of Federalism. Was this a McMahon slight of hand or was he protecting the smaller and thus the majority of the states and simultaneously advocating Federal dominance over the states economically by controlling their funds flow. Maybe it really was just 'politics as usual'.

It seems that a convenient starting point for exploring Federal-State Financial relations is the amendment to S105 of the Constitution. The resulting change became S105A.

The original **S105** reads

> *"The Parliament may take over from the States their public debts as existing at the establishment of the Commonwealth, or a peroportion thereof according to the respective numbers of their people as shown by the latest statistics of the Commonwealth, and may convert, renew or consolidate such debts, or any part thereof; and the states shall indemnify the Commonwealth in respect of the debts taken over, and thereafter the interest payable in respect of the debts shall be deducted and retained from the portions of the surplus revenue of the Commonwealth payable to the several states, or if such surplus is insufficient, or if there is no surplus, then the deficiency or the whole amount shall be paid by the several states."*

From the Federation Convention debates we know that the public debt of the states was in reality, quite high, and even though the prevailing interest rates were relatively low, the debt service could account for a significant proportion of the surplus cash flow available from the Commonwealth to the States.

PUBLIC DEBT OF THE STATES AT FEDERATION

New South Wales	65,332,993	48.00.0
Victoria	49,324,885	42.04.6
Queensland	34,349,414	70.07.9
South Australia	26,156,180	70.16.5
Western Australia	11,804,178	66.04.11
Tasmania	8,413,694	46.03.1
TOTAL	195,381,344	52.02.10

One of the challenges of Federalism is that the States retain their independence and by all accounts the main requirement is that of financial independence. However the framers of the Constitution were mindful of precedents overseas and took into account , in writing S105, the situation in the USA and Canada, which were the most comparable to the Australian situation.

In the US constitution the war debts, (rather than the ordinary debts) of the various states following Confederation, were embraced by the Union—

"All debts contracted and engagements entered into, before the adoption of the Constitution, shall be as valid against the United States under this Constitution as against the Confederation."

In the Canadian Constitution, the preference was that " Canada shall be liable for the debts and liabilities of each Province existing at the Union"

Clause 105 of the Australian constitution was so contentious that it changed many times from the Melbourne and Sydney Conventions of 1891 to the Adelaide session of 1897 and to the Melbourne session of 1898 whilst the final version of 1900 was different again. The arguments were over the key words of 'shall take over' or 'may take over'; the 'whole' or 'proportion thereof'. Equality between the states was the name of the game in the Debates and no one state was going to get advantage in any respect. " The 1891 draft Constitution provided a complicated system for the immediate post-Federation period(the first five years), with returns of the surplus based on amounts contributed. In respect of the subsequent period(the second five years), it provided merely that the surplus should be returned ' in the same manner and proportions until the Parliament otherwise prescribes. The Adelaide session of the 1897-98 Convention produced an even more complex three-stage system; with revenue returned per state contribution, minus expenditure for Commonwealth functions, followed by a 'book-keeping' period which recorded interstate customs: and a final stage with expenditure charged and surplus distributed on a state per capita basis. Commonwealth expenditure during the first three years was to have a strict ceiling. The next Melbourne session adopted a modified system for revenue distribution, similar to that adopted in Adelaide but allowing the Commonwealth, after five years, to pay the surplus 'on such basis as it deems fair' . The *Braddon clause* was adopted in the final draft—a section requiring the Commonwealth to return three-quarters of all its customs and excise revenue to the states in perpetuity. The S96 was added in the final draft giving the Commonwealth power to make grants to the states on 'such terms and conditions as the Parliament thinks fit'. " (Federation: The Financial Settlement P371—Cheryl Saunders). The delegates at the debates assumed ' that at the time of Federation, the bulk of Commonwealth revenue would come from customs and excise. It was also assumed that the Commonwealth would have relatively little to do and therefore relatively few expenses.' (Saunders).

Because universally free trade and commerce between the states was the supreme target and compromise, select committees were formed to calculate the likely financial impact of Federation. It was in New South Wales that the doyenne of free trade movement (Edward Pulsford) disagreed with the conclusions of the Colonial statistician—T. Coglan (ie the conclusions that the Conventions had been relying on). Pulsford computed a much greater impact on the state finances as a result of Federation than had Coglan, and wrote numerous articles challenging Coglan's conclusions but mainly to an audience of one, Sir George Reid, who was the only delegate to take up Pulsford's doubts. Although Finance Committees were formed at both the 1891 and the 1897-98 Conventions, and one entire chapter of the Constitution (Chapter IV) is devoted to 'Finance and Trade', few in 1901 felt that an entirely fair and workable system of 'fiscal federalism' was contained therein.

LaNauze in his 1970 book 'The Making of the Australian Constitution' records "the long debates concluding in the undramatic fashion may well seem ,seventy years later, to be interesting more for their omissions than for their affirmations since the structure they created was not to endure. The premiers were sorely troubled by the problems of finance; they were alert to the interests of their states while sincerely anxious to arrive at a conclusion fair to all; they were conscious that finance would be a central question in the coming public campaigns, and they must be able to reassure electors that their own states would not be crippled".

The delegates were blinkered in limiting their debate to only two main concerns—the distribution of the commonwealth surplus, and limiting commonwealth 'extravagance', but there was no equation of 'extravagance' with 'diminution of states power'. It took Alfred Deakin a further four years to proclaim that it would be by its financial power that the Commonwealth would restrict, and ultimately dominate, the States. As La Nauze concludes (P215) " At the Convention the vision of the chariot wheels of the central government had not yet appeared. They simply must prevent the Commonwealth being 'foolish'; they did not yet see it as potentially dangerous."

After the states had ceded power of direct taxation to the Commonwealth, it was George Reid (as reported by Lang in 'The Great Depression') who observed that it was the Braddon clause that was likely to induce a Federal Treasurer to resort to expanding direct taxation since, in contrast to customs revenue, he could retain the whole of the proceeds. But the delegates also did not see the future role of income taxes in the finances of the Commonwealth.

Let us now jump forward to the first challenge of the Section 96. 'As a result (writes Gordon Greenwood in ' The future of Australian Federalism P277) of the *Uniform Income Tax* case there is also a new appreciation of the significance of section 96 of the constitution—"the Parliament may grant financial assistance to any state on such terms and conditions as the Parliament thinks fit".

The Commonwealth had previously made considerable use of this section to persuade states receiving grants for specific purposes to implement a policy of which it approved. This was allowed because the Commonwealth could impose conditions on which it could pay a grant to the states. Thus through the technique of the grant-in-aid the Commonwealth has been able to influence policy on a number of matters upon which the Commonwealth under the constitution could not legislate. For example, in *Victoria v. the Commonwealth* 38 C.L.R. (1926) , 399, the High Court held that the Federal Aid Roads Act of 1926 (qv) was 'a valid exercise of the power conferred on the Commonwealth Parliament by Section 96 to grant financial assistance as the Parliament thinks fit'. In addition to the payments recommended by the Commonwealth grants commission, which operates under S.96, the Commonwealth has made grants with conditions for such things as road construction (where the roads will be placed), housing (matching contributions, specifications and decentralisation), and assistance to wheat farmers (for grain storage and movement).

Under the *States Grants (Income Tax Reimbursement) Act* **1942,** the Commonwealth provided that a state which wished to qualify for a grant under the Act must agree not to exercise its power to impose an income tax.

> *Section 96 reads " During a period of ten years after the establishment of the Commonwealth and thereafter until the Parliament otherwise provides, the Parliament may grant financial assistance to any state on such terms and conditions as the Parliament thinks fit. "*

Conciliation and Arbitration Disagreements

The Commonwealth's power of conciliation and arbitration was considerably enlarged as a result of radical judicial interpretation as set out in **The Engineers Case**. Isaacs, J, in delivering judgement, declared that S51 (xxxv) is expressed i*n terms so general that it extends to all industrial disputes, in fact, extending beyond the limits of any one state, no exception being expressed as to industrial disputes in which States are concerned* (28 C.L.R. p. 150*)*

One result of this interpretation is to be found in a subsequent case—***Clyde Engineering Co. v Cowburn*** (37 C.L.R. P466), which was subjected to an analysis by W. A. Holman wherein he declared

> *"The Commonwealth Parliament could apparently only put an end to the operation of an award of the Arbitration Court by the heroic step of abolishing the court in toto . . . . There is now, therefore, in Australia, no general legislative power on industrial topics at all. The State has a permitted power—so long as the Arbitration Court does not move—but there is no absolute power anywhere.*
>
> *The spectacle of a community of 6,000,000 people finding their ultimate authority on industrial matters not in any parliament, but in a court, is a striking one. So far as my knowledge goes no similar state of things can be found in any other part of the civilised world. It is a somewhat bewildering thought, that the return to British methods of interpretation and to British authorities, should have resulted in so singularly un-British a situation.* (Holman—The Australian Constitution: Its Interpretation and Amendment-1928—P58)

Section 109 sets the scene in the event of an inconsistency between State and Federal legislation.

"When a law of a State is inconsistent with a law of the Commonwealth, the latter shall prevail, and the former shall, to the extent of the inconsistency, be invalid"

Dixon, J., summing up the principles of interpretation adopted by the High Court, declares that if S.109 invalidates a law of a state, in so far as it would vary, detract from, or impair the operation of a law of the Commonwealth, even this wide-embracing rule is not capable of automatic application.(Dixon, J in ***Stock Motor Ploughs Ltd v. Forsyth*** 48 C.L.R. P 136 , quoted by K.H. Bailey 'Inconsistency with Paramount Law'). This concept was further tested when it was held in **Whybrow's Case** that 'there was no inconsistency between a state law fixing a minimum wage and a Commonwealth industrial award fixing a higher minimum (Bailey).

Under a different Arbitration decision, (Greenwood P371)reports that 'despite the specific inclusion within the Conciliation and Arbitration Act, 1904, of employees of state railways, the High Court held in the *Railway Servant's Case* (4C.L.R.—1906—P488 *The Federated Amalgamated Government Railway and Tramway Service Association v. The NSW Railway Traffic Employees' Association)* that State Railways were a state instrumentality and, therefore, exempt from the operation of the Commonwealth Arbitration Court. This interpretation was overthrown in the **Engineer's Case** (qv) when industry was divided artificially into two camps according to whether it could be classified as private or governmental.

Mr Justice Higgins (an active participant from Victoria in the Federation Debates) used the Engineers Case decision in the *Wheat Lumpers' Case* **(26 C.L.R.—1919—P 460** *Australian Workers Union v Adelaide Milling Co Ltd)* when he held that

"so far as the two states (Victoria and New South Wales) are concerned their operations were governmental and not trading, and that, therefore, the Commonwealth Court of Conciliation and Arbitration had no power to hear the dispute" Higgins further asserted that wheat marketing was an industrial operation and that industrial operations carried on by a state was not excluded from the jurisdiction of the Commonwealth court. This Wheat Lumpers Case provided additional proof both of the impossibility of distinguishing between the nature of work performed by state and private employees engaged in the same industry and of the illogical stance of permitting dual jurisdiction over any one industry. Higgins, J. gave this additional opinion

> *"Some men, employed by the state, were carrying or moving bags of wheat to a stack, and other men, employed by shipowners and others, were carrying or moving the same bags to the ships. Under the doctrine hitherto adopted, the Court of Conciliation was able to conciliate or arbitrate as to the one set of men and unable to do so as to the other set.*

Contrasts as to the conditions of the respective sets of men were sure to arise and did arise but the courts could not prevent the unrest which the contrasts caused"

The Financial Agreement

During the depression years in 1930-1932, the working of the Financial Agreement enabled a greater measure of co-operative action (Maclaurin 'Economic Planning in Australia') The **Financial Agreement** has been used to ensure that all governments carry out their public debt obligations. The Loan Council , formed as a result of the Financial Agreement, was an extra-Parliamentary body utilised as a means whereby policies finding favour with the banks could be imposed upon all state governments. Such a policy involved considerable loss of independence to both Commonwealth and states, moreover the staters under the Financial Agreement might suffer even more serious inroads upon its independence. N. Cowper in *Studies in the Australian Constitution* writes (P141) ' If a state failed to observe the terms of the agreement it could be compelled to do so by Commonwealth legislation, which authorises the seizure of state revenues and the control of state servants. Cowper concludes that if Jack Lang had won the July 1932 election and defied the Commonwealth enforcement legislation (**Financial Agreement Enforcement Act 1932)** the federation might have come perilously close to disruption or civil war. Going back to the post-Federation period, the Commonwealth revenue suffered from the decline in imports but as the states had certain expenditure obligations, the Commonwealth revenue was recovered through new revenue raising measures such as the ten percent tax on income from property, the primage duty on imports and the sales tax, and in addition the Commonwealth was helped by the suspension of War debt payments to Britain. The depression found Commonwealth revenues largely intact but state revenues were down whilst state expenditures due mainly to high unemployment were increased substantially and the adverse exchange rates, which caused, mainly in New South Wales and Queensland, an increase in expatriated payment of interest (NSW in 1933 paid an exchange of 2,430,000 pound, compared with 2,000,000 pound paid by the Commonwealth)

The Effect on Federalism

The founding fathers had wanted as a basis of Federation, the retention by the states of as much independence as was compatible with the surrender of limited powers to the Commonwealth. The decline in state power has been both visible and substantial (R.W.G. Mackay ' Studies in the Australian Constitution'). According to Greenwood, it is now of sufficient magnitude to threaten the status of Federalism within Australia. This is even more challenging when it is accepted that if a Federal system is to function effectively, it must be capable of preserving the independence of the states.

The Nova Scotia Jones Commission in 1934 found that

"A federation defeats its primary purpose, if, through its constitutional arrangements or by policies instituted by the national government, it accomplishes the debilitation of one or more of the political communities of which it is composed". Greenwood concludes that

"Federalism has not given that protection to the states which was expected of it. Indeed, during the war period of 1914-1918 the extension of Commonwealth activity through a liberal interpretation of the defence power was so far-reaching that the 1929 Royal Commission on the constitution could declare in its report that the Commonwealth had functioned as a unitary state. (Report P120) It seemed as though the construction, says Greenwood, placed upon the defence power meant that in wartime the Commonwealth might . . . *pass an law or give executive authority to make any regulation which it considers necessary for the safety of the country.* (Report of the **Royal Commission on the Constitution, 1929 P120).**

The Immunity of Federal Public Servants

The first case before the High Court, in which the doctrine of the immunity of instrumentalities found expression was that of **D'Emden v Pedder (1C.L.R.—1904—P112).** An attempt had been made by the Government of Tasmania to collect stamp duty on the salary of a federal public servant. The Commonwealth Attorney-General claimed that one government was by implication forbidden to interfere with the action taken by another, provided such action was within its constitutional powers. Marshall, C. J. opined that

"There is a plain repugnance, in conferring on one government a power to control the constitutional measures of another, which other, with respect to those very measures, is declared to be supreme over that which exerts the control".

Federalism in Action

From the first, it can be seen, the Commonwealth was in a dominant financial position. It was given not only the exclusive right of imposing duties of customs and excise but also the power to tax in all other fields. The states still retained their powers of taxation, but their relinquishing the tariff revenue removed their most important source of revenue, and since (says Greenwood P80) over all other sources of taxation the Commonwealth possessed concurrent powers, the states were at the mercy of the Commonwealth whenever it chose to invade any field of state taxation. Greenwood completes his argument with " whether the financial division of power within a federation is satisfactory can only be judged in relation to the functions which the various units have to carry out . . . . It is upon the application of this test that the inadequacy of the financial structure becomes apparent, for while the Commonwealth was given superior revenue resources, the states retained the more expensive responsibilities, such as land settlement and the provision of the majority of the social services. (also refer to 'The working of Federalism in Australia-March 1935).

Such a position of superiority was probably difficult to avoid. Given the transfer of collection of tariff revenue as a means of uniform customs rating for each Colony, the Convention debaters had little choice but to either hand over the largest revenue stream to the Commonwealth and demand a fair share to be returned or risk state disagreements well into the future by retaining this discriminatory tax and allowing the Commonwealth the chance of raising its own revenues by a growth tax of some other type. Income tax had not been considered at that time, and it must be remembered that import duties fell in the 1900s thus requiring the Commonwealth to underpin the revenue stream to the states by sharing with them some of this other revenue being raised by the Commonwealth from the transfer of this power from the states under the Constitution. The grants and Loans Commissions were established in response to the need to have a revised Financial agreement, both occurring within the first 30 years of federation. It was a serious dilemma, and one which could have been anticipated a little better and a resolution structured into the Federal constitution. The debates of the Finance Sub-committee were not recorded but we know that the serious depression of the 1893-4 period during which many banks closed and the 'land bubble' burst (Michael Cannon—Boom and Bust), left the Colonial governments struggling with delicately balancing their needs for revenue, and it could be that the 1891 Convention in Melbourne was the precursor to simply allowing the new Commonwealth powers to be more extensive and powerful, in the area of financial responsibility than might have been the case if the country had not been in the grip of such a serious condition.

Four tables show the particular plight of the states following federation. Total revenue by each state and revenue per head of population show the amount each state was giving up in tariff revenues in favour of the Commonwealth.

Table 1

REVENUE PER HEAD OF POPULATION 1889

Colony	Taxation	Land	Public Services	Other	TOTAL
NSW	2.8.6	1.18.9	3.2.11	0.14.0	8.4.2
Vic	3.7.11	0.11.2	3.10.9	0.7.3	7.17.1
Qld	4.7.4	1.13.1	2.11.10	0.9.9	9.2.0
SA	2.4.3	0.10.10	3.9.7	0.16.7	7.1.3
WA	4.10.6	2.0.7	1.11.3	2.4.0	10.6.4
Tas	2.16.10	0.9.6	0.17.9	0.7.2	4.11.2
Ave	**3.2.0**	**1.1.9**	**2.19.4**	**0.10.11**	**7.13.11**

(Source: Wealth & Progress of NSW—1886-87)

Table 2

GROWTH OF CAPITAL IN AUSTRALIA 1788-1888

	Amount of Wealth	*Increase in 25 years*
1788	0	Colonisation
1813	1000000	1000000
1838	26000000	25000000
1863	181000000	155000000
1888	1015000000	834000000

(Source: Wealth & Progress of NSW—1886-87)

Table 3

PUBLIC REVENUE 1889 ('000)

Colony	Taxation	Land	Public Services	Other	TOTAL
NSW	2677	2137	3347	775	9063
Vic	3749	616	3909	400	8675
Qld	1734	656	1029	194	3614
SA	711	174	1118	266	2270
WA	194	87	67	94	442
Tas	422	71	132	54	679

Table 4

TAXATION PER HEAD IN THE COLONIES—1881 AND 1889

	1881	1889
NSW	2.6.7	2.8.9
Vic	2.6.1	3.7.11
Qld	2.19.2	4.7.4
SA	1.19.2	2.4.3
WA	3.13.1	4.10.6
Tas	2.6.1	2.16.10
Ave	**2.9.4**	**3.2.0**

(Source: Wealth & Progress of NSW—1886-87)

Does Federalism have a Future?

We might ask where lies the future of Federalism? Did the founding fathers make a reversible error? Has the current concept of Federalism altered our life irreversibly? The realistic answer to each of these questions is a resounding 'NO !'. Obviously a constitution must be a living, ever changing document. What was written in the late 1890s must be applicable today even though few(if any) people today would recognise or understand the world of 100 years ago, nor would the people of yesteryear have anticipated the constantly changing world, or have foreseen the problems facing today's generations. In a little over 100 years since conception the constitution is still relevant and applicable. Obviously it has been updated (or amended) from time to time (more often opposed than approved) but as a living document it governs us today in almost as wholesome a fashion as the forefathers wanted. The dependence of the States on the Commonwealth in Financial terms is still as strong as it ever was and why should we not try to have a over-lording organisation that retains ultimate authority for setting standards and in turn regulates the states that might become miscreants or wayward, in the need for fiscal responsibility, and depart from acceptable paths. Surely the Commonwealth has that marginal monopoly on political wisdom and understands, more so than the generally parochial state politician what is best for the country as a whole? Federalism is a concept whose time has past but remains as a continuing goal and way of life as a relationship between the two tiers of governing. Most people think in terms of the Commonwealth managing the 'big picture', with the state being closer to the people but managing more of the socio-economic factors that regulate and effect our everyday life. The financial relationship between the Commonwealth and the States is largely settled and no major disputes are looming on the horizon. We can rest easy that after 100 years of constitutional government and 100 years of co-existence between big brother and little brother the relationship has been ironed out to almost everyone's satisfaction. The High Court has done its job, its judgements are set in stone and we live by their words. But events keep changing, hopefully for the better. The new role of government is to make constant improvements by fine tuning. For instance the Government still offers a better social welfare safety net for the people; a progressive and growth tax system for the states ; a worker sponsored conciliation court where both sides can share power and not repeat the 1960s where the Commonwealth gave over their conciliation mission to the employer representatives and the workers lived or died by the loudest voice; we might have not had a 'law of the sea' dispute for 30 years, but today we face a burgeoning environmental debate that could send the states and the Commonwealth to the poor house. We have been negligent for so long, that future generations will be paying off our extremes for many years. Rather than putting the bite on the government purse, we are going to be entering the phase where joint responsibility means sharing the burden—' work for the dole'; 'mutual obligation'; 'landcare and the greening Australia' will all soon become the catchcry for the answer to the environmental issue together with a simple solution of—'increase the GST rate for a few years; make the farmers pay a third of the cost; share the burden; user choice, user pays. Will this be the face of future Commonwealth-State relations? A fight for every dollar, selling off all the state assets, limiting the overseas debt, living within our means? This really is Big Brother coming to a place near you!

CHAPTER 5

A HISTORY OF FREE TRADE PARTIES IN NSW

As has been discussed in the introduction to this collection of essays, there are seven topics, which loosely inter-relate to each other. For instance the final essay, that on the History of Public Accounts, out of necessity includes a reference to the financial negotiations and debates leading to Federation, and the post-Federation handling of the Financial clauses of the new Constitution and the arrangements for the sharing of the surplus revenue as set down in the Braddon clause. The McMahon Biography includes references to his understanding of Federalism, and whilst he was Treasurer, his handling of the Commonwealth-State Financial relations in particular, the Commonwealth Grants Commission and the Uniform Taxation Legislation—both topics had caused a divide on the interpretation of Federalism and a rift in Commonwealth state Relations. McMahon had exposed a philosophy on Federalism which cannot be supported in practice, which practice especially deteriorated whilst he was Treasurer. Another link is the reminder that McMahon was a prominent member of the Liberal Party of Australia, which was a successor (by name change) to the original Free trade Party in NSW, the Nationalist Party of Joe Lyons and the 'All for Australia 'Party of McMahon's uncle, Sir Samuel Walder. The second essay in this collection relates to the History of the Free Trade Party in NSW, which was influenced greatly by Henry Parkes and Sir George Dibbs, as well as that august member of the Beckett family, Edward Pulsford. This movement was epitomised in NSW by The Free Trade Association, of which Pulsford was the Secretary and the Editor of its publication, the

Free Trade Journal (1900-1901). So there is an interesting link between at least five of the essays—McMahon, Free Trade, Commonwealth-State Financial relations, and the History of Public Accounts, and, of course, the Beckett Family History which includes great uncle Edward Pulsford. The other two essays relate to the Commonwealth Heads of Government meetings since 1945 and the South Pacific Regional Forum, which are examined for relevance and opportunity.

An analysis of the Free Trade Movement is probably an unusual topic for an essay but it tries to fit into the mould of this collection which generally surveys political and economic events in Australia's history. NSW has traditionally been a Free Trade State whereas Victoria has always supported (from the earliest Port Phillip settlement) the need for protection. This essay follows the growth and multiplication of the various Free Trade Parties and associations in the Colony and then the State of New South Wales.

An addition to the story on the development, chiefly by Henry Parkes and George Dibbs, both of whom became the public face of 'free trade' in New South Wales, of the Free Trade Party, is the extensive writing by Edward Pulsford (1844-1919). Pulsford was the founder and Secretary of The Free Trade Association of New South Wales, and the editor of the Journal of the Association (published 1900-1901) as well as the writer of many articles published in the Sydney Morning Herald, and the Melbourne Argus. After a significant contribution to the Federation movement, Pulsford was elected a member of the Senate in the first Commonwealth Parliament in 1901, and remained active in that state's house until 1910.

The most resplendent member, by marriage, of the Beckett family, is the Honourable Edward Pulsford, a distinguished elected member of the first Australian Senate. The family genealogy is important to understand. The writer's mother (Alice) was the only daughter of her mother (Constance Brown). Constance had a sister (Blanche Brown).

An Englishman by birth, he was to marry into the family in 1919 to Grandmother Brown's sister, Blanche Elsbeth. Mother Alice(Bailey) Beckett,(born 1911) was the only daughter of the Bailey family. Constance Pleasance Brown had married Alfred Bailey in 1888. The other issue of this marriage was William (Bill) Alfred Bailey, (born 1909). Blanche was widowed late in the year 1919 (29th September), not long after the marriage took place on 2nd March, 1919.

Edward Pulsford (1844-1919) had been born in Staffordshire, England, the son of a Baptist Minister. He was educated privately, but by 1870 , Edward and his Father, James, were in business as commission agents in Hull. In 1884, Edward transferred his business activities to Sydney, whilst James transferred to New York, as Secretary of the Liverpool, London Insurance Company.

Pulsford continued his active support of the free trade movement and established the Liberal Association of New South Wales, originally intended as a forum for liberal economic ideas, but in the election of February 1887, it became the first free-trade party machine.

Remaining its Secretary until 1901, Pulsford was its principal organiser and propagandist, publishing a range of newspaper articles, essays and pamphlets in defence of the free-trade cause. His writings have been preserved in the Mitchell Library. His writing was not restricted to advocacy of free trade. In 1884 he wrote '*Thoughts and suggestions on the commerce and progress of New South Wales*'. His controversy with Timothy Coglan (Colonial Statistician, commenced with the publication of this work, which countered some of the contents of the first Coglan (official) publication, the '*Wealth and Progress of New South Wales*'. Pulsford was an active Federationist, and as such his second and somewhat larger controversy with Coglan took place over the question of the probable cost of Federation to New South Wales.

He was a contributor to Webster's International Dictionary as well as being a regular correspondent on financial and commerce matters to numerous Colonial newspapers the and from 1890-1898 the proprietor of the Armidale Chronicle. He was appointed as adviser on the Colony's politics to Sir George Dibbs, but in 1895, Sir George Reid appointed Pulsford to the Legislative Council, after winning resounding electoral endorsement for a policy of free trade and direct taxation.

Having made a significant contribution to the Finance Committee of the Federation Debate, Pulsford organised in 1900 the Inter-colonial Free Trade Conference in Sydney which set up the Australian Free Trade Association to fight the first Federal Elections. He was President of the NSW Branch and edited a weekly newspaper *Our Country* for nine months from 1900-1901. Copies of this publication remain in the Mitchell Library. Pulsford was elected to the Senate in 1901 and held his seat until 1910. His next work *Commerce and the Empire(1903)* argued the case for bringing 'all parts of the Empire into line with British fiscal policy', and 'condemned the delusion of Imperial preferences'. He was a fervent free trader and a 'no tariffs' advocate. His last work, an update of the *Commerce and the Empire (1914 and after)* was published in 1917, but its reviewer W.G. McMinn (an eminent Australian constitutional expert) claims " though much more readable than the earlier work, it was a much more polemical (argumentative and quarrelsome), the product of long experience becoming clouded by the petulance of an aged, and increasingly derided prophet"

As a legislative Councillor he opposed the Henry Parkes poll-tax (1895) on Chinese, and voted against the 1901 Immigration Restriction Act, and supported unrestricted immigration against the then tide of the White Australia movement.

Pulsford had first married in Hull in 1870 and the union produced three sons. His second marriage to Blanche Brown in 1919 produced no heirs. After his death in 1919 he was buried in Gore Hill cemetery following Anglican rites.

Pulsford 'is most notable as one of the last survivors in Australia of the spirit of nineteenth-century liberalism' (McMinn) . Blanche died in 1948, a widow for 30 years.

Dean Jaensch commences the first chapter of his 1994 book 'The Liberals' with an unambiguous statement "The Liberal Party is 100 years old." We will try to trace some of that history.

Alfred Deakin was converted in 1884 from a free trader by David Syme to the protectionist cause and employed as a journalist on 'The

Age' newspaper. Deakin became Chief Secretary in the Conservative Liberal Coalition which governed Victoria from 1886 to 1890. Michael Cannon in his book 'The Land Boomers' wrote " When the Treasury had been emptied, when the trust funds had been drained of more than one million pounds, when the public was at last beginning to doubt the wisdom of extravagance as a method of government, a large group of members rebelled and voted Gillies and Deakin out of office" Deakin was to make a successful comeback in the federation movement and later, in federal politics. Deakin's decision to align himself with the free Trade movement in 1909 in order to retain government was regarded as a 'sell-out'. Sir George Reid had published, in 1875 his 'Five Free Trade Essays', a statement of Liberal beliefs and his opposition to the protectionist position. In the first Parliament after Federation, Deakin sat on the Government side and Reid faced him as leader of the opposition. This came about because at the March 1901 elections, the Protectionists won 44% of the vote whilst the Free Traders won only 36% and the new Labor Party secured 19%. The seats , according to Colin Hughes in 'A Handbook of Australian Government and Politics 1890-1964', were allocated as follows—Protectionist 32, Free Trade 26, Labor 15 and Independents 2. Reid did not win Government until August 1904 when some protectionists crossed the floor, later encouraging a truce between the Free Traders and Protectionists. This peace came about by a split within the Protectionist movement between Liberals and Conservatives in 1904. The Protectionist vote declined dramatically from 44% in 1901 to only 30% by 1906. The two non-labor parties—the Free Traders and the Protectionists fused into one party following Reid's retirement in 1908, and the Fusion Ministry soon took the name Liberal Party, to be led in 1910 by Alfred Deakin, but he lost to the Andrew Fisher Labor Party later in 1910. The name changed routinely in the following years—anti-Labor was too narrow, but the tags Liberal, Conservative, Nationalist and United Australia all followed the conservative politics of the day to be led by the likes of Deakin, Joseph Cook and Billy Hughes. Non-Labor was a suitable synonym for reference purposes to define their opposition to Labor. The non-Labor parties soon adopted the mantle of protectionism in its general platform. In a major speech at Adelaide in March 1906 (Sydney Morning Herald 30th March, 1906), Deakin identifies the developing principles of Australian Liberalism and stated ' The Liberal Party , in this country, considers that the adoption of a well thought out and scientific system of protection for the development of native industries is the first essential. In this respect we ought to claim the unqualified support of the Labor members. The beginning of the prosperity of the labouring classes is to be found in the protectionists system'.

A CHRONOLOGICAL SUMMARY

1857 post-responsible government Acts, select committees recommend consideration of federal union and recommends consideration of uniformity including uniform tariffs.

1884—Pulsford arrives in NSW

1885 Pulsford & Wise—Free-trade & Liberal Association of NSW

1889 George Dibbs forms new government defeating Henry Parkes. 'Free Trade Party' wins election

1890 The Melbourne Conference of the Federation Conventions was attended by representatives of all Colonies. Sir Samuel Griffiths (Queensland Opposition Leader) contended that a federal tariff, though desirable , was not absolutely essential, and that Federation without inter-colonial free trade would be better than no Federation at all.

1890 2nd Melbourne Conference where the serious 'lions in the path', were the differences of population, and the differences of fiscal policy, and so the differences at the convention were (1) between large states and small states, and (2) between a high tariff policy and a low tariff policy.

1891—'compromise led by Henry Parkes'. Federal taxation powers were granted to the Commonwealth, on condition it was uniform taxation in all the colonies, and upon adoption of uniform tariffs, trade between the Colonies must be free.

1891—Commonwealth Bill of 1891 was difficult to get approved in NSW Legislature because Reid placed free trade before Federation and Henry Parkes had lost his majority backing. Edmond Barton took up the reins and led the Federation movement in NSW.

1893 Barton formed the Australasian Federation League in Sydney. Henry Parkes stood aloof claiming he was the rightful head of the Federation Movement.. George Reid called a meeting of the Free Trade Party acted suspiciously of the new League and resolved that no new alliances would be formed on the question of Federation, but left it to individual members as to how they would act

1894 Geo. Reid replaces Dibbs as leader of Free Trade Party and Premier of NSW.

It was a brave and unusual person who thought in terms of free trade before 1851. From 1812 the Colonial Governor of New South Wales had been given the right to raised revenue for the Colony by applying a custom duty or tariff to goods imported into the Colony. This revenue was firstly contributed to the Gaol or Police Fund and then to the Orphan School Fund. These were the only revenues directly raised by and available to the Governor and no-one, other than the Colonial Secretary in London was going to interfere with that revenue, used to build the first gaol in Sydney Town and then build a school and generally care for the orphaned children, of which there were many, roaming the Colony. Trade, free of tariffs or duties was not a concept considered in the desolation and indeed destitution of the Colony.

Self-government came with the Act of 1855 and this new opportunity to the Colonists opened the door to the idea of unity, among and between the Colonies. Of course there were many stumbling blocks, the first being the difference in population between the Colonies. By 1860, the two older Colonies had burgeoned with people and fiscal growth, si that Melbourne Town in the Colony of Victorias had shot ahead of Sydney in the number of people. The discovery of Gold had brought great wealth, great population growth and economic independence to both Victoria and New South Wales. Gold had also been discovered in Queensland and Western Australia, and to a lesser extent in South Australia. Even Tasmania and New Zealand shared in the news of discovery. With self-government had cone mighty things for the Colonists—new wealthy, new discoveries, rural towns, railways, telegraph services, faster sailing ships, postal services, new schools, more newspapers, and a better quality of life. Imports grew to match the increasing exports of wool, wood, minerals, coal, gold and even some manufactured goods. But the Colonial Governments with their new legislatures had all imposed customs duties and tariffs as the mainstay, along with licences, fees and fines, for revenues to be used to improve their Colony. Other revenue items soon became available as a result of short—term overseas borrowing. These funds had been used to build the railway lines, build new water sources, develop sewerage systems, and develop the mineral wealth under the ground. Interest had to be paid on all these borrowed funds and the operating expenses had to be met but there was generally a surplus available to add to consolidated revenue.

With all imports being subjected to duties and with the start of inter-colonial trade being subjected to duties there was growing concern as to what effect a Federal Union would have on the revenue stream of each Colony. The early Federation meetings between Premiers and politicians determined these were the most important questions, but most agreed that Federation was a major challenge with the outcome justifying the hard work necessary to prepare for it. Free Trade was still an idea wanting development but the nagging dilemma behind the concept was—How do you replace the revenue raised from duties with other sources of revenue? When the debate really hotted up in the late 1880s, the philosophical question of free trade or protection was much easier to answer than the 'how to achieve it' question. The relocation of Edward Pulsford to Sydney from Hull, England was to accommodate his and his father James, business interests. As commissioned agents it was easy to understand their strong support for free trade. This support led Edward to develop a keen interest in the Free-Trade & Liberal Association of New South Wales. Pulsford and his friend B.R. Wise established this organisation, originally intended as a forum for liberal economic ideas., but the election of 1887, the Free Trade Party candidates were fielded. Pulsford was the Party's secretary and principal organiser , promoter and propaganda writer. He was full of ideas for developing free trade and wrote newspaper articles, pamphlets and well documented research papers in support of his goals for national free trade. So this was the start of the Free Trade movement in Australia. It was an idea whose time had come with Federation and was warmly embraced by many Federalist leaders.

'All the Colonies imposed import duties for revenue raising purposes; but as trade developed, these tariffs began to wear a protective aspect'. (Quick & Garran *The Annoted Constitution of Australia*).

The main thrust of the Federation movement was to encourage free trade, without duties or tariffs between each State, and adopt a common tariff for all goods coming into the Country. From 1887 the Free Trade Party organised meetings, developed policies, wrote publicity materials and organised candidates in all state and Commonwealth elections. The public face of the movement was George Dibbs and the George Reid. Pulsford never stood for election to the Legislative Assembly of New South Wales, but was appointed to the Upper House, or Legislative Council. After Federation, he sought election as a New South Free Trade Party Candidate to the Commonwealth Senate and remained a member until 1910.

CHAPTER 6

FOREIGN INVESTMENT TO THE RESCUE

EXPLAINING THE COLONIAL ECONOMIC DRIVERS 1788-1856

In order to understand the growth of the colonial economy, we must understand the economic drivers that underpinned, sustained and supported the colonial economy. There are at least six, if not seven, such economic drivers. They include the factors of (a) population growth, the (b) economic development within the colony, the (c) funding sources such as British Treasury appropriations and the (d) revenues raised from within the local economy (for example, taxes and duties on imports) and (e) foreign investment (both public and private). The traditional concept of growth within the colonial economy comes from (f) the rise of the pastoral industry. A seventh driver would be the all-important Land Board, which played such an important role within the colonial economy The Land Board played an important role in co-ordinating crown land policy, controlling land sales, squatting licenses and speculators, re-setting boundaries of location, establishing set aside lands for future townships and for church and school estates, carrying out the survey of millions of acres of land transferred by grant and sale, and offering terms sales for crown lands and being responsible for the collection of repayments, rents, license fees, quit-rents and depasturing fees. In addition the land board was vested with road reserves for hundreds of miles of unmade roads but important rights-of-way that would well into the future protect access to remote pastoral and farming properties. The main thrust of published material about the Land Board is in conjunction with crown land sales policy, but the Board had a much larger role and the overall Board policies sand performances are what are to be reviewed here.

Although an important factor it is no more important that our other five motivators of the colonial economy between 1802 and 1856. Why have I selected these two specific dates? 1802 was when Governor King first imposed an illegal, but justified and well-intentioned impost on the local free community to build a local gaol to replace one burnt to the ground through a lightening strike but which the British would not replace. The local residents thought a more solid and durable prison was a worthwhile community investment. At the other end, the year of 1856 signalled the first real representative and responsible government in the colony, and although it was not the end of the colonial era, it was certainly the end of Britain's financial support of sand for the colony and as such the colony was expected to stand on its own two feet.

These six factors will be discussed as mechanisms for 'growing the colonial economy between 1802 and 1856'

One consideration that must not be forgotten is the externally enforced pace of colonial expansion, particularly through the organised rather than the market-induced inflow of both convicts and assisted migrants. What this means is that instead of market forces requiring additional labour and human resources, extra labour and resources were imposed on the colony and there was an obligatory process of putting these people to work, in many cases by creating a public works program and pushing development ahead at an artificial pace rather than at a time and rate suited to the local economy. In much the same way, the 'assignment' system in the 1810-1830 period forced landowners to create clearing and development programs in order to utilise the labour available rather than only develop land as demand required.

1. Population growth including immigration of convicts & free settlers

The reason the colonial society did not change very much in the 1820s is that relatively few immigrants arrived. During 1823, Lord Bathurst, Colonial Secretary, sent instructions to Governor Brisbane (Macquarie's successor) altering the administration of the colony of NSW in most of the ways Commissioner Bigge had recommended in his reports.[1] One result of the Bigge Reports was that Macquarie was officially recalled to Britain even though he had canvassed his retirement before Bigge's arrival in 1819. Macquarie was distressed by the Bigge Reports and took very personally the recommendations made for change. Although there were many implied criticisms Macquarie considered that the public perception was that he had not acted properly in his role as Governor. Macquarie set to and compared the circumstances of the colony at the time of his arrival in 1810, with the great achievements he had made through 1821. In hindsight, Macquarie had accomplished much, mostly by means of arrogantly pursuing a series of policies without the pre-approval of the Secretary or the Government in London.

The arrival of only a few immigrants was because Bigge and the Colonial Office believed that only men of capital would emigrate. Labourers and the poor of England should not be encouraged and, as these people rarely had money to pay for the long passage to Sydney, few of them arrived.[2] Although the numbers were small, few of them came unassisted. In 1821 320 free immigrants arrived and this increased each year; 903 in 1826; 1005 in 1829, but slipping to 772 in 1830. Mostly they were family groups with some financial security.

---

[1]   Commissioner J.T. Bigge had been sent by Bathurst to Enquire into the State and Operations of the colony of NSW in 1819; the House of Commons had demanded an inquiry into the colony and had threatened to hold one of its own; Bathurst pre-empted a difficult government situation by appointing Bigge with a very broad and wide-ranging terms of Enquiry. Bigge held two years of investigations in the colony and reported to the Commons in 1823 with the printing of three Reports.

[2]   Australian History – The occupation of a Continent *Bessant* (Ed)

In 1828, the first census (as opposed to musters) of white persons in NSW was taken. 20,930 persons were classified as free and 15,668 were classified as convicts. However, of the free persons, many had arrived as convicts or were born of convicts. In fact, 70% of the population in 1828 had convict associations. However, by 1828, one quarter of the NSW population was native born; 3,500 were over 12 years of age

There was another side to this migration of unregulated souls. Shaw writes" The cost of assistance, the unsuitability of many emigrants, their ill-health, and the numbers of children and paupers that were sent – all these gave the colonists a source of grievance".[3] A large part of the problem was that the English wanted emigration – but those they wished to see emigrate were not welcomed in the colony. A growing opinion in the colony was that free migrants could not work with convicts; the convicts by themselves were too few and with growing expense; therefore transportation must stop and immigration be encouraged. However, immigrants of a good quality were not those the English wanted to send; its preference was for the paupers and the disruptive in the society. To stop transportation would be "attended with the most serious consequences unless there be previous means taken too ensure the introduction of a full supply of free labour". [4] In the next five years, the number of free immigrants increased so much that transportation could be stopped with little political backlash. Between 1835 and 1840, the colony was quite prosperous (it was a case of boom and bust—the great depression came in 1841); sales of crown land were large, and consequently the funds available for assisting immigrants were plentiful.[5]

---

[3]   Shaw, A.G.L. *The economic development of Australia* p.44
[4]   HRA Bourke to Colonial Secretary *Governor's despatches* 1835
[5]   The British Treasury had agreed to put 50% of land sale proceeds into assisting immigrants with shipping costs; a further 15% into assisting Aborigines' and the balance was for discretionary use by the crown. These percentages changed in 1840 when all sale proceeds were spent on immigration but the land fund still ran out of funds in 1842 and no further assistance was made to immigrants other than by the colonial government borrowing funds in the London market through its own credit.

In 1838, land revenue was over £150,000 and assisted migrants numbered 7,400; in 1839, land revenue was £200,000 and assisted migrants 10,000; in 1840 revenue was over £500,000 and assisted migrants 22,500.

Between 1832 and 1842, over 50,000 assisted and 15,000 unassisted migrants arrived in NSW; or they might have arrived as convicts, and over 3,000 arrived that way each year. Thus between 1830 and 1840 the population of the whole of Australia increased from 70,000 to 190,000, with 130,000 of those in 1840 being in NSW. Of these 87000 were men and 43000 were women; 30,000 had been born in the colony; 50,000 were free settlers, 20,000 were emancipists and 30,000 were convicts.[6]

2. Foreign Private Investment

We need to make the distinction between foreign public investment, and foreign private investment. The British Treasury appropriated specific funds for infrastructure programs in the colony, such as public buildings, churches, gaols, roads etc.

One reason that local colonial taxes and duties were imposed on the colony was to give the governor the funding source for discretionary expenditures in order to improve his administration. There were many instances of expenditures which could not be covered by the British funds, such as a bounty to recapture runaway convicts, building fences around the cemeteries and whitewashing the walls of public buildings (for instance barracks) in the settlement. The British Treasury would have considered such items of expense as being unnecessary. Road repair and maintenance was intended to be covered from toll receipts but they were never sufficient to make necessary repairs. Governors Hunter and Bligh did little to improve public and community buildings, roads and bridges and by the time Macquarie arrived in the colony in 1810, there was a major backlog of building work and maintenance to be undertaken. Macquarie expanded the local revenue tax base in order to give himself more flexibility in pursuing improved conditions for the settlers and the population at large.

---

[6]   Shaw *ibid*

Although Macquarie did not specifically seek new free immigrants for the colony, word of mouth circulated that the colony was in a growth stage and worthy of being considered for either immigration or investment. Usually one accompanied the other. The first private investment came with the immigrants. Free settlers would either cash up in England or transfer their possessions to the colony, and this small level of private investment was the start of a major item of capital transfers to the colony.

However, private capital formation took many forms; the early settlers, bought or built houses, they built or bought furnishings; they had carriages and often employed water conservation.

As the system of land grants was expanded and farming was encouraged the spread of settlement required a combination of public and private investment.

The government had to provide roads and townships, and the settlers had to provide pastoral investment. This pastoral capital formation consisted of five main types of assets:

> Buildings – residence, outbuildings, wool shed or grain storage
> Fences – stockyards, posts and rails
> Water conservation – dams, tanks, wells
> Plant – cultivators, tools
> Stocks – food, clothing, household items, materials for animal care and general repairs—livestock

Stephen Roberts offers an interesting insight into the colony of 1835.[7]

"It did not need much prescience to foresee the whole of the country united by settlement – so much had it outgrown the coastal stage of Sydney town. It was a new Australia – a land of free settlement and progressive occupation – that was there, and the old convict days were ending.

Both human and monetary capital were pouring into the various colonies and transforming the nature of their population and problems. Convicts

---

[7] Roberts, S.H *The Squatting Age in Australia 1835-1847 (published 1935)*

no longer set the tone; even autocratic governors belonged to a day that was passing, and instead, the country was in the grip of a strangely buoyant, and equally optimistic, race of free men". .

As part of our private capital formation, we must remember the growth of human capital and the needs for specific labour. Capital requires labour with a specific role. The establishment and expansion of farming meant more than shepherding and ploughing. There was a considerable demand for building skills, for construction and maintenance of equipment such as drays and carts, harness making and repair, tool-making etc. It became important, in order to support and sustain capital growth and economic development to be able to employ labour with multi-skills. This was a new phenomenon for the colony, especially since Britain did not develop these types of broad skills and self-motivation in its criminal class. The Rev. J.D. Lang sought a temporary answer by specifically recruiting 'mechanics' in Scotland as immigrant for the colony.

3. British Public Funding transfers

Public Capital formation is obviously different to private capital formation. I have given an example of rural-based private capital formation elsewhere in this study and will do so again here, in order to demonstrate both types of capital investment.

Private capital formation took many forms; the early settlers, bought or built houses, they built or bought furnishings; they had carriages and often employed water conservation techniques, which included tanks or earthen dams.

As the system of land grants was expanded and farming was encouraged the spread of settlement required a combination of public and private investment.

The government had to provide roads and townships, and the settlers had to provide pastoral investment. This pastoral (rural-based) capital formation usually consisted of five main types of assets:

Buildings – residence, outbuildings, wool shed or grain storage

Fences – stockyards, posts and rails
Water conservation – dams, tanks, wells
Plant – cultivators, tools
Stocks – food, clothing, household items, materials for animal care
and general repairs—livestock

Public capital on the other hand was a socio-economic based government asset, and included:

Roads, bridges, crossings, drainage, excavation and embanking, retaining walls
Hospital, storehouses, military barracks, convict barracks, Court-house, police posts, government office buildings
Market house, burial ground, Church, tollhouse, military magazines.

Obviously the list can go on and on.

Major Public Works in NSW 1817-1821

Roads
Sydney to Botany Bay
Sydney to South Head
Parramatta to Richmond
Liverpool to Bringelly, the Nepean and Appin
Buildings
Sydney
A military hospital; military barracks; convict barracks; carters barracks; Hyde Park
Toll-house; residences for the Supreme Court Judge, the Chaplain and the
Superintendent of Police; an asylum; a fort and powder magazines; stables for
Government House; a market house; a market wharf; a burial ground; St. James
Church
Parramatta
All Saint's church spire; a hospital; a parsonage; military and convict barracks; a
Factory; stables and coach-house at Government House; a reservoir
Windsor
St. Matthew's Church; military barracks; convict barracks
Liverpool
St. Luke's church; a gaol; a wharf; convict barracks

4. Economic Development

K. Dallas in an article on *Transportation and Colonial Income* writes, "The history of economic development in Australia is concerned with the transplanting of British economic life into a unique and novel environment. All colonial societies resemble each other in the problems of transplanting, but only in Australia was there no indigenous communal life vigorous enough to influence the course of future development"[8]

Dallas in the same article declares, "The economic effects of the transportation system are usually misunderstood. The real development of Australia begins with the pastoral industry and the export of wool in the 1820s. Until then, penal settlements were a base fore whalers, and made the pastoral possibilities known to English capitalist sheep farmers earlier than they would otherwise have known."[9]

Since this is such a major point on which much disagreement exists, an analysis of its merits is required. No less authority than N.G. Butlin, J.Ginswick and Pamela Statham disagree and they record in their introduction to 'The economy before 1850 "the history books are preoccupied with the pastoral expansion in NSW. It is reasonably certain from the musters that a great many complex activities developed and Sydney soon became not merely a port town but a community providing many craft products and services to the expanding settlement".[10]

The next section of this study outlines the remarkable contribution of Governor Macquarie between 1810 and 1821, most of the physical development taking place before the arrival of Commissioner J.T. Bigge in 1819. The table of infrastructure and public building development below confirms that the greatest period of economic development in the colonial economy took place under the Macquarie Administration and did not wait until the spread of settlement and the rise in the pastoral industry (which brought with it so many economic problems) in the late 1820s and 1830s.

---

[8] Dallas, Keith *Transportation & Colonial Income* Historical Studies ANZ Vol 3 October 1944-February 1949
[9] Dallas *ibid*
[10] The Australians: Statistics Chapter 7 'The economy before 1850'

IMPACT OF THE COLONIAL ISOLATION DURING THE 1800S

The question of isolation was of positive benefit to the British authorities because the concept of creating a *'dumping ground for human garbage'* was synonymous with finding a *'penal wasteland that was out of sight and out of mind'*.

However the disadvantages to the Colonial authorities were numerous

There was the tyranny of distance—the huge risks, of frightening transportation by sailing ship to a land hitherto unknown, uncharted and unexplored, promising huge risks and great loss of life.

Food preservation during the voyage and in the Colony was a challenge with no refrigeration or ice. The only preservatives being salt and pickling.

Communications between Sydney and London made exchange of correspondence, obtaining decisions and permission tiresomely long. It often occurred that the Colonial Governor wrote to a Colonial Secretary, who during the twelve months of round trip, had been replaced with another person.

Laws and justice, in the Colony, were to be based on British law, but in reality, local laws became a mix of common sense and personal philosophies eg Lt Governor Collins, as Advocate-General in the Colony desperately needed law books to practice, but they were never sent. Bligh, as Governor, ruled virtually as a despot and tyrannical dictator, knowing that a sea trip of seven months was between him and any admonishment or complaints being heard.

Factors Affecting British Investment in the Colony

A number of factors affected the level of capital investment into the colony – many were ill informed and relied on delayed newspaper reports on activity in the various settlements.

    a.   The offer of assisted migration

b. The failing economic conditions in Britain
c. Economic expansion for the pastoral industry due to successful exploration in the colony
d. The settlement at Port Phillip and the eventual separation of Victoria from New South Wales would promote great investment opportunities
e. The rise of the squattocracy
f. The crash of 1827-28 in the colony shakes British Investors
g. The Bigge's' Report of 1823 breathed new life into capital formation especially with Macarthur sponsoring the float of the Australian Agricultural Company
h. Further along, the good credit rating of the colonies (and there being no defaults on loans) encouraged larger investments and loans into the colonies
i. Shortage of Labour in the colony and the offer of land grants to new settlers became a useful carrot to attract small settlers bringing their own capital by way of cash or goods or livestock with them.
j. Two other steps had important consequences, one in the colony and the other in Britain. In 1827 Governor Darling began to issue grazing licenses to pastoralists, and the terms were set at 2/6d per hundred acres, with liability to quit on one month's notice. From this movement grew, writes Madgwick in Immigration into Eastern Australia, the squatting movement and the great pastoral expansion, and the idea of the earlier Governors that the colony of New South Wales should be a colony of farmers was thus abandoned. The concurrent event was the floating of the Australian Agricultural Company in London. Development by the AAC and by the free settlers brought increasing prosperity. Exports tripled between 1826 and 1831.
k. There is a connection between availability of factors of production and the level of investment. In the early days of the colony, labour was present—bad labour, convict labour, but still labour. The governors had demanded settlers with capital to employ that labour and develop the land. They proposed to limit land grants in proportion to the means of the settler. Governor Darling declared (HRA ser 1, vol 8) that 'when I am satisfied of the character, respectability and means of the applicant settler in a rural area,

he will receive the necessary authority to select a grant of land, proportionate in extent to the means he possesses.

Under Macquarie the colony had boomed with new buildings, new settlements, new investment and lots of convicts. Under Brisbane the needs for economic consolidation and new infrastructure would be addressed, together with an appeal for free settlers.

Some significant events took place during the Brisbane guardianship

The British were intent on accessing every available trading opportunity with the colony, and formed in Scotland *The Australia Company*

A road was built to connect the Windsor settlement to the new settlement at Maitland. This decision opened up the Hunter River district to new farming opportunities

The responsibility for convicts was transferred from the Superintendent of Convicts to the Colonial Secretary, although this move was to be reversed within the next decade

The first documented discovery of gold was made. It was hushed in the colony lest convicts run off to find their fortunes

In Bigge's third and final report, he recommended extra colonial import duties and less British duty on imported timber and tanning bark

The most significant event of all was the confidence placed in Bigge's favourable opinion of the potential of the colonial economy by the London Investment community and the resulting subscription of one million pound for the Australian Agricultural Company. The subscription was accompanied by a grant of one million acres of land around Port Stephens and the allocation of 5,000 convicts, but also brought inflation to livestock prices and availability throughout the colony.

J.F. Campbell wrote about the first decade of the Australian Agricultural Company 1824-1834 in the proceedings of the 1923 RAHS.

"Soon after Commissioner Bigge's report of 1823 became available for public information, several enterprising men concerted with a view to acquire sheep-runs in the interior of this colony, for the production of fine wool.

The success which attended the efforts of John Macarthur and a few other New South Wales pastoralists, in the breeding and rearing of fine wool sheep and stock generally, as verified by Bigge, gave the incentive and led to the inauguration of proceedings which resulted in the formation of the Australian Agricultural Company.

The first formal meeting of the promoters took place at Lincoln's Inn, London, (at the offices of John Macarthur, junior).

Earl Bathurst, advised Governor Brisbane in 1824 that . . . .

His Majesty has been pleased to approve the formation of the Company, from the impression that it affords every reasonable prospect of securing to that part of His Majesty's dominions the essential advantage of the immediate introduction of large capital, and of agricultural skill, as well as the ultimate benefit of the increase of fine wool as a valuable commodity for export.

The chief proposals of the company are:

> The company was to be incorporated by Act of Parliament or Letters Patent.
> The capital of the company was to be 1 million pound sterling divided into 10,000 shares of 100 pound each
> A grant of land of one million acres to be made to the company
> That no rival joint stock company to be established in the colony for the next twenty years
> That agents of the company would select the situation or the land grants.
> The shepherds and labourers would consist of 1,400 convicts, thereby lessening the maintenance of such convicts by an estimated 30,800 pound or 22 pound/per head/ per annum.

The Royal Charter of 1824 forming the company provided for payment of quit-rents over a period of twenty years, or the redemption of the same by paying the capital sum of 20 times the amount of the rent so to be redeemed. These quit-rents were to be waived if the full number of convicts were maintained for a period of five years. No land was to be sold during the five-year period from the date of the grant".

Being important that the investment be seen to have the support of strong leaders in Britain, and democratic governance, the company operated with· One Governor; · 25 directors; and 365 stockholders (proprietors). The old English structure was retained, that of, Governor and his Court, with the directors being the members of the Court whilst the Governor was the Chairman of the Board or Court

Leading stockholders included

- Robert Campbell
- Chief Justice Forbes
- Son of Governor King
- Rev'd Samuel Marsden
- John MacArthur
- Each Macarthur son, John Jr, Hannibal, James, Charles, Scott & William John Oxley. The Colonial-Surveyor (Oxley) had recommended the area of Port Stephens as an eligible spot for the land grant. The local directors inspected and approved the site but John Macarthur was extremely critical of the selection, the management plan and the extravagance of the first buildings.

This venture was the first major investment into the colony and set the scene for later developments. In 1825 the Van Diemen's Land Company was chartered by the British Parliament and granted land on the northwest corner of the territory.

Both the A.A. Coy and the VDL Coy still operate today after nearly 180 years of continuous operation, a record beaten only by the operation of the Hudson Bay Company in Canada.

Sir Timothy Coghlan was the colonial statistician whilst he was involved in preparing the series 'The Wealth and Progress of New South Wales 1900-01'. He was later appointed as Agent-General in London before compiling the 4-volume set of 'Labour and Industry in Australia'.

Circumstances in Britain contributed greatly to the climate of 'greener pastures' over the seas.

Conditions were never more favourable for emigration than they were during the 1830s. The decade had opened with rioting in the agricultural districts in the south of England. This was followed by the upheavals of the Reform Bill of 1832, the Factory Act of 1833 and the Corn Laws, which kept wages low and unemployment high. The Poor Law of 1834 withdrew assistance from the poor and re-introduced the workhouse. The Irish rebellion was creating both upheaval and poverty

These conditions were met by the enthusiastic reports coming from Australia of the progress being made in agriculture, commerce and the pastoral industry. The assistance granted to emigrants as a result of Edward Gibbon Wakefield's reforms made possible the emigration of people who had previously been prevented by the expense. It is almost certain that free passage would not have been a sufficient enticement if conditions in Britain had not been unfavourable. It is significant that years of small migration coincided with good conditions in England accompanied by unfavourable reports from the colony.

4. Creating Opportunities in the Colony

Availability of land and labour to yield profit on invested capital is the constant decisive condition and test of material prosperity in any community, and becomes the keystone of an economy as well as defining its national identity.

British Government policy for the Australian colonies was formulated and modified from time to time. Policies for the export of British capital and the supply of labour (both convict and free) were adjusted according to British industrial and demographic and other social situations, as well as the capability and capacity of the various colonial settlements top contribute to solving British problems.

By the 1820s there was official encouragement of British Investment in Australia by adopting policies for large land grants to persons of capital and for the sale of land and assignment of convict labour to those investors. Then followed the reversal of the policy of setting up ex-convicts on small 30 acre plots as small proprietors. The hardship demanded by this policy usually meant these convicts and families remained on the commissary list for support (food and clothing) at a continuing cost to the government. It was much cheaper to assign these convicts to men of property and capital who would support them fully – clothe, house and feed them.

We can ask, what led directly to the crash of 1827?

a.   Firstly, the float of the Australian Agricultural Company raised a large amount of capital, mostly from the City of London investment community, and this contributed to speculation and 'sheep and cattle mania instantly seized on all ranks and classes of the inhabitants' (written by Rev'd John Dunmore Lang) 'and brought many families to poverty and ruin'.

b.   When capital imports cease, the wherewithal to speculate vanished; speculation perforce stopped; inflated prices fell to a more normal level, and wrote E.O. Shann in Economic History of Australia 'because those formerly too optimistic were now too despairing, and people had to sell goods at any price in order to get money; men who had bought at high prices were ruined, and perforce their creditors fell with them'.

c.   In 1842, it was the same. The influx of capital from oversees, pastoral extension, and large-scale immigration, caused much speculation. The banks, competing for business, advanced too much credit. Loans were made on the security of land and livestock, which later became almost worthless; too much discounting was done for merchants. (Gipps, HRA Vol 23) In the huge central district on the western slopes, along the Murrumbidgee and the Riverina, the squatters triumphed, as was inevitable. He had the financial resources to buy his run – especially after the long period of drought. Four million acres of crown land was sold for nearly 2.5 million pound. The confidence of British investors was waning. A crisis in the Argentine and the near failure of the large clearinghouse of Baring's made them cautious. Stories of rural and industrial strife in the colony were not inducements to invest: and wood and metal prices were still falling Loan applications being raised in London were under-subscribed, at the same time, the banks were increasingly reluctant to lend money for land development, which was so often unsound.

5. Assisted Migration

The dual policy of selling land to people with sufficient capital to cultivate it, and keeping a careful check on the number of free grants was adopted after 1825. 'Yet the Colonial Office', says Madgwick, 'failed to administer land policy with any certainty (R.B. Madgwick 'Immigration into Eastern Australia'). There was no uniform policy adopted to encourage economic development in a systematic and rational way. The Wakefield system found new supporters. The principle had been established that the sale of land was preferred to the old system of grants. The dual system of sales and grants had failed to encourage local (colonial) purchases. They were willing to accept grants or even 'squat' rather than purchase land. Sales to absentee landlords and investors stepped up, and as can be seen from the following table, provided extensive revenue to the British Government to promote free and sponsored migration.

6. Successful exploration promotes new interest in the Colony

A period of rapid expansion followed the change in economic policy. Wool exports by 1831 were 15 times as great as they had been only 10 years earlier (in 1821). The increase in the number of sheep led to a rapid opening of new territories for grazing. It was the search for new land with economic value that underpinned most of the explorations. Settlers and sheep-men quickly followed exploration, and growth fanned out in all directions from Sydney town.

However, exploration was not the only catalyst for growth.

a. The growing determination to exclude other powers from the continent stimulated official interest in long-distance exploration by sea and by land and in the opening of new settlements. For instance, J.M. Ward in his work ' The Triumph of the Pastoral Economy 1821-1851' writes that Melville and Bathurst Islands, were annexed and settled between 1824 and 1827, whilst Westernport and Albany were settled in order to clinch British claims to the whole of Australia

b. When Governor Brisbane opened the settlement at Moreton Bay in 1824, it was to establish a place for punishment of unruly convicts and a step towards further economic development, and of extending the settlements for the sake of attracting new investment

7. Colonial Failures fuel loss of Confidence

The collapse of British Investment can be traced to one or two causes, or indeed both.

I. The British crisis of 1839 reflected the availability of capital for expansion by the Australian banks of that day – The Bank of Australasia and the Union Bank. These banks, three mortgage companies and the Royal Bank went into a slump due to shortage of available funds and deferred the raising of new funds until after the crisis. Stringency in the English Capital market had a serious impact on the capital raising opportunities in the colonies.

II. The second possibility is that the sharp decline was initiated by bad news of returns in the colonies, and that its role accentuated a slump with the dire consequences experienced in 1842-43. Recovery was delayed and made more difficult as there was 'no surplus labour in the colony'

It would be dangerous to imply or decide that every slump in Australia could be explained as being caused by economic events. British investment was independent then, as it is now, and so the more valid explanation of the downturn in British investment in this period is that negative reports from the colonies disappointed and discouraged investors with capital to place.

Most facts about public finance in New South Wales lead to the conclusion that it was disappointed expectations that caused the turn down in the transfer of funds. At this same time Governor Gipps (Sir George Gipps) was being pushed by bankers and merchants to withdraw government deposits from the banks and thus this action caused a contraction in lending by the banks which in turn caused a slow down of colonial economic activity. The attached statistics of land sales, registered mortgages and liens on wool and livestock reflects the strong downturn in the agricultural economy, which naturally flowed on to the economy as a whole.

CHAPTER 7

WILLIAM MCMAHON—
A BRIEF BIOGRAPHY

The Rt. Hon. William McMahon was Australia's 25th Prime Minister and the Liberal Party's 4th Leader. He still holds the record for the most portfolios administered (6) and the longest Cabinet career (21 years 1951-1972), and he became the 'father' of the House of Representatives by his service of 33 continuous years (1949-1982) on behalf of the electors of the Sydney metropolitan seat of Lowe.

McMahon had served his country militarily and politically for half his life, and met the challenge against odds to do so. Orphaned at the age of four, McMahon was raised first by his mother's family, then by an aunt and then by a guardian before returning to his mother's family (his mother's brother was Sir Samuel Walder). McMahon was separated for all his childhood from his siblings (brother, Sam, and sister, Agnes). He was left well off by his mother and then by his father (his solicitor father died when McMahon was 16), and attended a private school—Sydney Church of England Grammar School—before going to Sydney University and studying law. He claimed popularity came from his natty dressing, his being one of the lucky few to own a motor car, and also owning two race horses.

Upon graduation he worked his way up to a junior partner position with Australia's oldest law firm—Allen , Allen & Helmsley. His clients included both the Commonwealth Bank and the Bank of New South Wales.

McMahon's firm had briefed Garfield Barwick to challenge the Bank Nationalisation legislation brought down by Ben Chifley, and supported by the Chifley Attorney-General (H.V. Evatt). Sir Samuel Walder was a vice-president of the 'National Association of New South Wales' and negotiated its merger with the 'All for Australia' League to form the United Australia Party, and remain its Vice-President from 1933 to 1939. This was the predecessor of the Liberal Party of Australia, and it was Menzies who secured the merger of the many splintered parties to bring together the Conservative coalition.

McMahon suffered from a hearing impairment which stopped his World War service outside Australia. He spent the war years in northern Australia in an administrative role, rising to the rank of Major by the end of the war. Upon discharge he returned to Sydney University and studied economics, completing the four year degree in two years. Upon completion he travelled overseas for eighteen months studying both Christianity and socialism.

On his return, he claims to have met Jack Cassidy QC in the Sydney streets (Cassidy was on his way to a court hearing) and Cassidy asked McMahon to represent him at the preselection meeting for the Federal seat of Lowe. After his presentation McMahon says the ladies on the committee asked him if he personally would stand for the seat, and they would endorse him. It is unrecorded as to what Cassidy's response was, but McMahon then, having won the seat in 1949 for the Liberal Party, represented the same seat for the next 33 years until retiring in 1982.

McMahon came in the 22nd year of Federal Liberal Government over Australia (1949-1971). He came into office with inflation, unemployment and interest rates looking good. He had a 7 seat majority over the Labour opposition. Labour's leadership was becoming better organised, with reasonably pragmatic policies and enough media support to bring about a landslide victory in the December 1972 election. McMahon became the Liberal leader at the wrong time. The Party was in 'decline' and struggling with internal self-demolition. McMahon was just not the right leader for the time.

Harsh critics can be motivated by jealousy (Paul Hasluck claimed to have a passionate dislike, even contempt of the man); by frustration with opposite philosophies on key issues (McEwen decided not to accept McMahon as leader because of past conflicts over trade protection, sterling revaluation; or misreading the signs (Paul Kelly claims 'McMahon was unfit ever to become prime minister and the party that elected him was similarly unfit to govern' *The Australian Review of Books* 9th *April, 1997)*

Others, possibly those who either know the manner of the man (McMahon, and understand the commitment, dedication, loyalty, and total service to a cause, or even those who just share the limelight and therefore envy in some small way the achievements of McMahon, see him worthy of support and even praise. At the time of his death, his passing was remembered by many including Robert Hawke (as Prime Minister he recalled( ); John Howard who as Leader of the Opposition stated ; his former assistants as Treasurer, Senator John Stone and Senator ; his Country Party colleague, Ian Sinclair said ; and even the Government minister , Barry Jones, could muster a few kind words, along the lines .

Sir Alexander Downer wrote that McMahon

The two important political challenges McMahon met were firstly with McEwen and secondly with John Gorton.

Some of the more contentious issues handled were the conscription and national service and Vietnam; the question of state aid to church schools; the British entry into the Common Market followed by the revaluation of the Australian dollar after sterling moved;

McMahon made some little contribution to Liberal thought by writing a piece about party organisation for a collection of essays on the Australian Political Party System (S.R. Davies—Ed. 1954), and encouraging wide-reaching policy review and development within the Party.

McMahon entered the Menzies' ministry in 1951 , in just under two years of election to the House, and was to remain a Minister for the next 21 years. Before being elected to cabinet rank in 1958 as Minister for Labour & National Service, he served as Minister for Navy and Air (1952-1954), Social Services (1954-1956 , and as Minister for Primary Industry (with McEwen's support from 1956-1958). From 1964 to 1966 McMahon served as Vice-President of the Executive Council, a body of Cabinet under the Chairmanship of the Governor-General that deliberates on measures requiring the assent of the British Crown. He was a Privy Councillor from June 1966. His role as Minister for Labour & National Service brought him into conflict with the Waterside Workers Federation and the ACTU. His move to rid the WWF of its communist influence was partly successful and for a while the waterfront was peaceful. Not so the general industrial landscape. Neither widespread reform nor interference was in vogue in either Harold Holt's or McMahon's period as Minister for Labour. They were content to let major negotiations remain between the employer organisations and the unions. McMahon initially supported the Paul Hasluck preference to remain out of South Vietnam (this option was taken within the Foreign Affairs and Defence Cabinet Subcommittee) but the Full Cabinet. Pushed by Menzies opted for involvement and decided to send a squadron of RAAF aircraft to Cambodia and Army instructors to South Vietnam, both in response to a request by the United States. The US had determined that Indonesia was a hot-bed of discontent and likely to create major unrest in the region and the Australian involvement in Vietnam would somehow assist in a mutual deterrent.

Following Menzies' retirement in 1966, McMahon was elected deputy leader under the leadership of Harold Holt, and then appointed Treasurer in the Holt Cabinet.

His appointment to the Board of the Asian Development Bank in Manilla in 1968 and his Chairmanship of the Board in Sydney in 21969 had been preceded by appointment to the board of the International Monetary Fund in Washington from 1966 to 1969.

After the Liberal-Country Party Coalition had suffered a setback in the October 1969 election, John Gorton's position as Leader became under challenge in November that year. The challenge by McMahon and David Fairburn (the Minister for National Development) was defeated by the Party standing behind Gorton Following this move ,McMahon was removed as Treasurer and appointed as Minister for External Affairs. The appointment was viewed as a demotion, and as an act of reprisal by Gorton against McMahon's challenge, but it was also Gorton's way of trying to shake the McMahon power base. McMahon soon upgraded his new position, however, and remained a key figure in government. He organised the Department along lines of greater efficiency, renaming it the Department of Foreign Affairs, and changing his own title to that of Minister for Foreign Affairs.

McMahon had remained a bachelor until the age of 57, and in December 1965 he married Sonia Hopkins, the daughter of a textile merchant and a member of one of Sydney's wealthiest and most socially prominent families. Mrs McMahon is twenty-five years younger than her husband, is a former model and has also worked as an occupational therapist, a film producer's assistant, and a staff member of the Australian news and Information Bureau in New York. They had three children .

McMahon made a number of public declarations in support of 'federalism'. To the Liberal Party Federal Council on the 31st May, 1971, McMahon stated " I want to assure you that I do believe in a true Federal spirit. I don't believe in placing too much power in the hands of any one group for any great period of time". We may be forgiven for thinking this is the convenient concept of federalism, and to be used only for declaring one's support at a convenient time and in front of the right audience. It is not a statement one would make as a co-operative federalist. Before the Loan Council, McMahon's arguments were incompatible with the Financial Agreement between the Commonwealth and the States reached under the first amendment to the Commonwealth constitution (S105A) in 1928. The essence of federalism , contrary to the concept developed by S105A, is the complete independence of each government in its own sphere; it was also incompatible with the strict theory of responsible government. The first amendment gave exclusive control over all future loan raising except for defence purposes to the Loan Council (in effect a Premier's Conference attended by the Prime Minister). This revision to true state's rights and responsible government is conceded to be 'co-operative federalism' by W. G. McMinn (A Constitutional History of Australia-1979) McMahon too quickly embraced this new concept whilst pretending to be a fervent states righter and a Liberal Party traditionalism This concept transferred to a supra-government institution an important part of that financial control which a Parliament of the Westminster type is supposed to exercise over the executive. It was convenient and easier to concede a pragmatic approach rather than confront the Henry Bolte and Robin Askins of State politics. Practical federalism became apparent when the High Court in 1932 upheld (the Garnishee Case) the right of the Commonwealth to seize the revenue of the State of new South Wales, when that Government threatened to default on interest payments which it was obliged to make under the Financial Agreement of 1927 (as ratified by S105A of the Commonwealth Constitution.

This idea of practical federalism as supported by McMahon has another example. Whilst Treasurer, McMahon pushed hard for tied grants under S96 of the Commonwealth Constitution. This section gave the Commonwealth power to make grants to individual states without limit and subject to any conditions. The Federal Roads Act was the start of a run of legislation imposing onerous and anti-states right conditions on the States in exchange for commonwealth gratuities. Any State accepting funds under the Roads Act had to match the funds being made available, accept full responsibility for supervision of the project and agree to locate the roads under Commonwealth direction. Similar legislation provided money for the states to assist farmers in the purchase of rabbit-proof fencing. McMahon took this type of corrosion to State powers to a high art form during his Treasury years and set the scene for federal control of borrowing. So much for ' I do believe in a true federal system'.

The two smaller states (Western Australia and Tasmania) continued to be disadvantaged under Treasurer McMahon, whilst he gave demonstrable preferential treatment to New South Wales (Robin Askin—Liberal Coalition) and Victoria (Henry Bolte—Liberal Coalition). It was a negative reaction to this same disadvantage that led to Western Australia petitioning Westminster in 1933 for permission to withdraw from the Commonwealth.

Reaction from the Commonwealth came in the creation of the Commonwealth Grants Commission, a quasi-judicial body with power to investigate the financial problems of the three 'claimant States' and to recommend what special grants they needed. The main basis for claims to special assistance had been the contention that the smaller states were adversely affected by federal tariff policy and were therefore entitled to 'compensation'. But from its first report in 1934 the Commission, having found it impossible to assess the grants that were needed to 'compensate' the three States, adopted as the criterion their 'fiscal need'. McMahon saw nothing wrong in this 'cap-in-hand' ritual of the Premiers trooping to Canberra every year and returning home usually (except for the two most powerful states which held the most electors, the most federal electorates, and contributed the most revenues to the Commonwealth)disappointed. A Premier who has to justify to a Commonwealth officer the need for some particular expenditure must have his tongue very tightly in his cheek when he describes his State as 'sovereign'. McMahon's position regularly earned him negative reactions from the States for this approach to Federalism that was 'convenient ' , 'pragmatic' , 'co-operative' and 'corrosive' of State powers.

CHAPTER 8

THE DEVELOPMENT OF PUBLIC ACCOUNTS IN AUSTRALIA

It is accepted nowadays by Governments everywhere that budgeting, recording, reporting and financial transparency, are essential to our understanding and knowledge of the fiscal trends within the economic framework of the community. The development of public accounts within the first Australian Colony has a history as interesting as that of the exploration and development of the continent. The development of public or government accounts revolves around the first Governor's discretionary accounts, then the 'Blue Book' period, the Appropriation Bills prior to and following self-government and then Federation.

The Barter Economy (1788—1820)

In the instance of the earliest Australian Colony—that of New South Wales—this unplanned penal settlement did not recognise the use of coinage and this created the first accounting problem. Transactions were essentially by way of barter, bills of exchange, convict labour and survival by whatever means practical. Coinage came gradually—never in sufficient quantities to be of commercial value and always tied to artificial values imposed by the Governor of the day. For the payment of supplies, transportation, and other pre Colony arrival prisoner costs, the British Government paid for and accounted to its Treasury for all transactions. Due to these circumstances, recording in the Colony did not get under-way for at least ten years.

By the early 1800s, the Governor wanted to act a little more expansively, to build a Sydney town gaol, and also to create a fund for the support of deserving children left homeless. Thus came the first Colony (of New South Wales) government accounting—the Gaol and Orphan Funds—and the source of this revenue? A general levy on the Sydney dwellers did not raise sufficient funds, so the levy was extended to those people who had settled in the Parramatta, Hawkesbury and hinterland areas. When the gaol was finally built, in 1807, the name of this special reserve revenue was changed to the Police Fund, and maintained for a further period. Revenues for the Police Fund and the Orphan School Fund were then continued to be drawn from a moderate customs duty imposed on all imported goods into the Colony.

The Revenue raised for the Orphan Fund was also derived from fees on the entry and clearance of Vessels, and the payment for permits to land and remove spirits—both of these were first levied in 1800; further revenue was derived from the sale of licenses to retail liquor and from a duty of 1.5% on goods sold by auction (first collected in 1801); from a duty of 5% *ad valorem* on all articles imported, the produce of countries to the eastward of the Cape of Good Hope (first imposed in 1802) ; from fines levied by the Courts and Magistrates; from fees from grants of lands and leases, and ground (quit) rents on crown lands (Ground rents ceased in 1805). Other than 'quit' rents and crown land fees, all revenues were levied upon Colonial authority.

W.C. Wentworth in his 1817 treatise on the Colony writes that the Orphan Fund is 'devoted solely to the promotion of education amongst the youth of the Colony, whilst the Police Fund is used to support purposes of internal economy such as construction and repair of roads and bridges, the erection of public edifices, maintenance of the police and the cost of criminal prosecutions.'

The following is the sum total of revenue raised in 1805 (records from 1805 to 1810 are 'imperfect', according to the Colonial Treasurer of the time).

Table 1

1805 Revenues in Gaol and Orphan Funds:

(amounts are shown in ponds, shillings and pence)

Duties on Spirits	1569.11.3
Fees on Vessels, licenses	595.13.7
Ad valorem duty	531.10.3
Fines by courts	86.5.8
Other fees & charges	317.0.0
Total revenue raised in the Colony in 1805	**3,100.0.9**

Table 2

NEW SOUTH WALES PUBLIC FINANCE

Orphan, Gaol & Police Funds 1802—1821

Revenue

Year	Balances c/f	Customs	Total	Public Works Outlay
1802			900	
1803			5,200	
1804				
1805			3,100	
1806			1,900	
1807			1,200	
1808				
1809				
1810	0	1,384	3,272	2,194
1811	769	7,872	10,939	2,965
1812	5,016	5,579	13,494	3,259
1813	4,502	5,228	14,621	4,426
1814	6,016	4,529	13,325	4,993
1815	1,681	13,197	17,994	6,350

1816	3,327	11,200	17,782	5,582
1817	5453	16,125	24,706	7,048
1818	9363	17,739	31,008	6,219
1819	18900	22,579	42,968	17,131
1820	10725	27,891	44,507	14,700

The amount of customs revenue grew steadily from 1802 through to 1820. By 1820, Colonial revenue had grown to 44,507 pound of which 27, 891 pound was derived from customs and the balance from fees, fines, rents and sundry other items. This period of government record keeping was described, in a report to the Imperial Government, by James Thomson, the Treasurer in the Colonial Office of 1876, as 'being too imperfect to render the records of much value for statistical purpose, or for comparison with subsequent years' . A worthwhile reconstruction can be made from written reports by the Governors to the British Colonial Office and to others in the Parliament in London.

The 'Blue Book' Period (1822-1851)

The next distinguishable Public Accounts period saw definite improvement in the quality of output. The 'Blue Book' era, saw the commencement of a meticulous documentation and recording of every transaction made in and for the Colony. These records were kept in quadruplicate, two copies being sent to London and one to the Governor in the Colony and the last remained in the Colonial Secretary's office in Sydney. Other than for 1824, we have access today to all of these records, as well as to notes on the revenue raising categories used and the variety of expenditure classifications. It makes for imaginative reading and analysis. The Historical Records of Victoria have added a Volume 7 supplement which deals with the Public Accounts for that Settlement from 1831 to 1846. This writer's intention is to recreate a similar supplementary Volume for the Historical Records of New South Wales. S.G. Butlin's study of the Monetary System of Australia goes part-way to covering this early period but without an analysis of the 'Blue Book' records available. The name 'Blue Book' comes literally from the fact that the annual records were bound in blue covers and binding, in order to distinguish them from other Colonial Secretary's records of 'musters' (population counts), land grants, court decisions and the civil list records of government salaried 'employees', such as the Governor, military, judicial, surveyor, church clerics and other public officials.

Table 3—Civil List for 1792

		Pounds	/-	d.
Allowance to:	Governor	1000	0	0
	Lieut.-Governor	250	0	0
	Deputy Judge-Advocate	182	10	0
	Commissary	182	10	0
	Provost Marshal	91	5	0
	Secretary to the Governor	91	5	0
	For Stationary	20	0	0
	Chaplain	182	10	0
	Surgeon	182	10	0
	3 Mates ea 91/5/0	273	15	0
	Surveyor of Lands	182	10	0
	Lieutenant-Governor of Norfolk Island	250	0	0
	Assistant Chaplain	146	0	0
	Deputy Commissary of Stores	91	5	0
	Deputy Commissary of Stores at Norfolk Island	91	5	0
	Ten Superintendents of Convicts at 40/0/0 per annum cach engaged to serve three years after their landing	400	0	0
	Agent	150	0	0
	Arrears of Allowance for Secretary and Stationary from 10 October 1786 to 10 October 1792	667	10	0
	Upon Account for Payment of Fees upon the Receipt of Audit	200	0	0
	TOTAL	4,726	0	0

We also now have access to the British Colonial Office Records from 1788 onwards, which show the charges , made on account of the British Treasury for Convict Transportation, Victuals, Stores, and the Civil and Military Establishments. The last column in Table 4 shows the expenditure on account of the Commissariat.

Table 4
Colony of New South Wales—Public Finance

COLONY OF NEW SOUTH WALES—PUBLIC FINANCE
(Extracts from British Colonial Office Record 1788-1799)

Year 31 Dec	Convict Transport	Victuals	Stores	Bills	Civil establishment	Military	Marine	Pay & Allowances	Provisions	Total	Commissariat bills
1788	7393	261		4728	2877		2749				4346
1789	39588	21125	12853	891	2877	6847	3877				1331
1790	8203	1840	18402	1341	4559	6576	3853				920
1791	47356	25682	25603	13064	4758	9946	2611				744
1792	34234	17261	31140	2842	4726	10110	4275				4335
1793	21411	19762		11411	4658	10724	1996				13614
1794	15363	25470	12309	11217	4795	10228		4324	94618	98942	3289
1795	14909	36697	4392	3814	5241	10228					32103
1796	16156	31080	7931	10020	5241	13427					42101
1797	7703	7092	4030	78898	5524	16906	220				18857
1798	38900	12033	5169	26407	6157	19726	3032	5432	122552	129150	26281
1799	7672	6568	88	43448	6017	16481					41587

*Missing figures considered too unreliable

The commissariat is the source of government supplies for all settlers. This official table is misleading in a number of ways—one being that before 1799, the Colony was raising a growing share of its own revenue and certainly by 1810, based on the goal of being self-sufficient, there is ample evidence of this goal being substantially satisfied. The second problem with the Official Table is that the Commissariat was , by 1800, raising significant revenues, as the Commissariat was charging for the supplies provided, even if much of the 'income' was based on barter exchange. The Official figures also neglect to account for a , by now, major source of 'Government Revenue'—this being the output of the convicts. Once the convicts were directed and supervised in a productive way, with appropriate tools, equipment and resources being available, they produced all the bricks, tiles, stone block and coal for the Colony. They cut the timber, cleared the land, developed the roads, pulled the carts by hand since no horses were available for this type of transportation purposes. The convicts built the first huts, then the better quality homes, the military barracks, the church, the first hospital, the wharves; they unloaded the ships, handled the Government stores and contributed substantially to the work within the Colony. A convict was even the official scribe for the Governor at this time. For a number of years, ground cultivation and food production by convicts saved the Colony from starvation.

This contribution has never been recognised in the early financial accounts which were maintained simply on a cash accounting basis. It was not until the next stage of the Public Accounts record keeping that notation was even made of accruals of revenue (money's due but not received), or store stocks on hand (which would rightly be an offset to the expenditure in that prior period), and a recognition was made only in 1822 of the value of production of coal, by the Convicts, in the Colony.

N. G. Butlin wrote in " *The Historical Records of Australia*"—*Statistical Summary* that the British Government spent millions of pounds on establishing the Colony of New South Wales. This conjecture is not supported by facts found by this writer. If a careful analysis is made of the records available for this period, or even a reconstruction is made from other official documents, letters, reports etc where records are unavailable or non-existent, this proposition does not stand up to detailed scrutiny. One element missing from many traditional analyses is the concept of 'opportunity' cost, which should now be given recognition in the establishment of the 'cost to the British Taxpayers of establishing the Colony'. The main reason for the Colony being established in 1788, was that the American Colonies were no longer available as a receiver of British prisoners and the British gaols were still overflowing. The opportunity cost concept is relevant and important when the alternatives and choices confronting the British Parliament and its Ministers, are considered.

The choices become one of building more prisons in Britain, or adding to the hulks on the Thames, or transporting these prisoners away from Britain to another Territory. Obviously with the Napoleonic and other Wars raging, and there being a literal drain on the British treasury, the idea of transportation at a minimum cost was most attractive. If the pitch of Sir Joseph Banks, that any Colony in New South Wales would become self-sufficient quickly, proved soundly based, the economic opportunities for Britain in a new Colony were extensive. Even Governor Arthur Phillip wrote to the British authorities in 1794 that 'this Colony will be the best investment they would ever make'.

The earliest accounting from the Gaol/Police and Orphan School Funds through to the Blue Books reflects the real growth in the Colony and the road being followed to reach self-sufficiency. There were a number of distractions along the way; The revenue from the sale of Crown lands became a point of conflict between the British Treasury and the Colonial Governor and between the Governor and the Legislative Council. The commercial and dictatorial role of the Marine Corps and Military was another complication, which led to the *Rum Rebellion* and the mutiny against Governor Bligh. The rise of John Macarthur and the pastoral industry was an unexpected bonus and underpinned the export ability of the Colony, especially as importation of luxury consumable goods was being tied to the value of exports. The absence of currency and the growth of the barter system for goods, the payment of labour in spirits, the unrecorded output of convicts all led to the actual Public Accounts being coloured by such events and transactions, and in turn they became relatively misleading (without clarification or adjustment).

The next stage of development of the Public Accounts came shortly after the commencement of the Blue Book period and resulted from the

Imperial Legislation setting up a small level of (or the first step towards) self-government. In 1828 the British Parliament authorised the first nominated Legislative Council of 5 members to 'assist' (but not override) the Governor of the day. In 1834 the Colony was presented with the first 'Appropriation Bill', and this was a major step forward in budgeting, reporting and analysing the fiscal records of the Colony and exposing them to public scrutiny.

Appropriation Bills—from 1834

By the time the era of the Blue Books was over (this coincided with full self-government in 1851), the Colony had risen above clerical inconsistencies, errors in recording, problems with carry over balances from one year to the next and accounting for 'store' stocks at the end of an accounting period. The 'reformed' Public Accounts (following a review by the British Treasury in 1828) led to annual Appropriation Bills commencing in 1834 and these allowed the new nominated Legislative Assembly, to understand, challenge and (for the first time) overrule the Governor in the handling of revenue and its allocation to items of expenditure. This was surely the first time a 'line item veto' was used, in the western world. The Legislative Council maintained its interest in expanding the revenue base of the Colony (mainly through expanding and increasing customs duties and tariffs) at least until full self-government in 1851.

A Consolidated Revenue

The Colonial Treasurer of New South Wales wrote in the 1887 Financial Statements that " Prior to the passing of the Constitution Act in 1854, the Territorial Revenues of the Colony belonged to the Crown, but upon that coming into operation in 1855, they were placed at the disposal of the local Parliament, and together with the taxes, imposts, rates and duties were formed into one fund, under the title of the Consolidated Revenue Fund. In lieu of the Crown Revenues thus given up to the Colony, an annual Civil List of 64,300 pound was made payable to Her Majesty out of the Consolidated Revenues of the Colony." What this means is that the British Treasury allowed the offset of all direct British payments made on account of the Colony against revenues raised by the sale, rent or lease of Crown lands, hitherto reserved for exclusive allocation by the Crown.

A theory promoted by this writer is that the British Government obtained a 'net' surplus from the establishment of the Colony in 1788, through to the date of the last transported convict in 1842, rather than any acknowledgment that they 'invested' millions. This comes about by—on the 'plus' side ; the savings on housing prisoners in England (163,000 convicts were transported) + the transfer to Britain (without charge) of timber, and flax + the regular supply of the support product for their un-productive woollen mills + the benefit of output from the convicts + payment from Colonial revenue of the civil list and military personnel + proceeds from the sale of Crown lands:—on the other side; the expenses of operating the Colony for 60 years.

There was a major improvement in record keeping and reporting after self-government in 1855. The "Financial Statements of the Colonial Treasurers of New South Wales from Responsible Government in 1855 to 1881" set down the detailed accounting mechanism for recording classifications, and the compilation of budgets and reports to the local and British Authorities. The presented Reports contain the " explanatory memoranda of the financial system of New South Wales, and of the rise, progress and present condition of the public revenue".

This post-self government period was the necessary and important lead up to Federation. The Federation debates had included long and difficult discussions and negotiations within the Finance Sub-Committee of the Federation Convention arrangements. The essential items of negotiation revolved around firstly the matter of Colonial tariffs, and then in reaching a uniform rate of tariff (since each Colony had imposed their own rates of duties, even to the extent on inter-Colonial tariffs imposed and growing in significance as a source of revenue), compensating for the removal of inter-colonial tariffs, and sharing the surplus of the new Commonwealth treasury, between the States. These financial considerations have been accorded scant attention in the events leading up to Centennial anniversary of Federation, but have become part of the writer's considerations in the saga of Public Accounts in Australia. Post-Federation brought about new and exciting considerations for the recording and reporting of Commonwealth transactions, and the challenge was made more difficult for the States since firstly the Commonwealth poached some of the most senior and most experienced Treasury officials from the States and secondly, the States had to reconsider their revenue base since having lost direct tariffs and instead received a distribution of the Commonwealth revenues (after an appropriate and agreed allowance for 'collection' expenses.)

Postscript

The role of Public Accounts since Colonial days has been developing and emerging as successive governments and, in particular, Colonial Treasurers sought more and better ways of balancing the Colonial budgets and fulfilling the Government commitments in developing the railway, telegraphic, education and health infrastructure; they wanted to encourage population growth and regional development and try to remain within the limits of the yearly cash flow. Deficit funding was minimal and very short-term until the 1870s when events changed the nature of Government borrowing and international debt.

This is an early period of interesting and even exciting economic history and requires still further detailed study.

This article is based on the writer's volume covering ' The Development of Public Accounts in Australia—from the early Colony to Federation'.

The purpose of that volume was to fill in some of the gaps that occur in the general writings of this period and to reconcile some of the records held by the State Archives of NSW to events of the Colony. The 400 page Volume puts into context the key economic events of this first 100 years; discusses the confusion and conflict over the sale of Crown lands and the use of the resulting revenue; analyses the Blue Book period and the recording methodology set down by the British authorities and the Colonial Secretary's attempts to work within these guidelines.

CHAPTER 9

A BIOGRAPHY OF EDWARD PULSFORD

The Honourable Senator Edward Pulsford, an active Sydneysider from 1876 was a distinguished elected member of the first Senate in the Commonwealth of Australia Parliament. He was elected on a platform of supporting freetrade—the typical NSW *v* Victoria conflict of 'Freetrade'(NSW) and 'Protection'(Victoria). A supporter of Henry Parkes, a colleague of Sir George Dibbs and Sir George Reid, and a self-styled anti-protection and anti-immigration restrictions, he assisted the Federation movement by providing written submissions on his two pet projects, namely the abolishment of any artificial barriers to both trade and immigration.

An Englishman by birth, he was to marry, for a second time, in 1919 Blanche Elsbeth Brown. Blanche married Pulsford on 2nd March 1919 but was widowed a short time later (on the 29th September 1919).

Edward Pulsford (1844-1919) had been born in Burslem, Staffordshire, England, the son of a Baptist Minister. He was educated privately, but by 1870, Edward and his Father, James, were in business as commission agents in nearby Hull. In 1884, Edward transferred his business activities to Sydney, whilst James transferred to New York, as Secretary of the Liverpool, London & Globe Insurance Company.

Pulsford commenced his active support of the free trade movement, by becoming Secretary of the Freetrade Association, once he set himself up in Sydney and then established the Liberal Association of New South Wales along with the English educated (Rugby School) B.R. Wise. The Forum was originally intended as a forum for liberal economic ideas, but in the election of February 1887, it became the first free-trade party machine.

Remaining its Secretary until 1901, Pulsford was its principal organiser and propagandist, publishing a range of newspaper articles, essays and pamphlets in defence of the free-trade cause. His writing was not restricted to advocacy of free trade. In 1884 he wrote a thoughtful Tract *'Thoughts and suggestions on the commerce and progress of New South Wales'.* His controversy with Timothy Coglan (Colonial Statistician) commenced with the publication of this work, which contradicted some of the contents of the first Coglan (official) publication, the *'Wealth and Progress of New South Wales'.* Pulsford was an active Federationist, and as such his second and somewhat larger controversy with Coglan took place over the question of the probable cost of Federation to New South Wales.

Pulsford was a contributor to Webster's International Dictionary as well as being a regular correspondent on financial and commerce matters to numerous Colonial newspapers and then from 1890-1898 he became the proprietor of the Armidale Chronicle. He was appointed as a political adviser to Sir George Dibbs, but in 1895, after Dibbs lost the leadership position, Sir George Reid appointed Pulsford to the Legislative Council. Reid had won (in the 1896 elections) a resounding electoral endorsement on a policy of free trade and direct taxation .

Having made a significant contribution to the Finance Committee of the Federation Debate, Pulsford organised in 1900 the Inter-colonial Free Trade Conference in Sydney which set up the Australian Free Trade Association to fight the first Federal Elections. He was President of the NSW Branch and edited the Association's weekly newspaper *'Our Country'* for nine months from 1900-1901. Pulsford was elected to the Senate in 1901, representing the Australian Free Trade Association, and held his seat until 1910. His next work *Commerce and the Empire(1903)* argued the case for bringing 'all parts of the Empire into line with British fiscal policy', and 'condemned the delusion of Imperial preferences'. He was a fervent free trader and a 'zero tariffs' advocate. His final work,' The *Commerce and the Empire (1914 and after)*, published in 1917, was an update of his earlier work of the same name, but its reviewer W.G. McMinn (an eminent Australian constitutional expert) claims " though much more readable than the earlier work, it was a far more polemical (argumentative and quarrelsome), the product of long experience becoming clouded by the petulance of an aged, and increasingly deluded prophet". As a legislative Councillor he opposed the Henry Parkes poll-tax of 1895 which was imposed on the Chinese immigrants, and he voted against the 1901 Immigration Restriction Act, and supported unrestricted immigration against the then tide of the White Australia movement.

Pulsford first married in Hull in 1870 and the union produced three sons. His second marriage to Blanche Brown in 1919 produced no heirs. After his death later in 1919 he was buried in Gore Hill cemetery following Anglican rites.

Pulsford 'is most notable as one of the last survivors in Australia of the spirit of nineteenth-century liberalism' (McMinn) . Blanche died in 1948, a widow for 30 years.

The Pulsford philosophy can be separated into two distinct elements—one of unforgiving support for freetrade and then, equally passionate support for free movement of peoples, open immigration and total opposition to the policy of 'White Australia'.

He is on record as promoting both concepts, which in the late 1800s were not readily accepted. The Colony of New South Wales had grown into economic maturity based on the concept of Free trade and had readily adopted such policies in relation to Van Dieman's Land , New Zealand and South Australia. But the raising of sufficient revenue to meet the burgeoning needs of the 'Mother' Colony meant implementing taxation measures such as raising tariffs and imposing duties on imported, as well as on the inter-colonial transfers of goods. This policy was also that of Henry Parkes, George Dibbs and George Reid. Although all three were Federationists and took an active role in the federation movement, only Reid was to transfer his energy to the Federal sphere and become a successful leader.

The Freetrade movement grew from the inspiration of Pulsford upon his migration from England to Australia and his establishment of the Freetrade Association, along with B.R. Wise, a brilliant but eccentric English educated Australian. Pulsford was to assume the role of Secretary of the Association and carry out the secondary role of publicist and propagandist. This second challenge was one met by Pulsford with vigour and active participation in public discussion. He was a natural writer, reporter and publicist. The newspaper representing the views of the Association was widely read and well supported by advertisers. '*Our country*' was a tabloid size and usually contained around 20 pages. The front page generally contained the latest shipping advertisements, whilst the inside pages provided latest reports on the Federation Movement, facts about imports and exports and immigration. Pulsford never missed an opportunity to push his goals and ideas forward on any and all unsuspecting readers. His own writings were well publicised and given prominent showings. When he was nominated to the NSW Upper House—The Legislative Council—he used the weekly newspaper to set out his policies, and report each of his speeches in the Chamber.

He was a keen writer of tracts such as his 1892 effort ' The Rise, Progress and Present Position of Trade and Commerce in New South Wales' .(Printed in 1892 by Charles Potter-Government Printer). His books followed—'*Thoughts and Suggestions on the Commerce and Progress of New South Wales' (1895), and "Commerce and the Empire*' (1903) but shortly to be followed by a complete revision and update of '*Commerce and the Empire(1914 and after)*' in 1917. Whilst a Senator, he condensed a series of speeches on his opposition to the ' The Immigration Restriction Bill' (1901) into a tract entitled ' The British Empire and the Relations of Asia and Australasia—Immigration Restrictions in Australia' by Senator Pulsford (Printed by William Brooks and Company Limited—Printers and Publishers, Sydney 1903).

Although he was editor of 'Our Country' for only a short period—1900-1901—he left us with a wealth of views and opinions included in various issues of the weekly paper. For instance in the issue of March 2, 1901, the headline across the three column page read ' Mr Pulsford's Candidature for the Senate—A Speech by Mr Pulsford' The speech was then reported on the next three full pages. The following issue—March 9, 1901, saw a full page letter 'To the Electors of New South Wales'. His 'letter' is interspersed with quotation of poetry by Kendall (Henry)' *we waft goodwill from shore to shore*' and of Wentworth ' . . . . *fruitful commerce in thy lap shall pour/The gifts of ev'ry sea and ev'ry shore.*' His statement that 'Of course I believe in a "White Australia"is in total contrast and apposite to his views in the tract on the Immigration restrictions of 1903 " The 'fifties came with something of a rush under the spell of the gold discoveries. The spell of gold also caused thousands of Chinese to pour into the colonies of Victoria and New South Wales, and the problem of the relations of Asia and Australasia came into existence. The trouble has centred round the Chinese during the fifty years since it began, but for them it might never had existed in an acute form in Australasia, the whole of the other Asian immigration being relatively trivial." He later records(in the same article) the 'sad, shameful, but not unnatural climax to legislation, which treated with contemptuous indifference the feelings, hopes, inspiration, of tens and hundreds of millions of people' He was concerned at that stage with 'the people of China having been effectually blocked (the order was—'Slam the door'), the cry speedily arose to extend similar restrictions to the people of Japan; the people of British India; various other Asiatics; Polynesians, etc. The cry became a political asset to be realised on all possible occasions.'

So Pulsford's dilemma was 'A white Australia', 'unrestricted immigration' or selected immigration. He recalls that in 1901, 'the protests that were made against the character of the restriction proposals were swept aside, almost without the courtesy of acknowledgment. Finally, not content with insulting the people of India, Japan, China and elsewhere, the Federal Parliament proceeded to the wild extreme of prohibiting the employment of coloured persons on the high seas on board any vessel on contract to carry mails for Australia.' Pulsford writes that 'in 1901, federation having come about, the Commonwealth Government at once made the subject of Immigration Restriction for united Australia a matter of legislation. The Bill, which imposed the education test, admittedly intended to be applied only to the coloured races, was strongly opposed by myself in the Senate. I moved an amendment on the second reading condemning the bill on the same grounds as those on which I had condemned similar bills in the State of New South Wales, but, unfortunately, I could not get enough support to warrant my forcing the amendment to a division. In the course of my speech, whilst I was referring to 'our fellow subjects in India' an interjection was made by the leader of the Labour Party in the Senate. The interjection, and my reply to it, are thus reported in Hansard, November 13, 1901:-

Senate McGregor—The honourable senator is very fond of his fellow-subjects it appears.

Senator Pulsford—I am. I look upon the whole of the inhabitants of Asia as my friends. I am perfectly willing that they should be called my friends, and I hope, so long as God gives me breath, that I shall have the courage to stand up for what I consider to be right for them, as I shall stand up for what I consider to be right for myself, or for any other person

For a spontaneous statement of support for an anti-White Australia position, Pulsford was quite fluent and cogent—as he said, it was 'uttered on the spur of the moment, as evidence of the spirit and earnestness which I bring to bear on this subject.' All during the first session of the Senate, Pulsford had a notice of motion on the Business Paper, but no 'favourable opportunity offered for moving this motion, and was still on the paper when the session ended.'

Senator Pulsford—To move that, in the opinion of this Senate, it is desirable to—

(1) Make alterations in the Immigration Restriction Act so as to make such Act less offensive to Asiatics.

(2) Repeal the clause of the Postal Act under which the Postal Department is forbidden to give a contract to vessels carrying coloured crews.

Pulsford became friendly with the Japanese Consul in Sydney. At that time, all foreign delegations and representations to Australia were handled through London, leaving only consular contact in Sydney or Melbourne. The consul entered into frequent correspondence with any one who would listen or could make a difference in the Immigration Restriction debate. The Japanese representative, Mr Consul Eitaki, took every opportunity to write to Premiers in New South Wales and Victoria and even the Prime Minister, Edmund Barton, usually along the lines as included in his letter of November 25th, 1897

> "our position will be to obliging without losing the position we have attained in the esteem of the world. The people at home will never consent to being put under the same category with the Africans and the Polynesians."

The response that 'full and proper consideration will be given to your government's position' drew a further letter from the Consul dated 27th January, 1898.

> "I thank you sincerely for your kind note of December 10th. The tone of your letter takes a heavy burden from my heart. I beg you, and trust that you will kindly do your best for the sake of the good friendly relations between your Colony and Japan. In fact, there is no ground whatever that would induce Australia to object to Japan and the Japanese . . . .
>
> I hope earnestly that you will let me know any important development regarding the relation of the two countries; for, as a pioneer of the Japanese Consular establishment in Australia, I am truly interested in the good commercial relations that will grow up."

As a final word on immigration restrictions in the Colonies, Pulsford writes (The British Empire P23) " On 26th July, 1899, I moved the adjournment of the New South Wales Legislative Council to call attention to the fact that the Government was doing by regulation that, which, when done by Legislation, was disallowed by the British Government, and that such regulations were, therefore, *ultra vires*. The regulations specifically referred to members of the coloured races. The Government (of Sir George Reid) ultimately recognised that my contention was correct, and withdrew the regulations in question, but the withdrawal was resultless, as it was otherwise made clear to the officers, that the Act was directed only against coloured people." Pulsford exchanged correspondence with his friend the Japanese Consul and included the personal opinion that 'I have never wavered in my belief that the people themselves are far more in sympathy with Japan, and indeed with other Eastern peoples, than the legislation of their Parliaments would appear to indicate'

So it appeared that Pulsford was in favour of White Australia for election purposes in 1901 but in 1897-98 was opposed the immigration restrictions by stealthy under New South Wales regulations, and was equally opposed to the Immigration Restrictions Act of the first Federal Parliament which embraced the concept of White Australia and which was to 'influence' Australia's immigration policies until 1972, when Whitlam made his change to Government policy. The united non-labour parties of Free trade and Protection parties in 1901 introduced the Federal Legislation. The Fisher (the world's first Labor Government) Labor Government of 1907 endorsed and extended the legislation, and the Calwell Immigration Ministry of 1947 renewed and extended the policy again until Whitlam reversed and cancelled the policy of White Australia.

Again, on the topic of Free Trade, it seemed that Pulsford was equally as ambivalent as he was on White Australia. He wrote in his policy statement in 'Our Country' of March 9, 1901, that

"The question of the Tariff is far more than one of fiscal policy: it lies at the bottom of sound finance, honest government and true democracy, and it affects the friendly relations of our country with every other. A purely revenue tariff of about eight (8) million pound will be a burden quite big enough for Australia to carry without adding thereto the still bigger burden of a plunder tariff for the enrichment of a few people."

Pragmatism is moribund. On one hand Pulsford acknowledges the necessity of raising public finance by imposing tariffs but then claims a tariff is a plundering of national resources. He extends his contrariness to the protectionist policy of the United States of 1900. He claims that if the amount plundered by the United States by protected manufacturers were proportionately reached in Australia, such plunder would reach 20 million pound annually.

Agreeing that government revenue was a necessary evil , but not offering an alternative mechanism to a tariff on imports, Pulsford goes on to suggest that

"it is idle for anyone to pretend that there is nothing to choose between a revenue and a protective, or as I call it, a plunder tariff. The producers of Australia battling against a difficult climate, and with the width of the world separating them from their principal markets, have surely the right to exchange their hard-won products for the largest quantity of goods the world will supply, instead of being compelled to accept small quantities at the hands of protected manufacturers."

To conclude his election manifesto as published in 'Our Country' on March 2nd 1901, Pulsford claims that " As the principal promoter of the Inter-colonial Freetrade Conference held in Sydney a year ago, as the President of the New South Wales division of the Australian Freetrade and Liberal Association, and as editor of my Freetrade paper, 'Our Country', I have taken a very full part in the awakening of Freetrade throughout Australia. My engagements in this direction are still onerous, and will remain so right up to the day of polling. Under the circumstances I am precluded from giving that personal attention to my own candidature which I otherwise would give, but I do not think that I shall be allowed to suffer for my devotion to the cause of freedom in commerce. I ask you to vote for the selected Freetrade six (a ticket of 6 candidates representing the Freetrade Association), the whole six, and none but the six . . ."

Pulsford was pragmatic in the extreme. He argued for preserving the revenue derived from tariffs, but abhorred the fact that Freetrade could not be free with tariff barriers and protected manufacturing because of tariffs.

As a supporter of federalism, he disclaimed damage and indeed 'injury' done by Colonial tariffs to Britain. 'Commercial war' he roared is about to be declared by the Parliament against the rest of Europe. Pulsford's manifesto incorporated his Freetrade dichotomy " Now that Australia is about to sweep away protection between State and State, she ought to complete that splendid reform by sweeping away every vestige of that hateful policy from her international trade—a trade which is mainly with the British Empire. That Australia possesses the power to injure British Trade is the strongest reason why that power should not be used, since it is only by a generosity probably without parallel in the world's history on the part of Great Britain herself that Australia has obtained such power . When HRH the Duke of Cornwall and York opens the new Parliament, the Government is prepared to make him the mouthpiece for a declaration of commercial war against the rest of Europe. It is strange that gentlemen whose sincerity and loyalty to King and country cannot otherwise be called in question should submit themselves to such a course. "

The Pulsford suggestion to eliminate tariffs as a revenue item is 'economy in government'.

"Economy is a necessity of the times. The eight million pounds which has to be collected through the Customs is felt to be a heavy burden, but the burden which really strains Australia is interest. Roughly, it may be taken at 15 million pound, the very cream of our production. Though times are better than they were, there remains a stringency which is widely felt, and economy is both wise and compulsory. During the last 15 years (as an MLC) I have often raised my voice on behalf of economy in government, and I shall feel compelled to insist upon it on the part of the Commonwealth."

His other measure of economy is to restrain undue military development.

'While rejoicing at the felling of unity that ,marks our race wherever resident

I do not forget that Australia's main defence is her remoteness from the rest of the world.'

In an 1892 series of articles on "Capital and Finance in Australasia" for the Sydney Morning Herald, Pulsford suggests that the rush of new capital coming into the country in the form of Government borrowing, local council borrowing, private borrowing overseas and transfer of capital by immigrants(the total of all sectors amounts to over 200 million pound during the five years 1886-1890) was excessive, but more excessive in Victoria where borrowing per head of population was 51 pound but in NSW was only 43 pound. This dispute over the economic prowess of NSW versus Victoria raged from the 1860s. When in 1854 Victoria was separated from New South Wales and began its slow journey of colonisation from Port Phillip, the political managers of NSW tried very hard to evidence the superiority of the Mother Colony in all respects. But gold fever in Victoria brought with it great riches, enormous population gains and great progress.

Pulsford in various writings tried to debunk the myth of Victorian dominance of the Australia landscape. He wrote of the wealth and progress of New South Wales and the decline of economy in Victoria. He chose a letter to the Editor of the Sydney Morning Herald by a Mr Staples , wherein Staples attempted to 'clear the air, get a clear view and properly appreciate the conditions which have surrounded the two Colonies of Victoria and New South Wales during the last quarter of a century, to put down the Victorian achievements overall by reflecting on the level of borrowing between the two. .

However a brilliant summary of the gathered facts were presented by Pulsford he had least had the honesty to say in conclusion, that the figures are based on somewhat obscure and approximate data, but clear enough to ' say with certainty that it is Victoria and not New South Wales that has had the greater impetus to prosperity by the expenditure of British Capital' (SMH 2/2/1901)

He discussed the revenue from land sales which had only latterly (1855) been added to consolidated revenue rather than allocated by the British Treasury, and concluded that the two colonies were approximately equal in the revenue created by these sales, but his bottom line argument is quite novel for these (or in fact, any) times. Pulsford draws comfort from the claim that protectionist policies in Victoria are holding back the growth of that Colony but admits that Victoria had 50% more population; the representatives of British capital headquartered themselves in Melbourne; more gold was found in Victoria; the development of railways was double in Victoria; Victoria was producing more than enough wheat for her own use; Victoria industry had invested over 27 million pound in other states and was taking one and a half million pound per annum in interest and profits; NSW was paying Victoria one million pound per annum in interest and profit.

"Let it be remembered(Pulsford says) that the blessings that have flowed to Victoria through the open door policy of New South Wales are not due to her own closed door policy, since Victorians admit that access to New South Wales markets had been to them a source of great prosperity, but the closed door policy was a cause of depression to New South Wales."

However, the superiority of New South Wales remains and is still more marked, concludes Pulsford.

What an enormous enigma Pulsford shows himself to be. On the one hand, I am in favour of White Australia, and free trade and the bounteous wealth of New South Wales, and a proud devotee of the Colony, and worthy to represent her in the Federal Parliament. On the other hand, I am in favour of open immigration, of tariffs only for revenue purposes, of not injuring Britain in our trade war in Europe but of relying on Britain for defence and foreign policy matters.

But his manifesto (Our Country March 9, 1901 P4) states that :-

"the state rights of New South Wales exceed those in importance of any other state. Questions such as the (location of the Australian) capital, the rivers, the railways, the finances, military and naval services, postal and telegraph services, public debts, inter-state commerce, all present points where the interests of this state may conflict with other states. In those matters, the wide knowledge I posses of commercial and financial affairs, and of economic law, fits me, I submit, to watch the interests of new South Wales. At the same time I should expect that New South Wales would wish her affairs watched in no churlish spirit but with the broad-mindedness worthy of the leading State and her past history."

Would the real Edward Pulsford please stand up?

Pulsford had an extraordinary knowledge of facts relating to the commercial; side of the Colonies but relied on his friendship with Timothy Coglan, the Colonial Statistician, to assist in the gathering and collation of the facts. Coglan wrote his classic 'The Wealth and Progress of new South Wales' in 1892, whilst Pulsford, using the same facts wrote 'The Rise, Progress and position of trade and Commerce in New South Wales' in 1892.

Pulsford's expostulation in his thesis if masterful, full of relevant facts but also passionate. As W. G. McMinn wrote (refer above) his writings became clouded by the petulance of age', but more so, he was clouded by a fiery spirit and commitment to a cause that blinded all objectivity and perfect analysis. His thesis on the parochial world of NSW Commerce and

Industry is a brilliant, thorough and inspirational study of Australian commercial conditions and trends in three main periods from 1788 to 1871. It is a classic statement of opportunities leading to wealth and power. That it was published privately rather than by the Government printer and sold for One Shilling suggests a hidden profit motive. It was largely circulated and ran into a second printing in 1896. The 51 page work was a spirited defence of Australian industry. It reflects innovation, entrepreneurial ability and a 'craft' generated by the need to get things done, inspite of not having the right or all the equipment. Included in the thesis are fine supporting tables and data gathered by Timothy Coglan, the Colonial Statistician. The work treats with gentleness the moral question of gold discovery in the 1850s, the vexed concern of different railway gauges between Victoria and New South Wales, the development of international shipping, the intake of convicts and the rise of wealth in all Colonies.

Practical Politics

Pulsford stood for election to the NSW Legislative Assembly and the Senate, with only the latter being successful, but he was appointed to the NSW Legislative Council.

The last week of the Federal Election campaign in 1901 saw Pulsford and George Reid at the Paddington Town Hall. The campaign was one of 'every man for himself'. Pulsford led one of the very few 'tickets' in the country when he paraded a full complement of 6 candidates for the Senate ticket on behalf of the Freetrade Association. But there was no Liberal or National Party organisation in those early days. There was a Labor Party originating in Queensland and New South Wales which came together after the 1892 Shearer's strike in the Darling Downs area of Queensland, and there was a National Liberal Party led by Alfred Deakin in Victoria but these two 'parties' were limited in both candidate numbers and name recognition, and were without any coordinated policies (mainly because the Victorians were protectionist and the NSW/Queensland groups supported free trade). Even the Federation movement did not provide the rallying point for centralised party machines. It was not until Menzies coordinated the non-Labour factions (there were 41 registered parties of a conservative, nationalist outlook that merged into one Liberal Party of Australia in 1944) that party politics began to look real.

No where does Pulsford define the concept or reality of 'Freetrade', and yet it's in need of definition if we are to understand the apparent conflicts contained within Pulsford's speech at Paddington. One such conflict arises in his analysis of the American scenario. For instance Pulsford quotes Carnegie (from his *Triumphant Democracy*—1896) where he writes " Truly, here is the most magnificent exhibition of freetrade which the world has ever seen".

"In the United States—a veritable world in itself—settlement and development on a gigantic scale have been possible, and have been achieved because no internal tariff restrictions stood in the way."

But Pulsford also quotes the protectionist system policy of the United States of 1900. He claims that if the amount 'plundered' by the United States by applying high tariffs to imports and thus protecting U.S. manufacturers were proportionately reached in Australia, such plunder would reach 20 million pound annually(instead of only the 8 million pounds projected for the next twelve months.

In another conflicting analysis, Pulsford talks about the 'natural protection of imports—" Taking goods of all descriptions together, there is probably an all-round natural protection of 25 percent to the Australian manufacturer."

'Of course (Pulsford writes), where the bulk is great and the value small, the freight and charges become very heavy. Thus, salt costs about 200 percent on its shipping value to bring to Australia. This meant a 200 percent natural protection to any salt producer in Australia. Yet we have found a heavy customs duty asked for by people making salt locally. On kerosene it reached 50 to 100 percent; soda crystals 50 percent; stoves and grates 70 percent; woodenware, earthenware and ordinary glassware 100 percent; drapery goods 30 percent and ladies straw hats still higher. There is probably overall an all-round natural tariff protection of 25 percent to the Australian manufacturer.

Pulsford then quotes, with some level of affectation the concept of differential tariffs. Pulsford did not lean towards the Edmond Barton concept of differential tariffs, which he (Pulsford) was inclined to call 'conscience' money, which the protectionists wished to pay away to Great Britain. Mr Barton was inclined to =favour a 'preferential' duty system. Pulsford responded that 'freetraders were not called upon to consider such policies because they held out the same freetrade flag which the United Kingdom did. This scheme of preferential duties (said Pulsford) could not be carried out without inflicting great injury on ourselves.'

He refers to the many secret tariffs coming about by applications from industry for increases of protective or the imposition of new protective duties. 'In Victoria in the 1880s, the Minister for Tariffs and Customs received 300 applications for increases of protective duties or the imposition of new protective duties. If 300 applications for increases could be made in one state, what number was likely to be made at a time of forming a protective tariff for all Australia?'

Pulsford lists the statesmen he believes are committed to freetrade. In fact he goes one step further and protests that 'all the great statesmen of the reign of Queen Victoria were freetraders. Peel, Bright, Cobden, Palmerston, Russell, Gladstone, Salisbury, every one of them was a freetrader. Likewise the great historians were so—Macauley, Buckle, Lecky.'

Geoffrey Serle in his contribution to the A.W. Martin (Editor) *'Essays in Australian Federation'* wrote (Chapter 1—**Victoria's Campaign for Federation**)

"A New South Welshman at the Chamber of Commerce meeting in Melbourne suggested that 'It is all very well for Victoria . . . . to say to her neighbours—"Pull down your fences, and we will have a fair fight" but other delegates, in sorrow rather than in anger, denied they were wolves in sheep's clothing.

More significant still, at this first Congress of Chambers of Manufacturers in Melbourne late in 1888 there were strong demands for uniform legislation on such common interests as the estates of deceased persons and insolvents, the recovery of debts, partnerships, patents, trade-marks, insurance etc. In introducing the federal question, the President, Robert Reid, a Melbourne merchant, deplored the 'great darkness which still prevails in Victoria' on fiscal matters. Yet Edward Pulsford, the most able free trade propagandist, had difficulty in carrying a motion in favour of absolutely unrestricted free trade in all aspects. The President of the Chambers, Emanuel Steinfeld, moved a motion for a customs union only if each colony could retain its own tariff against the world outside Australia. After a rip-roaring speech by John Service, a delegate from South Australia, a resolution in favour of all colonies joining the Federal Council of the Federation movement was carried unanimously."

At the time of Pulsford's appointment to the New South Wales Legislative Council, the *Daily Telegraph* and the *Town and Country Journal* both ran short statements on Pulsford the candidate.

In the Daily Telegraph of June 16, 1894 ,accompanied by a 'pen and ink' sketch of Pulsford, was recorded this word picture of the candidate:—

"Mr Edward Pulsford

> Mr Edward Pulsford, a freetrade candidate was born in Burslem, Staffordshire in 1844. His father was a Baptist Minister. After a residence of about 30 years in Hull, the third seaport of the United Kingdom, Mr Pulsford came to Sydney in 1883. He became at once prominently associated with the freetrade cause in New South Wales. His writings on fiscal and financial matters are within the general knowledge of newspaper readers throughout the Colony. Mr Pulsford was a candidate for East Sydney in 1891, on the occurrence of a vacancy by the death of Mr Street. At the general elections , a few months later, Mr Pulsford again became a candidate for that district, but at the request of his Party, he retired. The Parkes Government, who had placed the cause of Federation before that of

Freetrade, seeking to secure both the rejection of Mr George Reid and the election of Mr Barton. Mr Pulsford was the first to call public attention to the number of electors who were being disfranchised under the new Electoral Act by removing from the constituencies for which they had qualified and obtained votes."

The Town and Country Journal of September 14, 1895 also included a sketch of Edward Pulsford, along with a photograph. The word picture reported as follows:—

"Hon. Edward Pulsford

The Legislative council for New South Wales has 10 new Councillors one of whom is the Honourable Edward Pulsford. Mr Pulsford is a native of England. He was born in Burslem, Staffordshire in 1844 and came to Sydney in 1883. He has a good knowledge of finance and the principles of taxation and has been a frequent contributor to the press on these subjects. For some years he was Secretary of the Freetrade Association of New South Wales, and did much to sustain the cause of Freetrade at a time when its supremacy in New South Wales was seriously threatened. He is now a newspaper proprietor, and in order not to endanger the freetrade interest politically has on more than one occasion retired from the field after announcing himself as a candidate, so that the party vote should not be split up among rival candidates. "

OBITUARY

(Sydney Morning Herald—September 30,1919)

Great Freetrader Dead—Ex-Senator Pulsford

One of the best informed and most widely known advocates of freetrade in Australia, ex-Senator Edward Pulsford, died suddenly at his home, Cromer, Edgar Street, Chatswood, yesterday. He had, apparently, been in good health until recently, and appeared yesterday morning to be as usual, but a sudden heart seizure proved fatal. He was 75 years of age and twice married. He is survived by a widow and three sons.—Mr J.E. Pulsford, Mr frank Pulsford and Mr H.S. Pulsford.

Senator Pulsford had been a consistent and most active advocate of freetrade ever since his arrival in New South Wales in 1884 from Hull, where he had been engaged in commercial pursuits. It is only recently that he followed up his works on the subject with a book on 'Commerce and the Empire'—the second of that title written by him—which was published in London. Therein he put forward with great clarity and ability the case for Empire freetrade, and the international dangers of protection. He argued that freetrade had been the dominating factor in the building of the Empire, and the establishment of its tremendous financial strength, and that it had done more than anything else to promote friendly relations with foreign powers. For the Empire to adopt a hostile fiscal policy, he urged, would undermine her financial stability and court a variety of dangers.

Within a year of his arrival in Sydney, Mr Pulsford was elected the Secretary of the New South Wales Freetrade Association, and he held that position for about six years. For his services in this cause in Australia in the pre-Federation days he was made an honorary life member of the Cobden Club in London. He worked hard for Federation, and when this was accomplished he retired from a seat he had in the New South Wales Legislative Council for five years, and was elected as one of the Senators for this State in the first Federal Parliament. He lost the seat in the 1910 election. He took a prominent part in convening the intercolonial Freetrade Conference, which was held in Sydney in 1900. As a result of this conference The Australian Freetrade Association was formed, and Mr Pulsford was elected President of the NSW division. For some years he owned

'The Armidale Chronicle' reported that Pulsford

"was an able conversationalist and contributor to the Press on financial, commercial and tariff topics. He was a native of Burslem, Staffordshire, England, and his father, the late James E. Pulsford, was for a time Baptist Minister at Burslem, and was afterwards, for a lengthy period, resident secretary in New York for the Liverpool, London, and Globe Insurance Company. Two of Mr Pulsford's uncles, the Revd Drs John and William Pulsford, were for many years leaders in Congregationalism in Edinburgh and Glasgow.

The funeral will leave Mr Pulsford's late residence at 2PM today for Gore Hill Cemetery.

CHAPTER 10

SOME HIGHLIGHTS OF THE INDUSTRIAL REVOLUTION IN BRITAIN

INNOVATIONS AND INVENTIONS

(The Industrial Revolution in Britain)

The Industrial Revolution in Britain was a series of events between about 1750 and 1850, wherein 'industrialisation' and manufacturing replaced agriculture and agronomy as the nation's main economic activity. With industrialisation came innovation, invention, increased—productivity, trade and standards of living. The revolution mainly affected manufacturing industry but had numerous sub-components such as population changes, and significant overhauls in the commercial, iron, transport, agricultural and textile industries. Its development depended on the unfettered response of private enterprise to economic opportunity.

The major outcomes were the higher wage rates achieved by labour, a trend to specialisation of labour, greater output, greater exports, development of national natural resources, and the export of technology and capital goods and capital funding.

'The industrial transformation in Britain, incorporated individual freedoms and initiative over compulsion and conformity, in addition to uplifting the role of land, labour and capital, as well as producing more goods, with a surplus for trade'.[11]

This is a brief study of the main elements and achievements of the Industrial revolution in Britain and because its time lapse coincided with the development and growth of the colonial economy in New South Wales, an examination will be made as to direct impacts on the colonial economy from the industrial revolution in Britain.

This study is broken down into various headings and sub-headings

Developing the economy through the Industrial Revolution

Changes brought on by the industrial revolution

1. Poverty
2. Dependence on agriculture
3. Lack of occupational specialisation
4. Low geographical integration

Components of the main industrial revolution

1. Demographic revolution
2. Agricultural revolution
3. Commercial revolution
4. Transport revolution
5. Textile industry revolution
6. Iron industry revolution

Chronology of Innovation

Changing Role of Labour
The Role of Capital
The Role of the Banks
Adoption of free Trade

---

[11]   This definition by Beckett in '*The economic History of New South Wales*' *(2002*-Colonial Press)

144

Modern economic growth depends on a continuing process of technical change. What the industrial revolution did was to increase substantially the flow of innovations embodied in the nation's economic activity and turn it into a continuous, if fluctuating, flow. One condition of an industrial revolution is a change in the attitude of mind of the representative producer. Another is 'innovation'. Dr Johnson claimed 'The nation is running mad after innovation'[12]

The complex process of economic change and growth that we named the industrial revolution—whether it concerned agriculture or transport or trade or manufacturing – was a process which called for a massive increase in the input of labour which in turn provided part of the need for that increase. The sustaining of the revolution depended on the unlimited response of private investment to follow economic opportunity and underpin economic innovation.

First, explaining a word used frequently in this study

---

[12] Quoted by Wilson & reader in *Men & Machines* (1958)

Defining 'Enclosure'

'In order to adopt the Norfolk four-course system, it was first necessary to alter the thousand-year-old layout of the arable fields. It was virtually impossible for an individual farmer to grow fodder crops on his strips of land in open fields, for at certain seasons (after harvest, for example) these fields were opened to grazing by the livestock of the whole community. The improving farmer, who grew clover and ryegrass or other legumes or a root crop, would simply have provided additional feed for his neighbours' as well as his own animals. Such an arrangement was possible, of course, if all the farmers cooperated, a rather unlikely but a not absolutely unknown state of affairs. On enclosed land, however, a farmer could cultivate these crops and benefit from his own efforts.

Consequently there was a rapid acceleration of the enclosure movement in England, sometimes by local agreement, or by Chancery decree (in the late 17th century), and by private acts of Parliament in growing numbers (18th century). Some 6,000,000 acres of English fields were enclosed between 1700 and 1845. '[13]

Developing the Economy through the Industrial Revolution

The central purpose of this study is to describe the process and period of the first industrial revolution in Britain[14], and determine the essential features of the economic changes and conditions prevailing before, during and following the designated period. However much of this selected period runs parallel to the occupation and growth of the colonial economy, so the question remains: Did the industrial revolution in Britain directly influence or impact on the colonial economy, and if so, how? Few references, if any, are made by Australian economic historians to the parallel timing of the early formation of the colonial economy and the struggles in Britain of the industrial revolution

---

[13] Extract from Britannica Encyclopaedia 2002
[14] This implies, and correctly so, that there was a second and subsequent industrial revolution

However there is a special relationship, one would think, between the growth of the English economy and the colonial economy. One linkage must be, the first industrial revolution, which is usually considered to have commenced around 1750 and prevailed for a century until about 1850. Both the starting point and the stopping point are difficult to statistically define as trends in output and national income at that time were highly influenced by seasonal variations and labour availability.

This does not imply that there is some definite process or event called an industrial revolution, which takes the same form in all countries in which it occurs. But it does imply that there are certain identifiable changes in the methods and characteristics of economic organisation, in those countries, which constitute a development of the kind that would be described as an industrial revolution.

Such changes can be identified in the following ways:

Widespread and systematic application of modern technology to the process of production for the market

Specialisation of economic activity directed towards production for national and international markets rather than for family, local or barter use.

Movement of population from rural to urban communities

Transfer of emphasis from family and/or tribe and more on corporate or public enterprise

Movement of labour away from production of primary (agricultural) products to the production of manufactured goods and services

More intensive use of capital resources as a substitute for human effort

Emergence of new social and occupational classes by ownership of the means of production other than land, namely capital'[15]

---

[15]   Phyllis Deane *The First Industrial Revolution CUP 1965*

Paul Mantoux [16] records that 'after 1782 almost every available statistical series of industrial output reveals a sharp upward turn. More than half the growth in the shipments of coal and the mining of copper, more than three-quarters of the increase of broad cloths, four-fifths of that of printed cloth and nine-tenths of the exports of cotton goods were concentrated in the last eighteen years of the century'.

Mantoux creates the current convention of dating the first industrial revolution from the 1780's as being the 'approximate date at which the annual percentage rate of industrial growth was first greater than two, a level at which it remained for more than a century'.[17] Professor W.W. Rostow[18] suggests an even more precise starting point, as 'the period 1783-1802 was the great watershed in the life of modern societies'. Thus the parallel development of the colonial economy, and the emergence of a nineteenth century economy, and the impact of the industrial revolution raise the spectre of a special relationship between the two.

Another purpose of this study is to examine the influence of the ongoing industrial revolution in Britain at the time of the first 50 years of the colony being established and determine if the transfer of convicts hindered or assisted the transfer of technology to the colony – at least for the period of transportation from 1788 to 1842. On one hand the growing availability of human labour in terms of convict numbers would have reduced the need for technological improvements, and reduce all 'production' and 'output' to a labour intensive arrangement. On the other hand until Macquarie encouraged government enterprise by way of the 'Timber Yard' and encouraged private entrepreneurs, all purchases for the colony were placed with British manufacturers through the Commissariat, which procedure also hindered the early transfer of manufacturing and industrial operations to the colony. However, when the Lumber Yard was put under pressure to produce more and more output for the growing economy, new technologies and practices, obviously based on knowledge transferred by newly arriving workers and supervisors from England and there became less emphasis on labour and more emphasis on productivity and output.

---

[16]   Paul Mantoux *The Industrial Revolution in the 18th Century 1961*
[17]   T. S. Ashton *The Eighteenth Century 1955*
[18]   W.W. Rostow *The stages of Economic growth 1960*

If we take our starting point as the middle of the eighteenth century, then we begin with pre-industrial Britain, though it is evident that the process of industrialisation had already begun. This conjecture raises the question of a further motive in the decision to transfer British prisoners from England to the new planned penal settlement of New South Wales. Did some clever analysts foresee the need for new or additional raw materials for post-industrial Britain and saw that possibility coming from the penal colony and the associated availability of unskilled labour, being the British prisoners whose labour was available to service the needs of Britain, in the penal colony.

A comparison of certain common elements within both economies can assist in determining the impact of the British economic cycles on the colonial economy.

Poverty

Professor Deane points out that in pre-industrial revolution Britain, average wages were between £8 and £9 per annum per head of population, whereas by the end of the 1750s the average had reached to between £12 and £13, per head of the population. As the revolution took shape in Britain, wages rose, based largely on skills, age and mobility, so, how was poverty, even if common to most economic societies, a factor in the economic cycles relative to the industrial revolution? In Britain, unemployment was relatively high. Even so, the average per head, per annum wage levels may not suggest a high standard of material well-being but they do indicate the existence of a national economic surplus, 'even if this was distributed through socially undesirable channels.[19] Professor Deane goes on to point out[20] that there is a famous controversy concerning the worker's standard of living during the industrial revolution, but at this stage the point to notice is that although the standard of life was simple, and sometimes disastrously vulnerable to climatic extremes in the mid-18th century, there was some economic surplus—some slack in the economy. However it is obvious that the English were better off that most of their contemporaries in other countries – the three richest countries in the world were Holland,

---

[19]   Deane, P. *Ibid* P7
[20]   Deane, P. *ibid* P10

England and France. Dorothy Marshall writing in her 1956 study of *English People in the 18th Century* concluded 'there is little evidence to show that the average member of the labouring poor was filled with bitter resentment or economic despair.

2. Stagnation

"Another characteristic of a pre-industrial community which distinguishes it from an industrial one is that its standard of living and of productivity is relatively stagnant. This is not to say that there is no economic change, no economic growth even, in a pre-industrial economy, but that such growth as does occur is either painfully slow or spasmodic, or is readily reversible. However, the ordinary man saw little evidence of economic growth within his own lifetime and no improvement that could not be eliminated within a single year by the incidence of a bad harvest or a war or an epidemic. In Britain the normal long-term rate of growth (before 1750) was .5 of a percent in real incomes and it was almost as common for the economy to slide into decline as it was for it to grow."[21]

3. Dependence on agriculture

A pre-industrial economy is obviously one in which the principal economic activity is agricultural production. This was the case in Britain before 1750 and was certainly the case in the colony of NSW before 1810. 'An underdeveloped country may be defined as a country with 80 percent of its people in agriculture and a developed country as one with 15 per cent of its employment in agriculture, in both cases giving or taking a little according to foreign trade."[22] Primarily agricultural families accounted for about 68 percent of the English population in 1750[23]. Most inhabitants of 18th century Britain lived in rural areas, though the towns were already beginning to expand.

---

[21] Deane, P. *ibid* P11
[22] Singer, H *The Concept of Economic Growth in Economic development (1960)*
[23] Deane, P *Ibid* Page 13

4. Lack of occupational specialization

Another obvious conclusion must be that a pre-industrial economy has little need of or planning for labour specialisation, whereas the industrialised economy has the need and use for specialised labour. Pre-industrial Britain was essentially unspecialised and the major industries were domestic industries subordinate to agriculture. There was mobility of labour and many mining employees moved from extractive industries to agriculture during harvest or planting time. It was at this time that Adam Smith urged the concept of 'division of labour'[24] and in essence the specialisation of labour. Adam Smith also concluded that in an industrialised economy the share of national income attributed to employees is generally over 50 percent, whereas in a pre-industrial economy this percentage will be generally less than 10 percent.

The low degree of geographical integration

Obviously a by-product of an agricultural economy and the low level of specialisation is the lack of integration among its regions. The general lack of mobility of labour is based on regionally based agricultural output as well as the lack of decentralised manufacturing activity.

'It is evident that the British economy of the mid-18th century displayed a number of features which can be recognised as characteristics of a pre-industrial economy'[25] In addition to any common elements there was certainly sub-elements of the main Industrial revolution. Gains and benefits achieved under and during the industrial revolution in Britain flowed to many countries and were widespread in the impact.

The demographic revolution

One of the features of an emerging industrial economy from its predecessors in the chain of economic development is that it enjoys sustained long-term growth of both population *and* output. The rate of growth of population depends largely on the rate of natural increase (the difference between

---

[24]   Adam Smith *The Wealth of Nations (1950)*
[25]   Dean, P *ibid Page 19*

the birth rate and the death rate). It was obvious in Britain that by the end of the 18th century the changes in both the birth rate and the death rate were such as to constitute a demographic revolution. Poverty, land enclosures and a brutal system of legal enactments in England tended to obscure the reality that a sizeable portion of the convicts were professional thieves hardened by repeated criminality. 'In the main they were working class, unskilled, town dwellers to whom law breaking had become a way of life.'[26]

Professor Deane concludes that there was a complex two-way relationship of cause and effect shaping trends of population growth and output. In the case of population, it was largely non-economic factors, which helped reduce the long-term death rate or raise the long-term birth rate. In the case of output, such factors as the growth of foreign markets and the widening of the technological horizon.[27] But there were other factors to be considered; such as the fact that new technology was introduced into a country that had labour, land and capital resources in reserve. If this was the case in 18th century Britain, it was slanted in a similar direction in the colony of NSW

Malthus observed

"During the last 40 years of the 17th century and the first 20 of the 18th, the average price of corn was such as, compared with the wages of labour, would enable the labourer to purchase with a day's earnings, two-thirds of a peck of wheat. From 1720 to 1750 the price of wheat had so fallen, while wages had risen, that instead of two-thirds the labourer could now purchase the whole of a peck of wheat with a day's labour.[28]

The Agricultural revolution

There were four unique features of the British agrarian revolution.

---

[26] John Malony *Penguin Bicentennial History of Australia* p.16
[27] Deane, P *ibid* P.34
[28] T.R. Malthus *Principles of Political Economy* 1838 *P.238*

Firstly, it involved farming in large-scale consolidated units in place of the medieval open fields cultivated in strips by serfs with rights of pasture, fuel (cut timber) and game on the overstocked common.

Secondly, it involved the extension of arable farming over heaths and commons and the adoption of intensive livestock husbandry

Thirdly, it involved the transformation of the village community of (largely) self-subsistent peasants into a community of agricultural labourers whose basic standards of living came to depend more on the conditions of national and international markets than on the state of the weather.

Fourthly, it involved a large increase in agricultural productivity. That is the volume of output produced by the full-time labour force in agriculture grew significantly.[29]

In Britain, the agricultural revolution took place when three related developments occurred. (1) The adoption of new techniques of production (2) enclosure, and (3) changes in entrepreneurial attitudes.

The agricultural revolution, as a division of the industrial revolution, contributed in a number of ways to the effectiveness of the primary transformation. (1) By feeding the growing population and in particular the population of the industrial centres; (2) by inflating purchasing power for the products of British industry, and (3) by providing a substantial part of the capital required to finance industrialisation and keep it going even through a period of major war.[30]

The commercial revolution

Ralph Davis, analysing British trade statistics between 1660 and 1700, [31] concluded that 'for most of its pre-industrial trading history, England came close to being a single export economy whereby wool or woollen cloth constituted almost the whole of English exports'. Even by the middle

---

[29] R. Nurske *Problems of Capital Formation in underdeveloped countries* (1953) (1953)

[30] Deane, P *ibid* P.50

[31] Ralph Davis *English Foreign Trade 1660-1700* p.150

of the 18th century, woollen textiles accounted for well over half the value of English domestic exports.

Is it any wonder that the first signs of the new Botany Bay settlement being able to sustain sheep production at a low cost and thus become a replacement for Spanish or German imports was so warmly welcomed and encouraged. English –plantations in the West Indies also opened up re-export markets to Europe and had it 'not been for the tropical products[32] with their elastic demand and growing markets in temperate regions, it would have been difficult to expand British trade with Europe'.[33] G.D. Ramsey analyses that the 'significance of the re-export trade in contributing to British economic growth and industrialisation lay predominantly in its indirect effect on economic organisation and opportunity. It was a direct source of incomes to groups of merchants and seamen' [34], and British re-export significantly supported the new colony of New South Wales, by being called upon to service all colonial supply needs, until the timeframe for ordering and receiving from the colonial commissariat through British merchants encouraged 'import replacement industries' in the colony and brought a new twist to the local manufacturing and agricultural industries.

Trade statistics can turn around very quickly as will be recognised by the immediate impact of colonial wool on the British textile market and the huge demand for imports by the Mills, to the point where a collection of Mill owners, combined to submitting a proposal in 1824 to Earl Bathurst for a land grant in Van Diemen's Land for wool production for sole export to Britain[35]; In 1750 grain accounted for 20% of English exports, but by 1800, Britain was a net grain importer. In 1750 woollens accounted for 46% of exports whilst by 1800, due to scarce source of raw materials, their share had fallen to 28%.

---

[32]   Such products as 'spices, tea, sugar, tobacco, cotton, indigo and dyewoods'

[33]   Deane, P *ibid* P.53

[34]   G.D. Ramsey *English Overseas Trade during the Century of Emergence* (1957) P.237

[35]   This was the beginning of the second land grant company – The Van Diemen's Land Company, formed by Royal Charter in 1826 and still in existence today. Refer Beckett, G ' The Economic History of the VDL Company 1826-1899'

There are at least six ways in which foreign trade can be said to have helped to precipitate the industrial revolution. (1) Foreign trade created a demand for the products of British industry; (2) International trade gave access to raw materials, which broadened the range of British products and cheapened British products in their destination market; (3) International trade provided poor and undeveloped countries with the purchasing power to buy British goods;

(4) It provided an economic surplus, which helped to finance industrial expansion and agricultural improvement; (5) It helped to create an institutional structure and a business ethic which was to prove effective in promoting home-trade; likewise, a more sophisticated set of attitudes to the role of government policy in promoting economic prosperity emerged (6) The expansion of trade in the 18th century was a prime cause of large towns and industrial centres.[36]

The Transport Revolution

The cheapest way of transporting bulky, weighty, goods was by water and Britain scored heavily in this respect by being narrow and insular – no part of the British Isles is farther than seventy miles from the sea—and by having a considerable length of canal system which is either naturally navigable or can be made so. It was this inland system of water navigation that provided the most spectacular innovations of the period. The first Industrial revolution grew on the basis of coal and iron and so it became necessary to move these heavy and bulky raw materials and the finished products quickly and cheaply around the country.

The transport revolution was the crucial factor in facilitating the cost reducing innovations necessary to sustain the industrial revolution.

The Textile Industry revolution

The cotton and iron industries are generally considered to be at the heart of the industrial revolution, that is the growth of modern manufacturing industry and all that this implies – large-scale units of production,

---

[36]   Deane, P *ibid* P.68

labour saving machinery, regimentation of labour, and specialisation of the labour-force We could also say that the demographic, agricultural, commercial and transport revolutions were the most important preconditions of successful industrialisation and the sustained economic growth that goes along with it The iron and cotton industries were two industries which first experienced the changes in technological and economic organisation that made Britain 'the workshop of the world'.[37] The term 'textile' industry is intended to cover both the cotton and woollen industries since both enjoyed similarities in machinery innovation, better quality and better-improved raw materials and indeed a growth of 'subcontractors' in 'cottage' industries able to prepare value adding to basic raw materials at a much lower cost. The invention that really laid the basis for the revolution in cotton was the water-frame, patented by Arkwright in 1769. This produced cotton yarn strong enough to serve as warp as well as waft and thus created a new product – a British cotton cloth that was NOT a linen mixture. Then came the 'jenny' and the combined effects of the water-frame and the jenny show up in the statistics of imports during the 1770s but it was not until the 1790s, after the American War that major increases in imports took place. Between 1780 and 1800 there was a 8-fold increase in raw cotton imports, but since the spun yarn was stronger and thinner, the raw material imports understate the increase in yardage and real value.[38] By the 1780s the volume of exports was 3-4 times the rate of twenty years earlier. By 1815 it was thirty times the volume of 1780. At this same time, exports of cotton textiles accounted for 40% of the value of British domestic exports, whilst woollen goods accounted for only 18 %. This situation caught the imagination of both businessmen and government and provided a dramatic lesson on the profitability of mechanisation. The factories, however, only provided a part of the immense increase in output that put cotton at the head of the British manufacturing industry – most of it was produced by a multitude of 'outworkers'. The tens of thousands of little men who operated jennies and looms in extensions to their cottages provided the industry with buildings and machinery which would have required hundreds of wealthy capitalists to set up on a factory basis. It was this situation more than any other that permitted the immediate expansion of capacity in response to

---

[37]   Rostow, W.W. *Stages of economic growth* p.53
[38]   W. Radcliffe *The origin of Power Loom Weaving* (1828) p.62

technological opportunities and market demand. Thus the costs and risks of the new industry were more widely spread that they would otherwise have been and were more readily undertaken because of this.[39] Obviously the cotton industry's success depended largely on its various factors of production, which were within the capability of the British economy to meet. It was labour-intensive rather than capital intensive, and there was a relatively abundant supply of 'skilled' (e.g. weavers) labour. The mechanisation and industrialisation of an industry had another benefit as well. It related to quality, and in the majority of marketing, when a commodity produced by British manufacturers was of 'good' quality it found a ready-made market. Its improved quality made it competitive with silk and linens and thus the market widened to mass proportions.

Another characteristic of the 18th century cotton industry was the fact that it was highly localised, as was the woollen industry. The reason for these concentrations is unclear but it is likely the concept of 'clustering' (cluster industries) is older than we think. Probably the most important reason for the cotton industry's ability to maintain its profits and hence its rate of investment was the fact that it enjoyed an almost inexhaustible low-priced labour supply. This sustained economic growth of the cotton industry between 1780–1850 is due, in part, to an increasing proportion of the incomes that it generated went to the entrepreneurs, who in turn ploughed back a substantial portion of their earnings into more plant and equipment. This meant two things: (1) the industry went on expanding its capacity to produce and increasing its economies of scale arising from the development of specialised ancillary industries in merchanting, bleaching, dyeing etc; (2) the industry went on improving its equipment even though radical changes in technique were not as rapid as they could have been, given the accessible range of inventions

The Iron Industry

Changes in the iron industry's system of production, which were involved in the industrial revolution, were less radical than changes in the cotton industry. The textile industry had been changed in organisation as well

---

[39]   Mann, Julia *The Cotton Trade & Industry* (1931)

as technology. The iron industry was already capitalistically organised.[40] Another feature of the industrial revolution in iron and steel, which distinguishes it from the cotton industry is that the former expanded on the strength of domestic raw materials, whilst the latter encouraged innovations which enabled British industries to turn from charcoal (a dwindling resource) to coal (abundantly available) and from imported to native ores. Whereas the cotton saved labour through mechanisation, the iron industry did so by economising in raw materials by using materials that were abundant in supply and cheap in place of materials that were scarce and expensive.

It was not until the middle of the 19th century that iron was used to construct railroads, locomotives, ships, machinery, gas and sanitation systems, which greatly expanded the range of its outlets. However, since prices fell steeply due to changes in production techniques, demand was too inelastic to permit a dramatic rise in sales.

Schumpeter[41], makes the case for a cluster of innovations during this period, which was decisive for three main reasons: (1) because they occurred at roughly the same period of time; (2) they came when Britain's naval superiority and contacts enabled her to take advantage of rising European and North American incomes, and (3) because they reinforced each other in certain important respects. The turning point in the industrial revolution took place in 1775 when James Watt's steam-engine made it possible to apply increased power for blowing the blast furnace and mechanical power for forging. 'There is no doubt of the immense importance of the steam engine to the iron industry.[42] The iron industry revolution gave value to British iron-ore resources, which had hitherto been so low grade that they were practically worthless. In addition to iron ore, the industry used large quantities of British limestone and British coal. The iron industry was the most important factor in the rising demand for coal in the first half of the 19th century, and also for transport facilities

---

[40]   Professor Nef *Essays in Economic History*

[41]   E. B. Shumpeter *British Overseas Trade Statistics (1697-1808)* (1960)

[42]   R.H. Campbell *Carron Company* (1961) P. 60

Good cheap iron was required for implements, ploughshares to lathes, for military and naval purposes for hardware, for telegraphic wire, for building purposes and for industrial machinery. The basis had been laid for the engineering industry to serve all British industry and supply the world with machinery during the 19th century, but the biggest contribution during this period was to the railways industry.

However, the iron industry played a role in British industrialisation that was both pervasive and stimulating. It provided cheaply and abundantly the commodity, on which, more than any other single material except coal, modern industry was to depend for its essential equipment

If the industrial revolution can be given a definition, there should be attached to it a fairly precise political and social philosophy and economic circumstance as well as a fairly precise timeframe. Within the main industrial revolution, there must be subsidiary components such as innovation, invention, entrepreneurship, speculation and development of private and government policies hitherto unknown – such as a new role of government, introduction of banking regulation, encouragement of capital creation, free trade, protection of patents, all of which created the environment to foster, encourage and prolong the industrial revolution. Some of these aspects will be considered in further detail.

A Chronology of Innovation

Key aspects of the timeframe include: (1) Changes in entrepreneurial attitudes to innovation (2) changes in the market environment (3) changes in the pace of invention

The period 1783-1802 is not unique as representing change during the industrial revolution. Population was in acceleration before reaching a later peak. The canal mania was preceded by an earlier unprecedented burst of construction activity and canal construction was followed a generation later by the more spectacular and important railway mania. The cotton and iron industries had begun to transform their techniques in earlier decades and by 1802 were still too small a part of total economic activity to carry the national economy along by their own weight. The upsurge in foreign trade, which characterised the period 1783-1802, was also important but not overly spectacular. It was a rebound from the abnormally low trade levels of the 1780s, caused by the American War

The Changing Role of Labour

An inevitable condition of successful economic development is the existence of an expanding, mobile and adaptable labour supply. As a factor of production, labour must be seen as a key ingredient in economic development together with natural resources, technical progress, accumulation of capital, and an increase in the labour supply.

In essence, the rate at which any economy can expand its output of food and services depends on four fundamentals: (1) The rate at which it can enlarge its stock of natural resources; (2) Technical progress also permits the production of larger output of goods and services with a given input of labour and capital; The third determinant of the rate of economic growth is the rate of new investment, and the fourth is the rate of expansion of the labour supply. The determinants are closely inter-related and it is usual not to be able to increase the national stock of natural resources or to introduce technical change without increasing the rate of investment. In the end, the capital required per unit of output may be smaller but at the outset the absolute amount of capital required for the productive process is almost invariably larger. The fact that British entrepreneurs in the late 418th century and early 19th century were able to increase industrial output and capacity without facing correspondingly increased costs due to a rise in the real wage-rate meant that the reward for successful innovation was largely shared between the investor and the consumer. Because in the early stages of the industrial revolution, the increasing population was largely due to the combined effects of a falling infantile death rate and a rising birth rate, the increment was largely composed of infants. Thereupon by about 1821 the active labour force was growing at a slower rate than the overall population. Another factor, which helped to increase the input of labour into the productive process, was the increase in the average number of hours worked per worker and per day. It was also fortunate for British industrialists that the demographic factors were operating in their favour throughout the crucial periods of the industrial revolution, and fortunate also that the technical progress took advantage of the demographic situation. It is not to be imagined that the pioneers of the industrial revolution found a factory labour force ready to use. The transition from agricultural or domestic industries with their seasonal routine, their variable pace and their family based organisation, to the monotonous, machine-driven, impersonal grind of factory work did not come easily to British workers. The early water-driven factories, generally situated in remote rural areas on the banks of streams, were constantly short of labour.

During the second phase of the factory age, within the industrial revolution, there was no cheap labour, but it was largely unskilled and relatively homogeneous and elastic in supply.

The Role of Capital

A second factor of production (the first being labour) whose development was crucial to the British industrial revolution was capital. What additions were made to the nation's capital in the 18ᵗʰ century? For example, the enclosure movement was associated with new investment in hedging, ditching, drainage and those sorts of works required bringing commons and wastelands into permanent cultivation. Urbanisation involved investment in buildings, street paving and lighting, water supply and sanitation. Improvements in communication entailed substantial capital expenditure on roads, bridges, river navigations and canals. These developments were taking place throughout the century though more extensively in the second half of the 18ᵗʰ century, and there was a marked acceleration over the last three decades in the pace of enclosures, of urbanisation and of canal building. But if the national capital grew faster between 1750 and 1799, so too did the national income and the population. If land is excluded from any calculation of the nation's capital, then man-made capital accounts for less than half of the remaining total – this consists mainly of industrial, commercial and financial capital (such as inventory or stock-in-trade, machinery, canals and foreign assets); additionally, public property accounted for about 33%, and farmer's capital for nearly 20% at the beginning of the 19ᵗʰ century. By the 1830s industrialists had been ploughing back profits at a higher than normal rate, or putting more savings into fertilizers, improved breeding stock, and farm machinery, than into enclosure of commons and waste. After the railway age, a very different picture emerges. New estimates put land in at 30%, but declining in relative importance, so that by 1885, land accounted for less than 20% of the total. Farm capital was also less important and declining in absolute terms by the fourth quarter of the 19th century

Railways were not initially a government instrumentality, but consigned to finance and development by private capital. As was the case for the railways, the bulk of the capital needed for the canal developments came from local businessmen who had a special interest in the success of the projected developments. There was much wastage of capital when speculators poured money into questionable projects. In addition to speculative losses, British capital was also being 'exported' and annual capital outflows represented between 3 and 4 percent of national product. More than £500,000 million was invested abroad between 1850 and 1870.

Another way of financing capital formation was to use inflation as a means of generating 'forced savings'. Inflation, sometimes uncontrollable, was a feature of the industrialising economy. Where prices are rising faster than wages, or profits grow more rapidly than either, and because prices (and profits) go on rising, industrialists are happy to plough this windfall back into capital formation.

The capital required for the industrial revolution was found not so much through national savings because the rate of demand for investment seems to have grown little, but from those who had resources to spare and had productive ideas for their use. In practice, the innovators used their own resources or those of friends and relatives. It was often possible for an industrious man to set up in business with very little capital and to build up his own resources until they were large enough to attract the interest of professional investors. Once the new enterprise was earning a steady profit it was usual to finance its continuance and its expansion by ploughing back the profits. Until the Joint Stock Company Act of 1856 established limited liability, incorporation was slow and expensive and required parliamentary sanction, and was rarely used except for schemes requiring abnormally large and unspeculative capital contributions – such as canals, docks, water supply, bridges, roads, gas supply and railways.

The Role of the Banks

The main determinant of the supply of money for the industrial revolution was the supply of gold, as the volume of coinage depended solely on the supply of gold, which in turn depended on the world supply and availability of gold and on the British balance of payments. If exports exceeded imports this generally implied an inflow of gold; conversely, if imports exceeded exports, the excess had to be financed by an export of gold. A system of credit, which depended so heavily on the state of confidence within the economy, caused instability in the economy when anything happened to disturb that confidence; though while the system was incompletely articulated it was still possible for a loss of confidence. This is what happened in 1797 when it was decided to lift the strain by breaking the link between gold and the money supply. The main reason for this decision was the fact that gold was flowing out of the country and there was no immediate prospect of stopping the drain. Apart from the general situation there were also some special circumstances, which precipitated the crisis of confidence. The first of such circumstances was the bad harvest of 17895. Britain's growing population could no longer feed itself when the harvest was below normal, and heavy imports of corn were required in the season of 1795/96. Abroad, the heavy expenditure on British fleets and armies, the subsidies to allies, the loans raised by allies on the British market, all created fresh pressures on the balance of payments, fresh reasons why payments to foreigners should exceed the value of receipts from foreigners and so have to be met by the export of gold. In 1821, the wartime emergency monetary system came to an end and Britain went formally and legally on to the gold standard. English monetary institutions at that time included: (1) a central joint-stock central bank – The Bank of England—which acted also as the government's bank and custodian of the nation's gold reserve; (2) about 60 London private banks of great strength; (3) about 800 small private note-issuing country banks uncontrolled in all matters except the denominations of the notes issued. Probably the English banks have never been so ready to assist innovation or finance long-term investment in industry as they were in the period 1770-1830 when the industrial revolution took shape. However during the period 1809-1830 there was 311 bankruptcies of country banks of which 179 took place in the two periods of 1814-16 and 1824-26.

Adoption of Free Trade

An elaborate system of tariffs designed to protect domestic industry from foreign competition was the focal point of a static economy where the major task of commercial policy was to maintain the *status quo*. *Innovation* and successful *industrialisation* provided opportunities for expansion, and encouraged a less restrictive commercial policy. Even as late as 1850, agriculture was still the major British industry. Whatever affected the level of incomes in the agricultural sector, affected the standard of living of more than a third of the population of Britain, during the first half of the 19ᵗʰ century. A second reasons for agriculture's dominance is due to an industry-wide increase in efficiency Farmers responded to extreme adversity by introducing cost-reducing innovations. The more inefficient farmer was forced off the land by a succession of crises from which there was insufficient time to recover, and those that were left were the fittest to operate in the industry. This higher efficiency resulted from increased investment in agriculture, in improved methods, and hence higher productivity.

The Changing Role of Government

Between 1780 and 1860 a great many restrictions on economic enterprise were done away with. Was this due to the 'triumph of the invisible hand'[43] or did it reflect the deliberate self-effacement of government in favour of a policy of complete laissez-faire? Was the British government really a passive agent in the British Industrial revolution? It was only when government took a more positive and serious role in the economy that it began to streamline its administrative machinery, to remove regulations that it was unable top enforce, and to formulate a considered view on what form its interventions should take and to sharpen its powers in the areas where it wanted to exert most influence. The beginnings of purposeful government economic policy go back to Pitt the younger.

'The odd thing was that a revolution in government, which represented the beginning of collectivism and of the modern welfare state, should have taken place in a community whose articulate political prejudices were flatly

---

[43]   Arnold Toynbe *The Industrial Revolution* (1884)

in opposition to such a development. It happened because of the existence of strong underlying pressures, which proved irresistible in the end.[44]

Nor was it only the central government that was strengthening its power and its will to intervene in the conduct of private enterprise. Local government began to assume wider responsibilities, especially in those larger populated urban areas.

Economic Growth and Economic cycles

The crucial perception that the economic life of *man* was a continuous economic change came in the century 1750-1850 when the scale of the British economy began to expand perceptibly and without limit, and this led to a sustained growth in incomes per head. Somewhere in the middle of the 18th century there is evidence that total national output began to grow-faster than it had done over the previous 100 years. We also know that population and prices and certain kinds of production and incomes and overseas trade, were growing much stronger than ever before. Were prices growing faster than the benefit from improvement in incomes, or was population growing faster than any improvement in production? In trying to assess the national rate of economic growth, the first assumption is that foreign trade (the best source of statistics for the 18th century) was of considerable importance to the economy, whilst an early conclusion is that there was growth in the total national product, in national productivity and in the standard of living (that is, a growth in real incomes per head. After a period of stagnation in output, prices, population, incomes and standards of living between 1700-1750, there was an upward trend in total national output dating from 1750.[45] It seems likely that the national rate of growth was slowed by the French wars before accelerating again in the 1820s and 1830s. In a pre-industrial economy, seasonal fluctuations are more significant than in an industrialised economy, because so much of economic activity is concerned with agriculture, fishing, seafaring and building – all of which are heavily influenced by climatic conditions – and only partly because one of the forms which technical progress takes is the

---

[44]   Arnold Toynbe *The Industrial Revolution* (1884)
[45]   National output in 1780-1799 was growing at the rate of 1.8% per annum, and output per head at a rate of .9% p.a.

adoption of methods and equipment which permit a more even utilisation of capacity and labour and an even flow of transactions throughout the year.

Two characteristics identify a trade cycle (1) an upward surge in economic activity that creates a crisis of confidence and a down turn: (2) a chain of interaction, which carries this disturbance from one sector to another and into the heart of the economy. The more interdependent, the economy the longer and stronger is the chain of the interaction and the greater the impact of the initial disturbance on the total national economic activity. In 1772, the failure of an important banking house caused a severe panic, and the American War brought a deep trade depression, followed by another boom in 1783, followed by another panic. The next panics took place in 1793 at the outbreak of the French wars and in 1797 on the occasion of a naval mutiny. There were crop and weather cycles, which produced sympathetic commercial cycles in pre-industrial economies, when agriculture was the chief economic activity and both trade and industry were dependent on the fortunes of agriculture. There is considerable evidence about the influence of harvests on levels of economic activity, especially where agriculture was the major industry. For the whole period 1750-1850, agriculture was Britain's number one industry. It probably absorbed half of the labour force in 1750 and more than 20% in 1850; it provided most of the nation's food; and in 1750 it made an important contribution to export trade, while by 1850 the harvest was so significant that it impacted on the balance of payments, on the level of imports and on the state of credit in general.

When harvest conditions were such that there was a dearth of agricultural products, the results could be pervasive. (1) There was a rise in raw material costs for a large number of industries; (2) high food prices and unemployment for agriculture workers, and thus reduced purchasing power for industrial products; (3) budget deficits due to a decline in output of dutiable commodities (which were mainly agricultural), which reduced government revenues and an increase in the food bill of the military which increased government expenditures; and (4) an unfavourable balance of payments due to a reduction in exports or an increase in imports of foodstuffs. War was another powerful factor in fluctuations of overseas trade. When war was imminent, merchants hastened to move goods before the trade lanes were closed and overseas business interrupted.

An expansion of the demand for exports produced three effects. (1) A condition of full capacity in some sectors; (2) an expectation of continued increase in output, and (3) an increase in profits. Each of these tended to stimulate an expansion of domestic investment.

Growth in the British economy has been cyclical rather than steady. The three main types of cycles are: (1) the single year seasonal cycles; (2) the trade cycles generally completed within a span of 9 years; (3) and the long waves which stretch over a period of 50-60 years.

Standards of Living

There are important discontinuities in the development process such that the growth of new kinds of industry require substantial initial expenditures on new capital assets (such as buildings, harbours, roads, canals, railway-lines, ships and vehicles, plant and machinery) before incomes begin to rise, and in the interim consumption may actually have to be reduced so that funds can be diverted to these capital expenditures. Since the evidence points to an increase in national output per head of the population, beginning in the 1780s, softened by the French and Napoleonic wars, it implies a rising standard of living, on the average. In general, the wages of workers in industry were higher than those in agriculture, so that as the proportion in industrial employment rose, the average money-wage grew.

There are three presumptions in favour of a rising standard of living, after the end of the war: (1) as industrialisation gathered momentum in the 1820s, employment became more rather than less regular than it had been in pre-war years; (2) the goods that tended to be omitted from the price indices, being largely manufactured goods, were more likely to be falling in price than the goods (mostly raw materials) that were included – and hence the price rises understated the post-war price fall; (3) the falling weight of taxation would, in the situation where most taxes were indirect and regressive, give perceptible relief to the working classes.

The Achievement

What conclusions can we draw from all of this? (1) There is no firm evidence of an overall improvement in working class standards of living between 1780 and 1820. If we take into account harvest failures, growing population, privations of a major war and the distress of post-war dislocation, we may conclude that average standard of livings fell rather than rose. (2) Beginning in the 1840s we find much stronger evidence of improvement in the average real incomes of the working class, evidence strong enough to observe a perceptible increase in real wage rates. In effect, the sustained growth of national product to which industrialisation gave rise tended to exert an upward pressure on working-class standards of living in three main ways: (1) by creating more regular employment opportunities; (2) by creating more opportunities for labour specialisation and hence hirer incomes than unskilled or semi-skilled workers could achieve; (3) the upward pressure on worker's standard of living operated through reductions in the prices of consumer goods and the widening of the range of products that could be found in the worker's 'basket of commodities'.

It would be generally agreed that Britain had been through an industrial revolution by 1850, though the revolution was not over. This implies that there had been significant economic changes, especially in three main ways differentiating the industrial revolution from the pre-industrial arena.

It differs in three ways:

(1) In industrial and social structure.

In 1850, more people were engaged in manufacturing than in agriculture. Nearly 3.25 millions of its work force were engaged in manufacturing compared with only 2 million in agriculture. Agriculture had also moved away from the owner-operator small plot syndrome found widely in the pre-industrial era. By 1851 more than 75% of all agriculture workers were paid employees. The term 'manufacturing' covers a wide range of activities, from cobbler to factory worker. However, the most significant difference between the labour forces of 1850 and 1750 was the degree of labour specialisation found in 1850. Also the distribution industry was the last stronghold of the traditional pre-industrial economy until well into the 19th century. Of course it had to adapt to the new industrialised economy.

(2) In productivity and in standards of living associated with higher productivity,

Over the century between 1750 and 1850, production per head is estimated to have multiplied nearly 2.5 times in Britain, and brought with it more than a doubling of the national standard of living.[46] Not all industries or community groups shared in this improvement. Certainly in industries like transport, textiles and iron manufacture, output per worker increased dramatically, though wages per worker rose only modestly. The large mass of labourers, with no skills, was probably better off in the up-phases of trade cycles than their forebears. Builders worked 52-64 hours per week according to season; a London compositor worked 63 hours per week all year round, as did the engineer and iron-founder. It seems that if the working classes earned more and spent more in 1850 than the labouring poor of the pre-industrial revolution, they paid for it in hard toil. The industrial revolution gave them a chance to better themselves by working harder.

(3) Rates of economic growth

The rate of growth of real national product was given by two factors: the momentum achieved in the sectors that were modernising and the rate at which resources were shifted from low-productivity, low-growth sectors to high-productivity, high-growth sectors. For gross national product as a whole, the peak rate of growth was not reached until the second half of the 19th century when industrial output was already showing a retarded rate of growth. In part, the slowness of the British rate of growth was an inevitable consequence of this being the first industrial revolution. Trail blazing is often slow whilst the economies that follow in the path had the advantage of uncertainties being removed.

---

[46]   Dean & Cole *British Economic Growth*

There were basically three main factors on which the rate of growth of an economy depends: (1) the rate of growth of the labour forces (2) the rate of capital accumulation, and (3) the rate of technological change. Technical progress proceeded at a leisurely pace in the British industrial revolution by comparison with later industrialisations. The transition from hand spinning-wheel to powered machines and from charcoal-fired furnaces to coal-fired furnaces took place rapidly only after crucial inventions in the last quarter of the 18th century, and the mainline railways were laid within a couple of decades after their economic justification of the 1830s. American inventiveness had begun before American industry began to compete with British manufactures on world markets. The Americans lived with a shortage of labour but an enterprising attitude characteristic of an immigrant community, and so were extremely receptive to labour-saving improvements. By 1859, less than a decade after the introduction of the sewing machine, there were five times as many in operation in the United States as in Britain. The corollary of a modest rate of technical progress is a slow rate of growth in the productivity of the economy. National product grew between 2 – 3 percent per annum during the 19th century, by about 1 ½ percent in the first half and by 2 ½ in the second half.

SUMMARISING THE COMPONENTS OF THE INDUSTRIAL REVOLUTION

Having tendered an overview of events and sub-components of the industrial revolution in Britain, a broad definition can be assembled.

There was a continuous flow of innovations, which often encouraged technological changes in associated industries eg. Steam benefited both industry and the development of the railways, as well as encouraging the search for natural resources such as coal and iron ore. Economic development of further natural resources followed

Technological change encouraged specialisation of economic activity especially towards large-scale production.

There was a movement from agricultural production to manufactured goods which, whilst not reducing the demand for grain and foodstuffs required agriculture to be more equipment oriented and more productive

There was a strong population growth based on higher live birth rates and longer life-spans

There was more intensive use of capital resources eg equipment, in lieu of labour and an expansion of capital formation

There was an upward turn in industrial output, and an expansion of trade, accompanied by an exporting of skilled labour and capital (both capital funds and capital equipment)

There was a general move to 'clustering' of like industries, economies of scale and continuous technical improvements

The economic surplus from new trade helped finance industrial expansion and general agricultural and industrial improvement.

Standards of living improved as did wage rates across all sectors of the economy.

There was an upward turn in industrial output

BROAD INDUSTRIAL REVOLUTION IMPACTS ON THE COLONIAL ECONOMY

Numerous studies have outlined the growth and development of the colonial economy from 1788. For example, N.G. Butlin (*Forming the Colonial Economy*), and indeed, N.J. Butlin, (*Foundation of the Australian Monetary System*), Hainsworth in *Sydney* Traders. Even Shaw, Fitzpatrick and Hartwell, in their individual ways, discussed many aspects of the colonial economy,

Now the similarity in the first twenty-five years of the colony of NSW with the British economy at the same time was that the average military pay (in both economies) was £50 per annum whilst the average salary of the civil servants was a like amount. Thus the average pay per head of population would have been during this 1788-1815 period approx £12.

Whereas in the colony the wages pressure came from availability of free labour, rather than the rising population of convict labour, in Britain wage pressure came from lack of skills and specialisation, lack of mobility, and inability to move from industry to industry or from agriculture to processing and factory work. In the colony employers, of all categories, preferred to equate the costs of maintaining convicts and their generally low productivity with the higher cost of free labour and their generally much higher reliability and productivity.

There is little question that the level of despair in the new settlement of New South Wales was tempered by the government support of both colonists and convicts in a welfare state; housing was generally provided and subsidised, whilst the Commissariat delivered food, supplies and rations to over 70% of the population until 1810. Despair, although not unheard of in Britain was diminishing as economic stability took hold and innovation in the manufacturing industry became accepted and almost routine; however, in the colony, despondency was essentially limited to those emancipists who were given a land grant of up to 30 acres, and taken 'off the store' could not apply his industry to developing the 'farmlet' even to subsistence level. The result was that usually they abandoned the farm and sought employment elsewhere.

It took Macquarie's interest in developing public infrastructure and the associated development of the Lumber Yard to establish the basis of manufacturing enterprise in the colony. It took over 100 years for the colonial economy to reach a balance between the manufacturing and agricultural sectors, mostly because economic growth was fuelled in and by agricultural production, alone. The wool industry in the colony led the continuous surge of exports, as well as foreign investment, overseas inspired speculation and employment growth in the colonial economy.

The colonial economy was influenced in its cycles by numerous factors – the overseas economy of Britain (in particular), local harvest affected by droughts and floods, the availability of labour and thus government policies on supporting or encouraging immigration, public development, and private investment. Inflationary pricing of goods and services was often artificially influenced by monopolies used by military officers and local speculators and entrepreneurs.

The colony of NSW responded to the focus of its employment being in Sydney town, by housing most of the population, even those largely engaged in agriculture within the County of Cumberland (i.e. that area of NSW between the Hawkesbury River, the Blue Mountains and the Shoalhaven River). This large area handled and managed all agriculture in the colony before 1813 and the exploration of a crossing over the Mountain range that guarded the western slopes and plains. Diversification into rural towns and villages was late in coming to the colony and followed improvements in roads and transportation. Macquarie deliberately encouraged growth of the rural sector by promoting public investment in roads, and decentralising services provided by the Commissariat in the colony.

Migration from Britain to the colony before 1850 usually encouraged the transfer of skilled workers and the colonial economy showed that the degree of specialisation of the labour force was one index of the degree of economic development achieved, along with the associated fairly complex market economy.

The colonial economy followed a similar pattern of specialisation – specialised labour even within agriculture but mainly in manufacturing and urban-based production.

These same characteristics pervaded the colonial economy before 1815, at which point, under Macquarie's aegis the economy naturally progressed towards wealth and improvement – a similar concept to that found by Adam Smith in Britain except that Smith claimed ' the annual produce of its land and labour is, undoubtedly, much greater at present than it was either at the restoration or the revolution.'[47]

Much the same changes occurred in the colonial economy, except that early demographics were 'transferred' personnel such as military and civil personnel. The numbers of free transferees grew from 529 in 1788 to 2553 in 1793. During the same period white convicts grew from 717 in 1788 to 3499 in 1793[48] The other interesting demographic factor in the

---

[47]   Adam Smith '*Wealth of Nations*' *Page 327*
[48]   *Australians – Historical Statistics* EC 1 – 14 P104

1793 colonial economy The settlements of Sydney and Norfolk Island had populations of over 3000 and 1100 respectively, however, convicts were in the proportion of five males to one female yet the birth-rate was rising. 1700 acres of land were under cultivation, and 3500 acres had been granted to 73 persons, livestock were in increasing numbers and convicts were being assigned to assist with agricultural production. Governor Phillip had adopted the policy of 30-acre farmlets, which Macquarie later found to be economically unsustainable. The colonial scene was largely influenced and coloured by the stain of the convict origins.'

It was Macquarie that gave initiative to an entrepreneurial rationale in the colony. He foresaw the need for local industry as a secondary means to utilise convict labour, rather than having them all supported by the agriculturalists and government. The rising flow of convicts had outstripped the ability to place them in productive enterprise, rather than have them end up as a 'servant' class. Macquarie's had been instructed to cut the cost of government support of convict labour, and anticipated a 'charge' to users of convict labour, buy taking convicts placed in private employment 'off the stores' – not only for food but also for bedding, clothing, boots and caps. He envisaged a government 'retail' store that would 'sell' these items to masters (of convicts) and therefore complete the cycle of convicts being supported, other than by government'. His encouragement of the entrepreneurial motivation commenced with a decision to employ convicts in all phases and aspects of government work. However, Macquarie's idea of government work was mostly built around the formation of public infrastructure, and to assist his efforts to improve the standard of living for existing residents and make immigration tom the colony and private investment in the colony more attractive to Englishmen. His plan was to create a simplistic manufacturing operation with the goal of (1) employing town-based government employed convicts, who were housed by the government in 'official' barracks; (2) produce requirements to maintain and expedite his public works program; (3) use a difficult class of government convicts to build roads, clear land and maintain government assets, and (4) to replace imports with local goods and avoid the lengthy (one to two years) order/delivery time for such items from Britain. To meet these goals, Macquarie established a series of government 'industries – e.g. government farms, for grain, vegetables, fruit and cattle; the Lumber Yard; the Dockyard; the Timber Yard; the Quarries; the Brick Yard and roofing tiles. Collectively these government industries employed over 3,000 convicts and supported all of the government building programs and had enough products left over for sale to private buyers.

It was Macquarie's plan, to create these industries and then turn them over to private entrepreneurs to carry on. However, most colonial entrepreneurs had a speculative and 'get rich quick goal' and were reluctant to partner government when private enterprise could do the job alone. Macquarie's goals with regard to public capital investment in infrastructure were largely met because of these government industries, and by direct association with the private sector, and the 'training' of convict labour in government enterprises, a private sector manufacturing industry did slowly emerge. It was market based and designed solely to satisfy the market place rather than anticipate the market, and be innovative. That trend would emerge as new ideas filtered through from Britain; a larger 'free' labour market was available and the travel time between Britain and its colony improved.

OVERALL SUMMARY

It is reasonable to conclude that the demographic, agricultural, commercial and transport revolutions were the most important preconditions of successful industrialisation and the sustained economic growth that went along with it.

The British industrial revolution was a spontaneous industrial revolution, not a forced change as some of its successors have been. Its development depended on the unfettered response of private enterprise to economic opportunity.

In examining the process of economic growth through technological change it is convenient to distinguish, as Shumpeter has done, between invention and innovation, for it is the latter, which is revolutionary in its economic effects, not the former. Invention is the basic original discovery, the crucial breakthrough in the realm of either theoretical or practical knowledge, which makes a change in productive methods possible. Innovation is the application of this new knowledge or the use of the new machine in practical economic activity.

One factor that facilitated economic growth was the response of businessmen to these changes through what is called 'technological dynamism' of the economy's entrepreneurs. Manufacturing industry generally led the way in innovation since the associated innovations in agriculture, commerce, and pre-railway transport were permissive factors that would have happened without the underlying revolution – that is, industrial evolution.

Other factors include: (1) The 18th century environment was generally favourable to technical change; (2) There were some sectors in which the generalised stimulus to expand output was intensified by an increasing technical difficulty in so doing. Innovations that broke through these technical limitations were particularly successful and particularly rapidly diffused; (3) the number of these sectors of highly successful, rapidly diffused technical change was rather few – they were limited (before 1820) to the cotton industry and to the iron industry. In addition there was the steam engine, successfully applied to a number of industries, but which was most important in cotton, iron, transport and mining, (4) those industries whose techniques had been revolutionised by the 1820s, but which accounted for a relatively small proportion of national income, continued to industrialise and develop new and better technologies.

The exodus of population from rural to town did not develop until the second half of the 19th century, although there was a growth of agricultural entrepreneurs and investors during the industrial revolution. The complex process of economic change and growth – called the industrial revolution – whether it concerned agriculture or transport or trade or manufacturing was a process calling for massive increase in the input of labour and in fact provided part of that increase. The factories gave full-time gainful employment to men, women and children – groups, which had rarely enjoyed more than seasonal or part-time paid work for, pay in the domestic industry era. This was not cheap labour, nor was it elastic in supply. The labour force at this time was largely unskilled (or at best semi-skilled) and was therefore relatively homogeneous.

The complex process of economic change and growth that is named the industrial revolution—whether it concerned agriculture or transport or trade or manufacturing – was a process which called for a massive increase in the input of labour which in turn provided part of the need for that increase. One thing that is clear about post-agriculture economic growth is that it depends on a continuing process of technical/innovative change. What the industrial revolution then did was to increase substantially the flow of these innovations embodied in the nation's economic activity and to turn it into a continuous, if fluctuating, flow.

The evidence suggests that most of the upward shift in the level of national investment, associated with the industrial revolution in Britain took place in the 3 to 4 decades beginning in the second half of the 1830s and ending in the late 1860s. One explanation for this relatively massive addition to the nation's capital was attributable to the great railway boom, which reached its peak in the late 1840s. Another sector – that of great investment in the cotton industry coincided with the employment of power-using machinery. Between 1830 and 1845, the number of spindles doubled and the number of power looms quadrupled. The mechanisation of the woollen industry peaked in the 1850s and 1860s. Investment in mines and the iron industry seems to have been closely allied to the railway boom. The triumph of the steam locomotive rather than the railways themselves fuelled the railway boom

By the 1850s new fields of coal and iron ore were being rapidly opened up in Scotland, Cumberland and Lancashire. But, above all, the middle decades of the 19th century were dominated by massive developments in transport. It was not only railways. There were ships, the construction of which doubled in the 1860s.

In summary, capital to finance the industrial revolution was accumulated from small individual savers (and investors). This required corporate enterprise and public issues of traded stock. It also required major changes in government policies, planning and approval of a vast range of new legislation. The massive social infrastructure capital used for canals, railways, street lighting and water-supply systems was possible due to promoters drawing on small personal and institutional savings from an economy that had begun to industrialise and grow. Later overseas governments and overseas railway corporations were able to tap the same sources partly because the precedent had already been set and the institutions were already there.

Among the structural characteristics that lie at the heart of every industrial revolution is the change in the position of the agricultural economy. From being the dominant industry of the pre-industrial economy, agriculture shifts to the ancillary position, which it takes in an industrialised economy. In the culmination of the industrialisation process, the ultimate cause was the radical change in commercial policy, which was symbolised by the repeal of the Corn Laws. What is particularly interesting is that this move came at the end rather than at the beginning of the Industrial revolution. At the beginning of the 18th century, Britain was exporting sufficient grain to feed a million people per annum – a surplus equivalent to the staple food supply of about 25% of its population. The growth of population, the increase of the non-agriculture labour force and a succession of bad harvests took away the nation's grain surplus. Grain exports dwindled to zero after 1765 and by the end of the century England was a net importer of corn. For the whole period 1750-1850, agriculture was Britain's number one industry.

Britain was endowed with plenty of labour, a limited and exhaustible amount of land and natural resources, a modest ability to save and invest and a government which preferred to leave economic development to the resources of private enterprise and so the British economy came through its industrial revolution with a relatively low growth-potential by comparison with most countries that industrialised later. By 1851 (the year of the British Exhibition) British manufacturers and their machinery were technically superior, but soon rivals emerged and succeeded when their governments showed willingness to assist the local industrialisation process – especially by using tariff policy in the interest of domestic producers.

So the end of British industrial supremacy was in sight.

Additional Notes (selections from Encyclopaedia Brittania)

The Corn Laws [49]

After 1791, protective legislation, combined with trade prohibitions imposed by war, forced grain prices to rise sharply. A bad harvest in 1795

---

[49]   This background explanation is sourced from Encyclopaedia Brittania

led to food riots; there was a prolonged crisis during 1799-1801, and the period from 1805 to 1813 saw a sequence of bad harvests and high prices. From 1815, when an act attempted to fix prices, to 1822, grain prices fluctuated, and continuing protection was increasingly unpopular. The Anti-**Corn Law** League, founded in Manchester in 1839, began to mobilize the industrial middle classes against the landlords, and the league's leader, Richard Cobden, was able to influence the prime minister, Sir Robert Peel. The failure of the Irish potato crop in 1845 convinced Peel to support the repeal of all Corn Laws, which was achieved in 1846.

It was the second quarter of the 19th century that the balance of power, economic and political, shifted from agriculture to the manufacturing industry. Over the preceding decades, both industries had often changed places in terms of importance, measured by the number of jobs they provided. Measured by the volume of incomes generated, the mining-manufacturing-building group of industries had taken the lead in the years of distress to the agriculture industry that had followed Waterloo; and in the second quarter of the century, agriculture's contribution to national income fell from 25% to 20%.

One of the myths that has grown up about the industrial revolution in England is that it happened in the absence of, rather than because of, government intervention, that government's role in the process was to eradicate itself as rapidly as possible in order to allow free enterprise to pursue its beneficent part in generating sustained economic growth. A famous passage by Adam Smith, in a chapter advocating free trade, provided the rationale for this legend by arguing that the maximisation of private profit by individuals involves the maximisation of national income.

The fact is that economic growth was not a process of steady improvement in standards of living for the mass of production. It was a process of economic and social change which often left certain sections of the population very much poorer than in the pre-industrial times and which made large sections of the population vulnerable to depressions in trade or industry or to variations in the state of the harvest.

The Industrial Revolution (as defined by the Encyclopaedia Brittania)

Some historians have questioned whether the term Industrial Revolution can really be applied to the economic transformation of late 18th—and early 19th-century Britain. They point out that in terms of employment the industrial sector may not have overtaken the agricultural sector until the 1850s and that even then the average unit of production employed only 10 people. Large, anonymous factories did not become common until the late 19th century. Other scholars have argued, rightly, that industry did not suddenly take off in the 1780s and that even in 1700 Britain was a more industrialized state than its European competitors. But, despite all these qualifications, the available evidence suggests that by 1800 Britain was by far the most industrialized state in the world and that, because of this, its rate of economic growth must have accelerated in the last third of the 18th century.

Perhaps the most powerful evidence one can cite for these statements (which are inevitably controversial, given the ferocity and rapid fluctuations of the debate on the Industrial Revolution) is Britain's ability to sustain an unprecedented growth in its population from 1780 onward without suffering from major famines or acute unemployment. In 1770 the population was about 8.3 million. By 1790 it had reached 9.7 million; by 1811, 12.1 million; and by 1821, 14.2 million. By the latter date, it is estimated that 60 percent of Britain's population was 25 years of age or below. By comparison, while a similar rate of demographic growth occurred in Ireland, there was no Irish Industrial Revolution. Partly as a result of this, Ireland suffered the great famine in the 1840s, whereas there was no similar famine in Britain.

To say this is not to deny the dark side of early industrialization. The conditions of work were often brutal, particularly for the young. Industrial safety was minimal, and environmental pollution and unguarded machines led to horrific injuries. Mechanization ruined the livelihoods of some skilled craftsmen, most notably the handloom weavers. Nonetheless, it is probable that without industrialization the social costs of rapid population growth in Britain would have been far greater.

Although it is not easy to account for Britain's early industrialization, some facts stand out. Britain, unlike its prime European rival, France, was a small, compact island. Except in northern Scotland, it had no major forests or mountains to disrupt or impede its internal communications. The country possessed a range of natural ports facing the Atlantic, plenty of coastal shipping, and a good system of internal waterways. By the 1760s there were already 1,000 miles of inland canals in Britain; over the next 70 years 3,000 more miles of canals were constructed. Britain was also richly endowed with coal and iron ore, and these minerals were often located close together in counties such as Staffordshire, Northumberland, Lancashire, and Yorkshire.

Most importantly perhaps, Britain could draw on an ample supply of customers for its goods, both at home and overseas. Its colonies fed it with raw materials while also serving as captive customers. And its expanding population meant buoyant demand at home even in wartime when foreign trade was disrupted. The best illustration of these advantages is the cotton industry. Its Indian settlements supplied Britain with ever-increasing amounts of raw cotton, and annual cloth production soared from 50,000 pieces of cloth in 1770 to 400,000 pieces in 1800. Much of this output in textiles was consumed by the home market. Some scholars have argued that the increased wearing of cotton (which could be easily washed) as distinct from woollen clothes (which could not) improved health conditions, thus contributing to Britain's population expansion. In modern history, the process of change from an agrarian, handicraft economy to one dominated by industry and machine manufacture. This process began in England in the 18th century and from there spread to other parts of the world. Although used earlier by French writers, the term Industrial Revolution was first popularised by the English economic historian Arnold Toynbee (1852-83) to describe England's economic development from 1760 to 1840. Since Toynbee's time the term has been more broadly applied.

The main features involved in the Industrial Revolution were technological, socio-economic, and cultural. The technological changes included the following: (1) the use of new basic materials, chiefly iron and steel, (2) the use of new energy sources, including both fuels and motive power, such as coal, the steam engine, electricity, petroleum, and the internal-combustion engine, (3) the invention of new machines, such as the spinning jenny and the power loom that permitted increased production with a smaller expenditure of human energy, (4) a new organization of work known as the factory system, which entailed increased division of labour and specialization of function, (5) important developments in transportation and communication, including the steam locomotive, steamship, automobile, airplane, telegraph, and radio, and (6) the increasing application of science to industry. These technological changes made possible a tremendously increased use of natural resources and the mass production of manufactured goods.

There were also many new developments in non-industrial spheres, including the following: (1) agricultural improvements that made possible the provision of food for a larger non-agricultural population, (2) economic changes that resulted in a wider distribution of wealth, the decline of land as a source of wealth in the face of rising industrial production, and increased international trade, (3) political changes reflecting the shift in economic power, as well as new state policies corresponding to the needs of an industrialized society, (4) sweeping social changes, including the growth of cities, the development of working-class movements, and the emergence of new patterns of authority, and (5) cultural transformations of a broad order. The worker acquired new and distinctive skills, and his relation to his task shifted; instead of being a craftsman working with hand tools, he became a machine operator, subject to factory discipline. Finally, there was a psychological change: man's confidence in his ability to use resources and to master nature was heightened

Economic growth and economic change involve an expansion of the flow of goods and services produced in the economy and change in its composition.

One way of assessing the achievements of an industrial revolution is to measure its consequences in terms of effects on standards of living. The process of industrial reevolution, should bring with it (1) a lowering of costs of production, booth in agriculture and industry; (2) a reduction in the amount of human effort required to produce a given unit of output, leading to an increase in the flow of goods and services available for consumption; (3) a rise in the standard of living and a rise in population growth. If the rising population is due, to a higher birth rate or lower mortality rate, then that condition brings with it a larger dependent population and a smaller proportion of the total population in active employment.

Navigation Acts

THE NAVIGATION ACTS in English history were a series of laws designed to restrict England's carrying trade to English ships, effective chiefly in the 17th and 18th centuries. The measures, originally framed to encourage the development of English shipping so that adequate auxiliary vessels would be available in wartime, became a form of trade protectionism during an era of mercantilism.

The first navigation act, passed in 1381, remained virtually a dead letter because of a shortage of ships. In the 16th century, various Tudor measures had to be repealed because they provoked retaliation from other countries. The system came into its own at the beginning of the colonial era, in the 17th century. The great Navigation Act passed by the Commonwealth government in 1651 was aimed at the Dutch, then England's greatest commercial rivals. It distinguished between goods imported from European countries, which could be brought in either English ships or ships of the country of origin, and goods brought from Asia, Africa, or America, which could travel to England, Ireland, or any English colony only in ships from England or the particular colony. Various fish imports and exports were entirely reserved to English shipping, as was the English coastal trade. The law was re-enacted in 1660, and the practice was introduced of "enumerating" certain colonial products, which could be shipped directly only to England, Ireland, or another English colony. These included sugar (until 1739), indigo, and tobacco; rice and molasses were added during the 18th century. Nonenumerated goods could go in English ships from English colonies directly to foreign ports. From 1664 English colonies could receive European goods only via England. Scotland was treated as a foreign country until the Act of Union (1707) gave it equal privileges with England; Ireland was excluded from the benefits of the laws between 1670 and 1779.

Although English tonnage and trade increased steadily from the late 17th century, critics of the navigation system argue that this would have occurred in any case and that the policy forced up freight prices, thus ultimately making English manufactured goods less competitive. At first, colonial merchants benefited from an assured market, but the tightening of the laws in 1764 contributed to the unrest leading to the rebellion of

England's American colonies; their achievement of independence made the first serious breach in the navigation system, and from then on exceptions were increasingly made. Enumeration was abandoned in 1822, and the navigation laws were finally repealed in 1849 and 1854.

The Agriculture Economy in Britain (pre-1750)

In modern history, the process of change from an agrarian, handicraft economy to one dominated by industry and machine manufacture. This process began in England in the 18th century and from there spread to other parts of the world. Although used earlier by French writers, the term Industrial Revolution was first popularised by the English economic historian Arnold Toynbee (1852-83) to describe England's economic development from 1760 to 1840. Since Toynbee's time the term has been more broadly applied.

The main features involved in the Industrial Revolution were technological, socio-economic, and cultural. The technological changes included the following: (1) the use of new basic materials, chiefly iron and steel, (2) the use of new energy sources, including both fuels and motive power, such as coal, the steam engine, electricity, petroleum, and the internal-combustion engine, (3) the invention of new machines, such as the spinning jenny and the power loom that permitted increased production with a smaller expenditure of human energy, (4) a new organization of work known as the factory system, which entailed increased division of labour and specialization of function, (5) important developments in transportation and communication, including the steam locomotive, steamship, automobile, airplane, telegraph, and radio, and (6) the increasing application of science to industry. These technological changes made possible a tremendously increased use of natural resources and the mass production of manufactured goods.

There were also many new developments in no industrial spheres, including the following: (1) agricultural improvements that made possible the provision of food for a larger non-agricultural population, (2) economic changes that resulted in a wider distribution of wealth, the decline of land as a source of wealth in the face of rising industrial production, and increased international trade, (3) political changes reflecting the shift in economic power, as well as new state policies corresponding to the needs of an industrialized society, (4) sweeping social changes, including the growth of cities, the development of working-class movements, and the emergence of new patterns of authority, and (5) cultural transformations of a broad order. The worker acquired new and distinctive skills, and his relation to his task shifted; instead of being a craftsman working with hand tools, he became a machine operator, subject to factory discipline. Finally, there was a psychological change: man's confidence in his ability to use resources and to master nature was heightened.

18th-century Britain, 1714-1815

The state of Britain in 1714

When George Ludwig, elector of Hanover, became king of Great Britain on Aug. 1, 1714, the country was in some respects bitterly divided. Fundamentally, however, it was prosperous, cohesive, and already a leading European and imperial power. Abroad, Britain's involvement in the War of the Spanish Succession had been brought to a satisfactory conclusion by the Treaty of Utrecht (1713). It had acquired new colonies in Gibraltar, Minorca, Nova Scotia, Newfoundland, and Hudson's Bay, as well as trading concessions in the Spanish New World. By contrast, Britain's rivals, France, Spain, and the Dutch Republic, were left weakened or war-weary by the conflict. It took France a decade to recover, and Spain and Holland were unable to reverse their military and economic decline. As a result Britain was able to remain aloof from war on the Continent for a quarter of a century after the Hanoverian succession, and this protracted peace was to be crucial to the new dynasty's survival and success.

War had also strengthened the British state at home. The need to raise men and money had increased the size and scope of the executive as well as the power and prestige of the House of Commons. Taxation had accounted for 70 percent of Britain's wartime expenditure (93,644,560 between 1702 and 1713), so the Commons' control over taxation became a powerful guarantee of its continuing importance.

Britain's ability to pay for war on this scale demonstrated the extent of its wealth. Agriculture was still the bedrock of the economy, but trade was increasing, and more men and women were employed in industry in Britain than in any other European nation. Wealth, however, was unequally distributed, with almost a third of the national income belonging to only 5 percent of the population. But British society was not polarized simply between the rich and the poor; according to writer Daniel Defoe there were seven different and more subtle categories:

1. The great, who live profusely.
2. The rich, who live plentifully.
3. The middle sort, who live well.
4. The working trades, who labour hard, but feel no want.
5. The country people, farmers etc., who fare indifferently.
6. The poor, who fare hard.
7. The miserable that really pinch and suffer want.

From 1700 to the 1740s Britain's population remained stable at about seven million, and agricultural production increased. So, although men and women from Defoe's 6th and 7th categories could still die of hunger and hunger-related diseases, in most regions of Britain there was usually enough basic food to go around. This was crucial to social stability and to popular acquiescence in the new Hanoverian regime.

But early 18th-century Britain also had its weaknesses. Its Celtic fringe—Wales, Ireland, and Scotland—had been barely assimilated. The vast majority of Welsh men and women could neither speak nor understand the English language. Most Irish men and women spoke Gaelic and belonged to the Roman Catholic Church, in contrast with the population of the British mainland, which was staunchly Protestant. Scotland, which had only been united to England and Wales in 1707, still retained its traditional educational, religious, legal, and cultural practices. These internal divisions were made more dangerous by the existence of rival claimants to the British throne. James II, who had been expelled in the Glorious Revolution of 1688, died 13 years later, but his son, James Francis Edward Stuart, the Old Pretender, pressed his family's claims from his exile in France. His Catholicism and Scottish ancestry ensured him wide support in Ireland and the Scottish Highlands; his cause also commanded sympathy among sections of the Welsh and English gentry and, arguably, among the masses.

Controversy over the succession sharpened partisan infighting between the Whig and Tory parties. About 50 Tory MPs (less than a seventh of the total number) may have been covert Jacobites in 1714. More generally, Tories differed from Whigs over religious issues and foreign policy. They were more anxious to preserve the privileges of the Anglican Church and more hostile to military involvement in continental Europe than Whig politicians were inclined to be. These attitudes made the Tories vulnerable in 1714. The new king was a Lutheran by upbringing and wanted to establish wider religious toleration in his new kingdom. As a German he was deeply interested in European affairs. Consequently he regarded the Tory party as insular in its outlook as well as suspect in its allegiance

Outline Of British Banking

A BANK is an institution that deals in money and its substitutes and provides other financial services. Banks accept deposits and make loans and derive a profit from the difference in the interest rates paid and charged, respectively. Some banks also have the power to create money.

The principal types of banking in the modern industrial world are commercial banking and central banking. A commercial banker is a dealer in money and in substitutes for money, such as checks or bills of exchange. The banker also provides a variety of other financial services. The basis of the banking business is borrowing from individuals, firms, and occasionally governments—*i.e.* receiving "deposits" from them. With these resources and also with the bank's own capital, the banker makes loans or extends credit and also invests in securities. The banker makes profit by borrowing at one rate of interest and lending at a higher rate and by charging commissions for services rendered.

A bank must always have cash balances on hand in order to pay its depositors upon demand or when the amounts credited to them become due. It must also keep a proportion of its assets in forms that can readily be converted into cash. Only in this way can confidence in the banking system be maintained. Provided it honours its promises (*e.g.,* to provide cash in exchange for deposit balances), a bank can create credit for use by its customers by issuing additional notes or by making new loans, which in their turn become new deposits. The amount of credit it extends may considerably exceed the sums available to it in cash. But a bank is able to do this only as long as the public believes the bank can and will honour its obligations, which are then accepted at face value and circulate as money. So long as they remain outstanding, these promises or obligations constitute claims against that bank and can be transferred by means of checks or other negotiable instruments from one party to another. These are the essentials of deposit banking as practiced throughout the world today, with the partial exception of socialist-type institutions.

Central banks, bankers to governments and "lenders of last resort" to commercial banks and other financial institutions carry on another type of banking. They are often responsible for formulating and implementing monetary and credit policies, usually in cooperation with the government. In some cases—*e.g.* the U.S. Federal Reserve System—they have been established specifically to lead or regulate the banking system; in other cases—*e.g.,* the Bank of England—they have come to perform these functions through a process of evolution.

Some institutions often called banks, such as finance companies, savings banks, investment banks, trust companies, and home-loan banks, do not perform the banking functions described above and are best classified as financial intermediaries. Their economic function is that of channelling savings from private individuals into the hands of those who will use them, in the form of loans for building purposes or for the purchase of capital assets. These financial intermediaries cannot, however, create money (*i.e.,* credit) as the commercial banks do; they can lend no more than savers place with them.

This article describes the development of banking functions and institutions, the basic principles of modern banking practice, and the structure of a number of important national banking systems. Certain concepts not addressed here that are nonetheless fundamental to banking are treated in the articles accounting and money.

Branch banking: the United Kingdom

If the United States banks can be taken as representative of a unit banking system, the British system is the prototype of branch **banking**.

Its development was linked to the growth of transportation and communications, for otherwise banks cannot clear checks drawn on other banks and effect remittances speedily and efficiently. The Scots favoured branch banking from the very beginning (the Bank of Scotland was founded in 1695), but at first they were not very successful—largely because of poor communications and the difficulty of supplying branches with adequate amounts of coin. Not until after the Napoleonic Wars, when the road system of Scotland had been greatly improved, did branch banking begin to develop vigorously there. As the Industrial Revolution progressed and as the size of businesses increased, the structure of English banking underwent a corresponding change. Greater resources were required for lending, and banks also needed more extensive interconnections in order to provide an increasing range of services. Where banks remained small, they were frequently unable to take the strain of the larger demand; they tended to become overextended and often failed.

The growth in size of banks was also greatly encouraged by legislation that encouraged joint-stock ownership, beginning in 1826. Joint-stock ownership, which reduced the risk to any individual, must be distinguished from limited liability, which did not become widely accepted until the failure of the City of Glasgow Bank in 1878 demonstrated the need for a legal device to protect the stockholder. The early joint-stock banks tended to remain localized in their business interests; it was only gradually (with the spread of limited liability and disclosure of accounts) that amalgamations began to convert the banking system in England and Wales into its highly concentrated modern form. The main movement was completed before World War I, though there was to be a further degree of concentration in the years after World War II. By these means, British banks were able to attract deposits from all parts of the country and to spread the banking risk over a wide range of industries and areas.

The business of banking

The business of banking consists of borrowing and lending. As in other businesses, operations must be based on capital, but banks employ comparatively little of their own capital in relation to the total volume of their transactions. The purpose of capital and reserve accounts is primarily to provide an ultimate cover against losses on loans and investments. In the

United States capital accounts also have a legal significance, since the laws limit the proportion of its capital a bank may lend to a single borrower. Similar arrangements exist elsewhere.

Functions of commercial banks

The essential characteristics of the banking business may be described within the framework of a simplified balance sheet. A bank's main liabilities are its capital (including reserves and, often, subordinated debt) and deposits. The latter may be from domestic or foreign sources (corporations and firms, private individuals, other banks, and even governments). They may be repayable on demand (sight deposits or current accounts) or repayable only after the lapse of a period of time (time, term, or fixed deposits and, occasionally, savings deposits). A bank's assets include cash (which may be held in the form of credit balances with other banks, usually with a central bank but also, in varying degrees, with correspondent banks); liquid assets (money at call and short notice, day-to-day money, short-term government paper such as treasury bills and notes, and commercial bills of exchange, all of which can be converted readily into cash without risk of substantial loss); investments or securities (substantially medium-term and longer term government securities—sometimes including those of local authorities such as states, provinces, or municipalities—and, in certain countries, participations and shares in industrial concerns); loans and advances made to customers of all kinds, though primarily to trade and industry (in an increasing number of countries, these include term loans and also mortgage loans); and, finally, the bank's premises, furniture, and fittings (written down, as a rule, to quite nominal figures).

All bank balance sheets must include an item that relates to contingent liabilities (*e.g.*, bills of exchange "accepted" or endorsed by the bank), exactly balanced by an item on the other side of the balance sheet representing the customer's obligation to indemnify the bank (which may also be supported by a form of security taken by the bank over its customer's assets). Most banks of any size stand prepared to provide acceptance credits (also called bankers' acceptances); when a bank accepts a bill, it lends its name and reputation to the transaction in question and, in this way, ensures that the paper will be more readily discounted.

The development of banking systems

Banking is of ancient origin, though little is known about it prior to the 13th century. Many of the early "banks" dealt primarily in coin and bullion, much of their business being money changing and the supplying of foreign and domestic coin of the correct weight and fineness. Another important early group of banking institutions was the merchant bankers, who dealt both in goods and in bills of exchange, providing for the remittance of money and payment of accounts at a distance but without shipping actual coin. Their business arose from the fact that many of these merchants traded internationally and held assets at different points along trade routes. For a certain consideration, a merchant stood prepared to accept instructions to pay money to a named party through one of his agents elsewhere; the amount of the bill of exchange would be debited by his agent to the account of the merchant banker, who would also hope to make an additional profit from exchanging one currency against another. Because there was a possibility of loss, any profit or gain was not subject to the medieval ban on usury. There were, moreover, techniques for concealing a loan by making foreign exchange available at a distance but deferring payment for it so that the interest charge could be camouflaged as a fluctuation in the exchange rate.

Another form of early banking activity was the acceptance of deposits. These might derive from the deposit of money or valuables for safekeeping or for purposes of transfer to another party; or, more straightforwardly, they might represent the deposit of money in a current account. A balance in a current account could also represent the proceeds of a loan that had been granted by the banker, perhaps based on an oral agreement between the parties (recorded in the banker's journal) whereby the customer would be allowed to overdraw his account.

English bankers in particular had by the 17th century begun to develop a deposit banking business, and the techniques they evolved were to prove influential elsewhere. The London goldsmiths kept money and valuables in safe custody for their customers. In addition, they dealt in bullion and foreign exchange, acquiring and sorting coin for profit. As a means of attracting coin for sorting, they were prepared to pay a rate of interest, and it was largely in this way that they began to supplant as deposit bankers their great rivals, the "money scriveners." The latter were notaries who had come to specialize in bringing together borrowers and lenders; they also accepted deposits.

It was found that when money was deposited by a number of people with a goldsmith or a scrivener a fund of deposits came to be maintained at a fairly steady level; over a period of time, deposits and withdrawals tended to balance. In any event, customers preferred to leave their surplus money with the goldsmith, keeping only enough for their everyday needs. The result was a fund of idle cash that could be lent out at interest to other parties.

About the same time, a practice grew up whereby a customer could arrange for the transfer of part of his credit balance to another party by addressing an order to the banker. This was the origin of the modern check. It was only a short step from making a loan in specie or coin to allowing customers to borrow by check: the amount borrowed would be debited to a loan account and credited to a current account against which checks could be drawn; or the customer would be allowed to overdraw his account up to a specified limit. In the first case, interest was charged on the full amount of the debit, and in the second the customer paid interest only on the amount actually borrowed. A check was a claim against the bank, which had a corresponding claim against its customer.

Another way in which a bank could create claims against itself was by issuing bank notes. The amount actually issued depended on the banker's judgment of the possible demand for specie, and this depended in large part on public confidence in the bank itself. In London, goldsmith bankers were probably developing the use of the bank note about the same time as that of the check. (The first bank notes issued in Europe were by the Bank of Stockholm in 1661.) Some commercial banks are still permitted to issue their own notes, but in most countries this has become a prerogative of the central bank.

In Britain the check soon proved to be such a convenient means of payment that the public began to use checks for the larger part of their monetary transactions, reserving coin (and, later, notes) for small payments. As a result, banks began to grant their borrowers the right to draw checks much in excess of the amounts of cash actually held, in this way "creating money"—*i.e.,* claims that were generally accepted as means of payment. Such money came to be known as "bank money" or "credit." Excluding bank notes, this money consisted of no more than figures in bank ledgers; it was acceptable because of the public's confidence in the ability of the bank to honour its liabilities when called upon to do so.

CHAPTER 11

POPULATION INCREASE, MIGRATION AND INVESTMENT AND ECONOMIC DRIVERS

Sex distribution

Australia has, since the first settlement of the continent in 1788, differed materially from the older countries of the world. Older countries, that are countries having an established civilised population, have, in general, grown by natural increase and their composition usually reflects that fact with the numbers of males and females being approximately equal, with a tendency for females to slightly exceed males. This slight excess arises from a number of causes

Higher rate of mortality amongst males
Greater propensity of males to travel
The effects of war
Employment of males in the armed forces
Preponderance of males amongst emigrants
Masculinity of the Population

"The changing population structure necessarily implied a radical alteration in the size of the male workforce in the total population. The increasing numbers of young males and of all females compelled this change as shown below.

Year	Workforce Males	% of Total Popln
1790	1784	77.7
1795	3692	79.1
1800	4555	74.1
1805	5981	70.7
1810	7100	63.0
1815	9575	61.4
1820	22822	71.1
1825	34565	71.4
1830	47180	69.4

MASCULINITY OF THE NSW POPULATION 1800 to 1855

Year	%
1800	44.91
1805	40.00
1810	31.16
1815	30.76
1820	41.81
1825	53.00
1830	52.06
1835	45.71
1840	34.25
1845	21.05
1850	16.13
1855	11.14

This compares with other countries in various years, which would create a guide and average for base purposes

Canada	1911	6.07
India	1911	2.24
New Zealand	1919	1.15
Australia	1919	1.00

Poland	1914	0.41
Hungary	1912	-0.94
Ireland	1915	-1.36
England	1917	-16.43

Age Distribution

During the first 80 years of settlement, the age distribution of the colonial population has varied considerably. Prior to1856, the distribution averaged as follows:

Males >15	31.4
Males 15-65	67.4
Males <65	1.17
Total	100%
Females >15	43.0
Females 15-65	56.2
Females <65	0.77
Total	100%
Persons>15	36.28
Persons 15-65	62.72
Persons <65	1.0
Total	100%

Sources of Race & Nationality

The primary distribution is between the aboriginal natives and the immigrants, who since 1788 have made the colony their home. Under immigrants would come not only the direct immigrants but also their descendants. For the first 60 years after settlement, the Aboriginal population was in decline (refer also to Chapter 3 of this study – The Aboriginal Economy of 1788). It is of interest to note that in the first census of the aboriginal population in 1911, the Commonwealth statistician made the following reference.[50] " At the census of 1911 the number of full-blood aboriginals who were employed by whites or who lived on the fringe of white settlement was stated to be only 19,939. In Queensland, Western

---

[50]   *Commonwealth Year Book 1901-1919* (1920) p.88

Australia and the Northern Territory, there are considerable numbers of natives still in the 'savage' state, numerical information concerning whom is of a most unreliable nature and can be regarded as little more than the result of guessing".

The academic studies by Dr. Roth, formerly Chief Protector of Aborigines in Queensland puts the number of full-blood aborigines in the 6 colonies at 80,000 in 1919"[51] As a matter of Commonwealth census policy no count was attempted of 'half-castes' as 'no authoritative definition has yet been given.

The predominant race of immigrants and their descendants is British. However, by 1900, the local born population had reached 83%. The figure in 1856 was calculated to be in the 52.5% vicinity. The other main birthplaces included Germany, China, Scandinavia, Polynesia, British India and Japan

From one aspect the total population may be less significant than in respect of the absolute amount than in respect of the density of its distribution. The total land area of the country is 2,974,581 square miles, and at the time of the Constitution of 1901, the country only had a population of 5,347,018 persons, with a density of 1.80. Even today that density is only a little less than 7. The comparative densities are, for the earliest period of statistics maintained (1919 – Statesman's Yearbook), Europe at 122.98, Asia 54.45. Americas 16.87 and Australasia 2.38

Some definitions

Natural Increase

The two factors, which contribute to the growth of a population, are the 'natural increase' by excess of births over deaths and the 'net migration', being the excess of arrivals over departures. In a new country such as the colony of NSW between 1788 and 1856, the 'net migration' occupies an important position as a source of increase of population especially as the

---

[51]   CYB *ibid* p.89

early imbalance of sexes and the shortage of females in the colony, allowed for only a relatively small natural increase.

Net Immigration

The quinquennial period in which the greatest net migration to the Colonies occurred is outside our study period but was that of 1881-85 with a total of 224,040, whilst the period 1901-05 departures exceeded arrivals by 16,793

Total Increase

The total increase of the population is found by the combination of the natural increase with the net immigration

Rate of Increase

The rate of increase in the early colony rose quickly but then steadied as migration took on a smaller 'net ' effect. After 1830 the average rate was only 4% but then declined steadily until by 1901, the rate was only 1.38. NSW always enjoyed the highest rate of increase and averaged over 5% before 1850 declining to 4.83 from 1860. The 1850s were a period of low natural increase and high net migration with the gold fields being the main catalyst.

Density of Population

Urban Population

One of the key features of the distribution of population in Australia is the tendency to accumulate in the capital cities. In every colony the capital city had a greater population than any other town in the colony. It was the hub and as such it carried certain features. The main population area was a port for international shipping. There were adequate fresh water sources servicing the population. In the early days of the colony of NSW the 'urban' population would have been close top 100%, but as Macquarie developed and serviced his regional towns, the urban percentage declined until by 1900, Sydney had only 41.38 % of the colonial population

Aboriginal population

The Commonwealth Year Book of 1901 reminds us that "The Commonwealth Constitution Act makes provision for aboriginal natives to be excluded for all purposes for which statistics of population are made use but the opinion has been given by the Commonwealth Attorney-General that 'in reckoning the population of the Commonwealth, half-castes are not aboriginal natives within the meaning of Section 127 of the Constitution', and should therefore be included in any census count."[52] This is one reason that the ABS (Australian Bureau of Statistics had so much doubt over the number of aborigines in the country – they had not been counted and would not be counted at any time until 1966. The ABS records guesses ranging from 150,000 to as low as 61,705 in 1925[53]

Enumeration

In colonial NSW, the system of 'musters' was the way chosen to count the convicts and the free settlers. The governor would 'gazette' or announce the date and place of the next muster, and usually commissariat officers would officiate at the count. The basis of the count was often widened to include a record of the number and type of livestock, of acres cultivated and would be used to verify the rations receivable by that family 'off the store'. In 1828 the muster system was replaced by the first 'census' where a more detailed record was made of the population demographics including ages, sex and birthplace of each inhabitant and whether 'free' or 'convict'.

Musters

J.C. Caldwell writes in the introduction to the Chapter on 'Population'[54] "For the first 40 years of the Australian colonies, our knowledge of population numbers is derived from the musters. Their major deficiencies

---

[52] Commonwealth Year Book #3– W. Ramsey-Smith ' *Special Characteristics of Commonwealth Population'* P.89

[53] 4The count in each state is estimated at 30th April 1915 by Ramsey Smith as NSW-6,580;Victoria 283; Qld 15,000; SA 4,842; WA 32,000; NT 3,000 for a total of 61,705

[54] Australians: Historical Statistics

are that of the omission of the native peoples. Even in 1800 the musters perhaps account for only 1 or 2 percent of the actual population".

IMMIGRATION AND INVESTMENT

The economic theory of 19th century British investment

Before we can complete the task of identifying capital formation by the British investor, both public (government) and private investment, let me review a piece by Sir T.H. Farrer (Bart) from his 1887 book *Free Trade versus Fair Trade*. The notation on the front-piece of the book shows the Cobden Club emblem with the words 'free trade, peace, goodwill among nations'. We will discuss Cobden a little later when we review the work of the Australian Senator Edward Pulsford, another outspoken supporter and devotee of the Cobden philosophy, and free trade and open immigration.

> *'The amount of English capital constantly employed abroad in private trade and in permanent investments, including Stock Exchange securities, private advances, property owned abroad by Englishmen, British shipping, British-owned cargoes, and other British earnings abroad, has been estimated by competent statisticians as being between 1,500 and 2,000 million pounds, and is constantly increasing. Taking the lower figure, the interest or profit upon it, at 5 per cent, would be 75 million pounds, and at the higher figure it would be 100 million pound.*[55]

Farrer equates this income figure to the spread of imports over exports and finds that the two compare. But then he argues there is the question of freights:

> *'A very large proportion of the trade of the United Kingdom is carried in English ships, and these ships carry a large proportion of the trade of other countries not coming to England. This shipping is, in fact, an export of highly-skilled English labour and capital which does not appear in the*

---

[55] Farrer, T.H *Free Trade or Fair Trade*

export returns of the 19th century, and considering that it includes not only the interest on capital but also wages, provisions, coal, port expenses, repairs, depreciation and insurance; and that the value of English shipping employed in the foreign trade is estimated at more than 100 million pound per annum, the amount to be added to our exports on account of English shipping, must be very large. [56]

He goes further,

' . . . add to this the value of ships built for foreigners amounting to over 70,000 ton per annum, worth together several millions, and all these outgoings, with the profits, must either return to this country in the shape of imports, or be invested abroad—I believe £50 million is too low an estimate of the amount of unseen exports. In addition there are the commissions and other charges to agents in this country, connected with the carriage of goods from country to country, but each of these items do not appear in the statistics of exports. I can only assume that we are investing large amounts of our savings in the colonies, such as Australia. [57]

The Farrer argument in favour of 'free trade' then turns to the 'fair trade' objections to foreign investments. He writes:

'When we point to the indebtedness of foreign colonies to England as one reason for the excess of imports, they tell us that we have been paying for our imports by the return to us of foreign securities; and at the same time they complain bitterly that, instead of spending our money at home, our rich men are constantly investing their money abroad, and thus robbing English labour of its rights here. [58]

---

[56]   Farrer *ibid*

[57]   Farrer *ibid*

[58]   Farrer *ibid*

But we know that is not the whole story. When British investors transferred capital to the colonies, it was not only in the form of cash (which would come from savings) but it was more often in the form of capital goods. Britain sent iron; the shipbuilders who make the ships to carry the goods and the sailors who navigated them. What happened when they reached the colonies?. They returned with grain, coal, wool timber making those commodities cheaper in Britain. The investor received interest or profits on the capital invested which would generally be greater than what could have been earned if it had been invested in Britain. That return can be spent on luxury goods, invested locally or re-invested overseas to begin the whole cycle again.

Based on the Farrer argument, it remains true that on the whole the transfer of British capital from an English industry that did not pay to a colonial industry which did pay, was no loss to England generally and caused no diminution in the employment of British labour. However, there are at least two drawbacks to colonial investment by a maritime power; one, in the event of a war, that returns would be open to greater risk, and two; that investors could more easily evade taxation by the British Government.

Obviously, since 1886 when Farrer constructed this argument, the world has changed and investment opportunities have changed. Britain has fallen from its pinnacle as a world power and international commercial leader and the improved collection of statistics now recognises movements of goods and investments on both current account and capital account. However, the concept helped put the Australian colony on the map and attracted enormous amounts of private capital into the colony to make it grow and prosper.

Farrer concludes his argument with this observation.

> 'The desire to make profitable investments, however valuable economically, is not the only motive which governs rich men; it's the love of natural beauty; interest in farming and the outdoor life; personal and local attachments; all of which are quite sure to maintain a much larger expenditure on English land than would be dictated by a desire for gain. Let these other motives have their way, as these investors

still contribute to the welfare of the toilers and spinners who produce the goods, and make a good return that in the end makes England wealthier.[59]

Factors affecting British investment in the Colony

A number of factors affected the level of capital investment into the colony – many were ill informed and relied on delayed newspaper reports on activity in the various settlements:

The offer of assisted migration

The failing economic conditions in Britain

Economic expansion for the pastoral industry due to successful exploration in the colony

The settlement at Port Phillip and the eventual separation of Victoria from NSW Wales would promote great investment opportunities

The rise of the squattocracy

The crash of 1827-28 in the colony shakes British Investors

The Bigges' Report of 1823 breathed new life into capital formation especially with Macarthur sponsoring the float of the Australian Agricultural Company

Further along, the good credit rating of the colonies (and there being no defaults on loans) encouraged larger investments and loans into the colonies

Shortage of labour in the colony and the offer of land grants to new settlers became a useful carrot to attract small settlers bringing their own capital by way of cash or goods or livestock with them.

---

[59]   Farrer *ibid*

Two other steps had important consequences, one in the colony and the other in Britain. In 1827 Governor Darling began to issue grazing licenses to pastoralists, the terms being set at 2/6d per 100 acres, with liability to quit on one month's notice. From this movement grew, writes Madgwick in *Immigration into Eastern Australia*, the squatting movement and the great pastoral expansion, and the idea of the earlier Governors that NSW should be a Colony of farmers was thus abandoned. The concurrent event was the floating of the Australian Agricultural Company in London. Development by the AAC and the free settlers brought increasing prosperity. Exports tripled between 1826 and 1831.

There is a connection between availability of factors of production and the level of investment. In the early days of the Colony, labour was available, bad labour, convict labour, but still labour. The governors had demanded settlers with capital to employ that labour and develop the land and they proposed to limit land grants in proportion to the means of the settler. Governor Darling declared (HRA ser 1, vol 8) that 'when I am satisfied of the character, respectability and means of the applicant settler in a rural area, he will receive the necessary authority to select a grant of land, proportionate in extent to the means he possesses'.

Let us examine some of these important elements commencing with the Bigge Report into Agriculture and Trade of the Colony.[60]

The Australian Agricultural Company

J.F. Campbell wrote about the first decade of the Australian Agricultural Company 1824-1834 in the proceedings of the 1923 RAHS:

> *'Soon after Commissioner Bigge's report of 1823 became available for public information, several enterprising men concerted with a view to acquire sheep-runs in the interior of this colony, for the production of fine wool.*

---

[60]   Bigge, John Thomas *Commissioners' Report into Agriculture & Trade in NSW – Report No. 1 1823*

The success which attended the efforts of John Macarthur and a few other New South Wales pastoralists, in the breeding and rearing of fine woolled sheep and stock generally, as verified by Bigge, gave the incentive and led to the inauguration of proceedings which resulted in the formation of the Australian Agricultural Company.

The first formal meeting of the promoters took place at Lincoln's Inn, London, (at the offices of John Macarthur, junior).

Earl Bathurst, advised Governor Brisbane in 1824 that.

"His Majesty has been pleased to approve the formation of the Company, from the impression that it affords every reasonable prospect of securing to that part of His Majesty's dominions the essential advantage of the immediate introduction of large capital, and of agricultural skill, as well as the ultimate benefit of the increase of fine wool as a valuable commodity for export."

The chief proposals of the company are:

i. The company would be incorporated by Act of Parliament or Letters Patent.
ii. The capital of the company was to be 1 million pound sterling divided into 10,000 shares of 100 pound each
iii. A grant of land of one million acres to be made to the company
iv. That no rival joint stock company to be established in the colony for the next twenty years
v. That the agents of the company would select the situation or the land grants.
vi. The shepherds and labourers would consist of 1,400 convicts, thereby lessening the maintenance of such convicts by an estimated 30,800 pound or 22 pound/per head/ per annum

The Royal Charter of 1824 forming the company provided for payment of quit-rents over a period of twenty years, or the redemption of the same by paying the capital sum of 20 times the amount of the rent so to be redeemed. These quit-rents were to be waived if the full number of convicts were maintained for a period of five years. No land was to be sold during the five-year period from the date of the grant.'

It was important that the investment be seen to have the support of strong leaders in Britain and democratic governance, and company operated with

A Governor
25 directors
365 stockholders (proprietors)
Leading stockholders included
Robert Campbell
Chief Justice Forbes
Son of Governor King
Rev Samuel Marsden
John Macarthur

Macarthur family members, John jr, Hannibal, James, Charles, Scott and William

John Oxley, the Colonial-Surveyor, had recommended the Port Stephens area as an eligible location for the land grant. The local directors inspected and approved the site but John Macarthur was extremely critical of the selection, the management plan and the extravagance of the first buildings.

This venture was the first major investment into the colony and set the scene for later developments. In 1825 the Van Diemen's Land Company was chartered by the British Parliament and granted land on the northwest corner of the territory. Both the A.A. Coy and the VDL Coy still exist today, after nearly 180 years of continuous operation, a record beaten only by the Hudson Bay Company in Canada.

Macquarie's bank

*Nothing quite engenders confidence in an investor like
the thought of a new bank opening for business. Less than
three months after his arrival in the Colony, Macquarie
foreshadowed his plan for a bank on the South African
model, as a 'remedy' to:*

' . . . be speedily applied to this growing evil' of private promissory
notes. With some exaggeration he explained that there was 'no other
circulating medium in this colony than the notes of hand of private
individuals' which, as he said, had 'already been productive of infinite
frauds, abuses and litigation'. He accordingly announced his intention to'
strongly recommend the adoption here of the same system of banking and
circulating medium as is now so successfully and beneficially pursued at
the Cape of Good Hope.'

By June 1810 Macquarie had developed his plan for 'The New South
Wales Loan Bank' as a government institution 'as nearly as possible on the
same system and principles as the Government Loan Bank at the Cape
of Good Hope'. There, he explained the government issued notes by way
of loan on the security of mortgages at 6 per cent per annum. He also
pointed out that in England the government borrowed on exchequer bills
at 5 %, so that the Cape was 11% better off. 'It appears to me' was his
conclusion, 'the most perfect model in all its parts that could be possibly
adopted here' By October 1810, he was willing to accept any alternative
form of bank which Liverpool (Secretary for the Colonies) might believe
to be 'better calculated to effect the desired object.

Obviously a Bank would form the foundation for a monetary policy in
the colony, and stop the use of Commissary receipt (store receipts) as an
exchange mechanism, promote a currency and an official exchange rate
for traders and cease to rely on bills drawn on the British Treasury to pay
for goods and services.

The British scene

Circumstances in Britain contributed greatly to the climate of 'greener pastures' over the seas. Conditions were never more favourable for emigration than they were during the 1830s. The decade had opened with rioting in the agricultural districts in the south of England. This was followed by the upheavals of the Reform Bill of 1832, the Factory Act of 1833 and the Corn Laws, which kept wages low and unemployment high. The Poor Law of 1834 withdrew assistance from the poor and re-introduced the workhouse. The Irish rebellion was creating both upheaval and poverty.

These conditions were met by the enthusiastic reports coming from Australia of the progress being made in agriculture, commerce and the pastoral industry. The assistance granted to emigrants, as a result of Edward Gibbon Wakefield's reforms, made possible the emigration of people who had previously been prevented by the expense. However, it is almost certain that free passage would not have been a sufficient enticement if conditions in Britain had not been unfavourable. It is significant that years of small migration coincided with good conditions in England accompanied by unfavourable reports from the colony.

Creating opportunities in the Colony

The availability of land and labour to yield profit on invested capital is the constant decisive condition and test of material prosperity in any community, and becomes the keystone of an economy as well as defining its national identity. British Government policy for the Australian colonies was formulated and modified from time to time. Policies for the export of British capital and the supply of labour (both convict and free) were adjusted according to British industrial, demographic and other social situations, as well as the capability and capacity of the various colonial settlements to contribute to solving British problems.

By the 1820s there was official encouragement of British investment in Australia by adopting policies for large land grants to persons of capital and for the sale of land and assignment of convict labour to those investors. The reversal of the policy of setting up ex-convicts as small proprietors on small 30 acre plots followed. The hardship demanded by this policy usually meant these convicts and families remained dependent on the commissariat list for support (food and clothing) at a continuing cost to the government. It was much cheaper to assign these convicts to men of property and capital who would support them fully – clothe, house and feed them.

Reasons for the crash of 1827?

a. The float of the Australian Agricultural Company raised a large amount of capital, mostly from the City of London investment community, and this contributed to speculation and, as noted by Rev John Dunmore Lang, 'sheep and cattle mania instantly seized on all ranks and classes of the inhabitants and brought many families to poverty and ruin'.

b. When capital imports cease, the wherewithal to speculate vanished; and speculation perforce stopped; inflated prices fell to a more normal level. In his Economic History of Australia, E.O. Shann wrote 'because those formerly too optimistic were now too despairing, and people had to sell goods at any price in order to get money; men who had bought at high prices were ruined, and perforce their creditors fell with them'.

c. In 1842, it was the same. The influx of capital from oversees, pastoral extension, and large-scale immigration, caused much speculation. The banks, competing for business, advanced too much credit. Loans were made on the security of land and livestock which later became almost worthless; too much discounting was done for merchants (Gipps, HRA Vol 23). In the huge central district on the western slopes, along the Murrumbidgee and the Riverina, the squatters triumphed, as was inevitable. They had the financial resources to buy a run – especially after the long period of drought. Four million acres of Crown Land was sold for nearly £2.5 million. The confidence of British investors was waning. A crisis in the Argentine and the near failure of the large clearinghouse of Baring's made them cautious. Stories of rural and industrial strife in the Colony were not inducements to invest: and timber and metal prices were still falling. Loan raisings in London were under-subscribed and, at the same time, the banks were increasingly reluctant to lend money for land development which was so often unsound.

Assisted Migration

The dual policy of selling land to people with sufficient capital to cultivate it, and keeping a careful check on the number of free grants was adopted after 1825. 'Yet the Colonial Office', says Madgwick, 'failed to administer land policy with any certainty (R.B. Madgwick Immigration into Eastern Australia). There was no uniform policy adopted to encourage economic development in a systematic and rational way. The Wakefield system found new supporters; the principle had been established that the sale of land was preferred to the old system of grants. The dual system of sales and grants had failed to encourage local (colonial) purchases. They were willing to accept grants or even 'squat' rather than purchase land. Sales to absentee landlords and investors stepped up and this provided extensive revenue to the British Government to promote free and sponsored migration.

The original plans and costs

A letter to Under Secretary Nepean, dated 23rd August 1783, James Maria Matra of Shropshire and London assists us in this regard. It was Matra, who first analysed the opportunity of using the new colony as a penal colony but his estimates were incorrect and ill-founded. He had advised the Government that it would cost less than £3,000 to establish the colony initially, plus a transportation cost at £15 per head and annual maintenance of £20 per head. In fact the transportation was contracted for the Second Fleet at £13/5/—per head and Colonial revenues from 1802 offset annual maintenance.

However, Matra made a significant statement in his letter to Nepean, when he pointed out that the prisoners housed, fed and guarded on the rotting hulks on the Thames River were being contracted for in the annual amount of £26/15/10 per head per annum. He also writes that 'the charge to the public for these convicts has been increasing for the last 7 or 8 years' (Historical Records of NSW—Vol 1 Part 2 Page 7). Adopting this alternative cost (£26/15/10) as a base for comparison purposes, the colony's benefit to Britain over a twenty-year period increased from

£140,000,000 to £180,000,000. This calculation assesses the Ground 1 benefit at £84,000,000. Benefit to Britain on Ground 2 is put at £70,000,000 (again over a 20-year period) which places the value of a convict's labour at £35 per annum. Matra had assessed the value of labour of the hulk prisoners at £35/17/-.

The valuation of convict labour in the new Colony should reflect the fact that convicts were not only used on building sites, but also on road, bridge and wharf construction. This would add (based on £35 per annum) a further £21,000,000.

The Molesworth Committee (a House of Commons Committee investigating transportation) concluded that 'the surplus food production by the convicts would feed the Military people and this, over a period of 10 years, would save £7,000,000 for the British Treasury. The benefits of grants of land to the Military etc can be estimated (based on £1 per acre) at over £5,000,000 before 1810.

From Governor King's Report to Earl Camden dated 15th March 1806 (which, due to a change of office holder, should have been addressed to Viscount Castlereagh as Colonial Secretary) that the convicts engaged in widely diverse work. The Report itself is titled *Public Labour of Convicts maintained by the Crown at Sydney, Parramatta, Hawkesbury, Toongabbie and Castle Hill, for the year 1805*. This work included:

Cultivation—Gathering, husking and shelling maize from 200 acres sowed last year—Breaking up ground and planting 1230 acres of wheat, 100 acre of Barley, 250 acres of Maize, 14 acres of Flax, and 3 acres of potatoes—Hoeing the above maize and threshing wheat.

Stock—Taking care of Government stock as herdsmen, watchmen etc

Buildings—
At Sydney: Building and constructing of stone, a citadel, a stone house, a brick dwelling for the Judge Advocate, a commodious brick house for the main guard, a brick printing office
At Parramatta: Alterations at the Brewery, a brick house as clergyman's residence

At Hawkesbury: completing a public school
A Gaol House with offices, at the expense of the Colony
Boat and Ship Builders: refitting vessels and building row boats
Wheel and Millwrights: making and repairing carts
Manufacturing: sawing, preparing and manufacturing hemp, flax and
wool, bricks and tiles
Road Gangs: repairing roads, and building new roads
Other Gangs: loading and unloading boats"
(Historical Records of NSW—Vol 6 P43)

Thus the total benefits from these six items of direct gain to the British amount to well over £174 million, in comparison with Professor N.G. Butlin's proposal that the British 'invested' £5.6 million.

However, one item of direct cash cost born by the British was the transportation of the prisoners to the Colony, their initial food and general well being. Although the British chartered the whole ship, some of the expense was offset by authorising private passengers, 'free settlers' to travel in the same fleet. A second saving was that the authorities had approved 'back-loading' by these vessels of tea from China.

Only limited stores and provisions, tools and implements were sent with Captain Arthur Phillip, the appointed first Governor, and his efforts to delay the fleet until additional tools were ready were met with an order to 'commence the trip forthwith'. This turned out to be a mistake as the new Colony could only rely on minimal farming practices to grow a supply of vegetables and, without the tools to scratch the land and remove the trees and vegetation, little progress was made. This was a potentially big cost to the fledgling Colony.

The Blue Book accounting records, as maintained by Governor Macquarie from 1822 include a reference to 'net revenue and expenses' which suggests an offset of all revenues against all expenses, and including as revenue certain convict maintenance charges, to be reimbursed by the British Treasury. Such reimbursement was accounted for and reported only once, in 1825, when £16,617 'the amount of the parliamentary grant for the charge of defraying the civil establishment' was recorded as a 'receipt in aid of revenue'. Prior to and after that date, there are only reports of payments and outgoings to the civil establishment, military and other personnel, without offset from reimbursement. Other notations in 1825 include revenues from rentals of government assets (Government outsourcing and privatisation obviously started back in 1825) such as:

Ferries	£1,584
Toll gates	£6,554
Gardens	£1,835
Mill	£1,749
Canteen	£910
Church pews	£1,296
Hire of convict 'mechanics'	£6,853
Slaughtering dues	£975
Duty on colonial distillation	£4901
Duty on imported spirits	£178,434
Duty on imported tobacco	£21,817

Even in 1822 the Colony was showing a small operating surplus. This surplus grew through 1828 until, other than for transportation of convicts to the Colony, the charges on account of the British Treasury were less than £100,000 for protecting, feeding and housing nearly 5,000 fully maintained convicts. Against this cost, the charge for housing, feeding and guarding this same number of prisoners in Britain would have been substantially higher since, in addition to the 5,000 fully maintained convicts, there were a further 20,000 being paid for by free settlers and used as supervised labour. Britain surely had found a cheap source of penal servitude for at least 25,000 of its former prisoners, and found a very worthwhile alternative to the American colonies as a destination for its prisoners.

Revenue from Crown Land sales and rents was used to offset Civil (Crown) salaries and expenses. The opportunity cost to the British Treasury includes not only the cost savings but also the lateral savings and benefits produced for England and the British Treasury. Some of the other advantages to Britain include:

- The build-up of trade by the East-India Company

- The advantage of a secure, in-house supply of raw wool, to keep the spinning mills occupied
- The opportunity cost of housing, feeding and guarding prisoners
- The use of convict labour in the new Colony, for such as
  Land clearing, farming, food production
  Road construction
- Building projects such as:
  Public wharves
  Barracks
  Public Buildings
- Productions of Materials supply eg brick & tile production.
- As unpaid day labour for the pastoral & agricultural industry.

We can assume that land grants in the Colony to men on the military and civil list were a form of 'fringe benefits' and they should be quantified as an alternative to paid remuneration for these people. Even land grants to emancipists were used as an incentive to increase food production.

We can quantify the 'value of direct gain to the British economy' of nearly £140,000,000, compared with the publicly recorded expenditure on transportation, supplies, and military personnel of £5,600,000, between 1788 and 1822. The purposes of trying to quantify these benefits are to challenge to traditional concept that 'the British invested millions of pounds in the Colony of New South Wales'. This is obviously only the case when the outlay is shown and not the on-going benefits for over 50 years, and indeed two hundred years. It is still arguable that the continent of Australia was, in the words of Captain Arthur Phillip 'the best investment Britain will ever make'.

Having established the parameters for studying British (private and public) investment in the Colony of NSW, the question must now be one of who else thinks this investment was of interest and relevance. N.G. Butlin did not complete his manuscript of *Forming a Colonial Economy* because his death in 1991. However his notes to that time were edited and assembled into the book form and we can learn a great deal about the British plans for the colony and its economic development. Butlin writes:

*'Even though, there may have been other imperial motives
behind the British settlement of Australia, there is no doubt
that the transportation of convicts to the Antipodes was a
convenient solution to social, judicial and budgetary problems
in Britain in the 1780s.'*

Butlin further deduces that 'Persons may move between countries (i.e.
immigration) when the capitalized value of the differential in expected
lifetime earnings abroad as compared with those at home exceeds the
transfer and relocation costs'. The good news of free immigration and
the capital transfer into the Colony was that between 1788 and 1800
21,302 'free immigrants' arrived. There are nine identified categories of
'immigrants' during this period.

- Military and civil officers and their families
- Former officials returning to the colony
- Convict families
- Indentured labourers
- Assisted immigrants
- Privately supported persons sponsored by colonials
- Free immigrants and their families

Given that Britain provided not only human capital but also fiscal resources
to support the people concerned, the volume and, nature of these resources
and access to them became interesting. However, it remains the case that
Britain, having put into place extensive levels of capital, certainly succeeded
in withdrawing a great deal of its early fiscal support and bringing the
Commissariat effectively under military control. Obviously another form
of 'investment' is public debt, and public borrowing, secured by the full
faith and credit of the Colonial government.

The 'works outlay' is another element of 'public investment' and it was
not fully accounted for until 1810 when Governor Macquarie arrived.
From that date, works outlay (i.e. capital expenditure from the local
revenue of the Colony) grew annually from £2,194 in 1810 to £14,700 in
1821. However, this is a small component of total works outlay or capital
expenditure since a Mr. Henry Kitchen, in a submission to Commissioner

J.T. Bigge, stated that his estimate of building construction under Macquarie was in excess of £900,000.

A table included in *Australians Historical Statistics* titled 'Gross Private Capital Formation at current prices' does not commence until 1861 and later in this study we will try to assemble data on both public and private capital formation from 1800 – based on a separate study of Colonial industrial, building and construction development. This table is derived from Butlin's 'Australian Domestic Product, Investment and Foreign Borrowing 1861-1938'. It appears that no previous studies have been undertaken of private or public Capital Formation between 1788 and 1861.

T.A. Coghlan is generally recognised as a significant contributor to Colonial economic history and he writes in Volume 1 of *Labour and Industry in Australia* of another phase of public investment and its encouragement in the colony, by favourable official policies. Coghlan writes:

> *'Under the Governorship of Macquarie the infant town of Sydney grew considerably. King had been the first Governor to grant leases there (Sydney), but as the leases were only for five years the buildings erected were naturally not of a substantial character. Macquarie granted a number of leases also, but gave permanent grants of land in cases where valuable buildings were to be erected, so that at the end of his term of office Sydney had grown considerably, having the appearance, according to W.C. Wentworth in his Historical and Statistical Account of the Colony, of a town of 20,000 inhabitants though its population, numbered only 7,000; and while the houses were for the most part small one-storied dwellings, it contained buildings, private and public, excellent both in construction and in design, and many stores where goods of all kinds could be bought. The Government Store continued in existence as a shop open to the public until January 1815, when Macquarie, considering that its purpose had been served as a means towards keeping down*

prices, closed it to all except the military and the convicts in government employment. [61].

So, having fixed the short-term land lease, Macquarie actively encouraged public and private investment in building and construction. Coghlan provides an insight into another Macquarie step to encourage investment. He writes:

'Until Macquarie arrived, the means of communicating between one part of the settlement and another was difficult, as all roads were poor. Macquarie had a passion for construction, and his roads were excellent. He made a turnpike road from Sydney to the Hawkesbury, completing it in 1811. Now goods and passengers did not have to be carried by boat, as previously was the case. A few years later he constructed the great road over the mountains to the western plains, and also extended his roads in other directions. With the construction of the roads, internal trade and all the industries dependent thereon developed. It took a further time before travelling by road was safe, as many convicts escaped and took to the bush, preying upon defenceless travellers; journeys to any part of the settlement was usually made in company and it was customary to make even the short journey from Sydney to Parramatta about 14 miles in parties. [62]

If we intend to extend our parameters to further analyse the types and amount of public and private British investment in the Colony of NSW, we will have to now review certain other matters:

- The development of private industries eg boat-building; timber harvesting and processing; agriculture sand pastoral pursuits, whaling and overseas trading – all of which were reasonably capital intensive operations which would have attracted both overseas investors and a local breed of entrepreneurs

---

[61] Coghlan, T.A. *Labour & Investment in Australia Vol 1*
[62] Coghlan *ibid*

- The development of building and construction in the Colony, including reference to the public buildings completed in the period, how much they would have cost and how they were paid for.
- We will try to assemble a table of public and private overseas (British) investment, and establish the background to debt in the Colony from overseas sources.
- We will attempt to recreate the level of investment in the colony by category by first identifying the various sources of both public and private investment and relating value to each one
- We will endeavour to track bank deposits and advances, which until the 1850s were generally in the negative (i.e. advances exceeded deposits and it fell to the local banks to accept British deposits for fixed terms of 1, 2 or 3 years. Banks advanced money by way of pastoralists' overdrafts, on city land and on stocks and shares. Land banks offered mortgages. Banks' liabilities before 1850 by way of term deposits from overseas depositors were almost 40 million pound.
- One gauge of how much money was flowing through the domestic economy is the volume of cheques, bills and drafts passing through the clearing-house. By the 1860s, this amount had risen to almost £6 million each week.
- Coghlan's *Wealth and Progress of NSW* for 1900 reflects on the source and disposition of public capital and can be tabulated as follows:[63]

Source of Funds

Treasury bills and debentures	8,168,554
Transfer from Consolidated Revenue	1,668,640
Sum Available for Expenditure	82,430,777

Use of Funds

Railways	40,450,473
Tramways	2,720,338

---

[63]   Coghlan, T.A. *Wealth & Progress in NSW 1900*

Telegraphs	1,255,600
Water supply and sewerage	9,878,833

Catalysts for immigration

Free immigration into the Colony – a new perspective

The need for education in the colony is an interesting pre-emptive to the need for free immigrants. Immigration would help solve numerous gaps in the colony—capital and labour, societal demands and the imbalance of men and women, the demand for a free enterprise economy and 'foreign' investment. The direct association then as now, between education and investment, knowledge and growth is unmistakeable. It was largely left to Macquarie to juggle the need for balance in the penal colony, but this was not a high priority and it was passed to Brisbane and then Bourke. Before migration could be practiced, thought Macquarie, I need to rid the streets of the waifs, orphans and unwanted children of a largely immoral society. Bligh had first drawn official attention to the deteriorating social fabric with three times as many 'kept' as married women and the dazzling count of illegitimate children compared with those that numbered in the legitimate category. Education would help, not only with this social dilemma, but also with the rampant illiteracy in the Colony—the three Rs were down to one R and 'riting was largely limited to an X on the spot.

Education, a construction program, local discretionary revenue raising and elimination of spirits as the currency of the day, were Macquarie's top priorities – only then could free immigrants be welcomed. Of course a bank would be helpful in cementing the colony as a land of opportunity. The English thought in terms of symbols even if they were thin. So, understanding the needs for education set the scene for a rational immigration policy.

The economy was at the top of the triangle pointing the way ahead. The fact that the Colony had no treasury was a disincentive to migration but Macquarie believed in balancing finely the needs of a despotic governor with the daily demands on government with the desire for free enterprise. Macquarie had decided that government had the need and responsibility to encourage and sponsor exploration, and it was the crossing of the mountain range west of Sydney town that inspired and commenced the first sustained economic expansion of the Colony. The pastoral movement led the way towards encouraging migration. The financing mechanism for the new policy was the sale of Crown or 'waste' lands and the boom and bust syndrome was set in place by speculators in both land and livestock. The market economy would be in tatters within 20 years of Macquarie's departure.

This is the story of the need for education and a sound economy leading to migration as a catalyst for growth in the 'new' economy.

Immigrants and Free Settlers

On 15th January 1793, Collins records that the *Bellona* transport ship had arrived in Sydney Harbour with a cargo of stores and provisions, 17 female convicts and five settlers, one of whom was a master wheelwright employed by the governor at a salary of £100 per annum. A second was a returning skilled tradesman who had previously been employed as a master blacksmith. All five settlers had brought their families. Collins conjectured that these first five settlers had received free passage, the promise of a land grant and assistance with farming, as incentives for becoming free settlers.

In *A History of Australia*, Manning Clark records that in 1806, 'a dozen families from the Scottish border area arrived as free emigrants and each received 100 acres of land on the banks of the Hawkesbury River in a place they called Ebenezer. They were devout Presbyterians, and were allowed to worship in the colony according to their own lights'. However the authorities were not prepared to tolerate the practice of the Catholic religion, because they saw it 'as an instrument of mental slavery, a threat to higher civilization, and a threat to liberty' (Clark Vol 1)

Developing immigration

Even by the census of 1828, NSW had fewer than 5,000 people who had come out voluntarily out of a population of 36 598. The Colony had attractions unavailable in the USA, free land and convict labour. Settlers were given freehold land for agriculture and pasture but it applied only to men who had immigrated as private citizens, military officers who had decided to stay and pardoned convicts who had been granted land.

In 1831 the British Government, against the opposition of many in the Colony, decided to stop giving away land grants to settlers, choosing instead to 'sell' the land and use some of the proceeds to sponsor migrants to the colony. The initial sale price was 5 shillings an acre. It was a way of inducing poor families to migrate and relieving the labour shortage. Between 1831 and 1840 about 50,000 prisoners were transported and about 65,000 free men and women chose to emigrate.

The balance of the sexes was more equal amongst emigrants than among convicts: but even South Australia, which was wholly an emigrant colony, had only eight females for every 10 males by 1850. In Australia as a whole there were fewer than seven for every 10. The resulting challenge was only partially met by Caroline Chisholm who met every convict and emigrant ship to stress the dangers to young unmarried women. Her main accomplishment was when she convinced the Colonial Office in 1846 to offer free passage to all families of convicts resident in the Colony. Her detractors claimed that the result of her efforts on behalf of convicts and poor emigrating families would be to create in the Colony an imbalance of Catholics In Australia, Catholics were already twice the proportion of the population that they were in England.

'Populate or perish'

The history of Australia is bound tightly into two aspects—the economics of colonisation and the story of immigration.

The first free immigrants who came out on the *Bellona* were given small land grants on Liberty Plains (the Strathfield-Homebush area). The first family to arrive included a millwright who had been on the hulks in Britain for a minor crime and been released. Major Grose, acting as the Administrator after Phillip's departure, observed 'from some dirty tricks he has already attempted, I fear he has not forgotten all he learned as a former prisoner. He is evidently one of those that his country could well do without'.

In his report *The State of the Colony in 1801,* Governor King wrote on the subject of free immigrants:

> 'Settlers are of two classes i.e. those who come free from England and those who were convicts and whose terms of transportation are expired, or who are emancipated. Of the first class, I am sorry their industry and exertions by no means answer the professions they made in England, several of whom are so useless to themselves and everyone about them that they were not only a burden to the public but a very bad example to the industrious. As they brought no other property than their large families, many have been and will continue an expensive burden on the public, or starve. The settlers are maintained by the crown for eighteen months and have two convicts assigned to each, which is very sufficient to provide against the time of doing for themselves, but that period too often discovers their idleness and incapacity to raise the least article from a fertile and favourable climate, after having occasioned an expense of upwards of 250 pound for each family, exclusive of their passage out The desirable people to be sent here are sober, industrious farmers, carpenters, wheel and mill wrights, who having been used to draw their food from the earth, secure sand manufacture it, would here find how bountifully their labour would be rewarded.'

It appears that King did not have a very high opinion of the potential for free migration to the Colony.

Phillip's successor – Governor Hunter—was instructed by the Colonial Office to 'encourage free settlers without subjecting the public to expense'. They were to be given larger land grants than the emancipists and as much convict labour as they wanted. Hunter observed in one of his submissions to the Secretary for the Colonies that 'free immigrants would not come to the country whilst the needs of the colony were supplied from Government farms'. Economic factors hit the immigration concept in 1801 when Hunter's successor, Governor King, wrote to the Duke of Portland, as Colonial Secretary, suggesting family immigration. It was declined on the basis that transporting a family would cost £150 and annual maintenance until they were self-supporting would cost £250 (HRNSW).

In 1802, the HRNSW records that free settlers (28 in one group) arrived by the *Perseus* and *Coromandel*. More arrived in the Navy ship *Glatton*, including a person supposedly bearing 'perfect knowledge of Agriculture, having held a very considerable farm in his hands, but which through youthful indiscretion, he found it necessary to relinquish'. The Governor was asked to place him 'above the common class of settlers'. The government, Governor King wrote 'was much imposed on' by these free settlers. The *Glatton* settlers were sent to the Nepean, where they were wrote King 'going on with great spirit and well applied industry'.

In 1804 King reported to Lord Hobart 'there were 543 free settlers supporting 351 wives and 589 children and utilising 463 convicts'. Further free settlers are recorded as arriving in the *William Pitt* in 1805, mainly because land and subsistence was being replaced by the lure of wealth coming from the fine wool being promoted by John Macarthur. This endeavour and attraction of wealth brought a different and probably better class of free settler – the Blaxland brothers arrived on a charter vessel with their families, servants and capital of over 6,000 pound. Again the governor received instructions. 'They are to be allowed 8,000 acres of land and the services of up to 80 convicts for 18 months at the commissary store's expense. Governor Bligh was given similar instructions in reference to a 'lady of quality' – a Mrs Chapman, a widow, Governess and teacher. Bligh was directed to 'afford her due encouragement and assistance'. The next governor, Lachlan Macquarie took a different stance – he discouraged free immigration, probably because the flow of convicts was almost overwhelming his administration. His position is not readily understandable. As a quasi social reformer and developer of free enterprise in the colony, one would have expected Macquarie to welcome free settlers for what social and economic values they could contribute. When the Bigge report was published in London, it raised the interest of men of wealth in the colony and a Lieutenant Vickers, an officer of the East India Company, volunteered to emigrate with 10,000 pound of capital, an unblemished reputation and a purity of private life ' not previously known in any class of society', and in return demanded privileges by way of land grants, livestock and a regular seat at the governor's table. Brisbane, as governor, was directed by Lord Bathurst as Colonial secretary to give Vickers 2,000 acres of land and a house allotment near Newcastle. Brisbane investigated Vickers and found him to be little more than 'an adventurer, a bird of passage, and boycotted by his fellow officers'. Marjorie Barnard concluded, 'Only distance made his deception possible'. Opportunities followed good publicity, and the floating of the Australian Agricultural Company in London in 1823 did much to promote the colony in Britain, and brought another spate of free settlers to the colony.

This then is the early trend in the free settler movement – it had not been seen yet as a government opportunity. But that was about to change. Lord Bathurst came along with an idea, urged by the Wakefield supporters and the rash of economists waging war on the increasing unemployment, poverty and lack of investment opportunities in Britain.

A privately sponsored scheme was funded by a loan to Dr. J.D. Lang by the governor in the amount of 1,500 pound, which brought out 100 selected 'mechanics' (semi-skilled labourers) and their families. Lang used a charter vessel to transport these immigrants, and the understanding was that the immigrants would repay their expenses from future wages. In 1831 this was an inspiring move to privatising a government policy.

Three factors were set to establish an on-going immigration policy. The three factors were bad times in England; shortages of skilled labour of both men and women in the colony; and the cessation of the assignment system.

A commission on Emigration was established in England to select and despatch suitable agricultural labourers. A plan to tax landowners of assigned convicts failed when the difficulty of collection was recognised. There were still 13,400 convicts on assignment in 1831.

The governor agreed that official funds would contribute 20 pound towards each immigrant family and try to recover it after the family settled. The collections were rarely made.

It was left to Governor Bourke to formulate a workable plan. The 'bounty system' relied on sponsored workers funded by government. The government paid 12 pound out of the 17 pound passage money. The Emigrants Friendly Society existed in Sydney to help and protect these sponsored migrants.

A more refined method was needed to select and sponsor these migrants. Glenelg reformed the financial side in 1837. He allocated the revenue from land sales in the colony as a means of affording immigration. The land as well as any revenue derived from its sale, lease or rental, had remained the property of the crown, not the colonial administration. Two-thirds of these funds were to be allocated to migrants by way of grants – 30 pound for a married couple, 15 for an unmarried daughter, 5 and10 pound for children depending on age.

The zenith of immigration success could be seen in the 1830s under Governor Gipps. Land revenue was high, the colony was prosperous and plenty of migrants were on offer and the colony could successfully absorb them. The severe drought at the end of decade (1838) cause land revenue to fall sharply. Gipps proposed a loan to the Land Fund in order to continue the immigration program. He requested of the British Treasury a loan of 1 million pound. The intention of floating the loan would ensure the repayment of the loan. English interest still dwelt on the export of her paupers and her unemployed. The response by Gipps to Lord John Russell's criticism of the Gipps approach to immigration was that the bounty system had caused the depression of the 1842-44 periods and not the reverse.

The Report of the 1837 'Committee on Immigration' opened up for opposition to the traditional White Australia policy.

"This committee was appointed to consider and report their opinion made to the government of New South Wales, for introducing into the colony certain of the Hill Labourers of India; and to consider the terms under which Mechanics and Labourers are now brought from Europe".

Summary

The British trait of pomposity came to the fore during the days of early migration to the colony. 'We are British, we are free, we are pure of spirit and more worthy than the prisoners already shipped' they thought' but we will take or families, our servants, our capital and relocate to the new colony, provided we are treated as privileged persons and given land, livestock and a seat at the governor's table'.

But establishing a class structure was not on the list of plans for Brisbane, Bourke Darling or Gipps. They hands their hands full keeping the economy moving forward and keeping the economy afloat. Although they were guided by an appointed Legislative Council, the governors role was an onerous one – balancing the ever-changing political scene in Britain with the ever-diminishing financial support coming from the British Treasury for colonial operations, and the growing relaxing of isolation of the colony in world events. Trading ships of many nations were daily arrivals into the splendid harbour. The other settlement under the governor's watchful eye was taking more and more time. It was fortunate that Port Phillip settlement was a net contributor to the New South Wales coffers, whilst Morton Bay, and VDL were still being supported out of Sydney. The huge influx of convicts made life difficult in the settlements. Finding places to put these people to gainful employment at little (if any) cost to the Treasury was growing more and more difficult. It was largely 'out of sight, out of mind'. Until they engaged in crime, or the landowners ran into hard times and suddenly the convicts were unwanted and thrown back onto the charity of the government. Free settlers were fine in theory but their growing influence in the political and financial arena of the colony, made both political and economic decisions difficult. The constant pressure to open up new land, build new roads, carry out surveys, create new settlements – was a continuing problem for the governor who kept demanding more and more money to run the colony. That placed pressure on raising more and more revenue, especially for public works, education, migration and government services.

Migrations soon became the life-blood of the colony. They brought their capital, their worldly goods, their ways of life, and over all made a valuable contribution to their new land. They were the basis of attracting new investment from the motherland. But migrants down through the years were always to be attractive in the Australian physic. This was to be a nation of immigrants, but society had to be built around the needs of this new world.

Special Events –Colonial Education & Immigration Policies

Synopsis

As the first of the special events to be examined, we can review the impact of both education and immigration, from the standpoint of the economy, the social framework, the political structure and look at the rocky road that was created by religious bigotry and factions within the colony. Naturally as a bi-product of the immigration policies, the transportation (of convicts) program was its first and most significant contributor. Education was a significant economic tool, as the rate of illiteracy within the colony fell from 75% before 1800 to 25% by 1830. The development of local industry was most dependent then, as it is still today, on a literate and educated workforce. Immigration of free settlers hastened the end of the transportation program and although the mass of people supported and approved of its cessation, the pastoralists, traders and merchants bemoaned the shortage of labour and the high price of skilled labourers arriving from Britain. Naturally the discovery of gold in the early 1850s drove those same prices and shortages even higher, since many in the population looked to find their fortune on the goldfields and gave up regular employment in order to move to the goldfields.

Immigrants and Free Settlers

Collins records that on the 15th January 1793, the Bellona transport ship, arrived in Sydney Harbour with a cargo of stores and provisions, 17 female convicts and five settlers one of whom was a master wheel-wright employed by the governor at a salary of 100 pound per annum. A second was a returning skilled tradesman who had been previously employed as a master blacksmith. All five settlers had brought their families.

Collins conjectures that these first three settlers had received free passage, a promise of a land grant and assistance with farming, as the incentive for becoming the free settlers,

Manning Clark (A History of Australia) records that in 1806, 'a dozen families from the Scottish border area arrived as free emigrants and each received 100 acres of land on the banks of the Hawkesbury River in a place they called Ebenezer. They were devout Presbyterians, and were allowed to worship in the colony according to their own lights'. However the authorities were not prepared to tolerate the practice of the catholic religion, because they saw it 'as an instrument of mental slavery, a threat to higher civilization, and a threat to liberty' (Clark Vol 1)

Developing Immigration

Even by the census of 1828, NSW had fewer than 5,000 people who had come out voluntarily, in a population of 36 598. The colony had the attractions unavailable in the USA, free land and convict labour. Settlers were given land for agriculture and pasture usage. This meant freehold land, and it only applied to men who had immigrated as private citizens, to military officers who had decided to stay and to pardoned convicts who had been granted land.

In 1831, the British Government, against the opposition of many in the colony decided to stop giving away land grants to settlers and chose instead to 'sell' the land and use some of the proceeds to sponsor migrants to the colony. The initial sales price was 5 shillings an acre. It was a way of inducing poor families to leave the country, but as well of relieving the labour shortage. Between 1831 and 1840 about 50,000 prisoners were transported and about 65,000 free men and women chose to emigrate

The battle of the sexes was more equal amongst emigrants than among convicts: but even South Australia, which was wholly an emigrant's colony, had only 8 females for every 10 males by 1850, and in Australia as a whole there was fewer than 7 in every ten. The resulting challenge was only partially met by Caroline Chisholm who met every convict and emigrant ship to stress the dangers to young unmarried women. Her main accomplishment was to convince the Colonial Office, in 1846, to offer free passage to all families of convicts resident in the colony. Her detractors suggested that the result of her efforts towards convict families and emigrating poor families would be to create an imbalance of Catholics in the colony, who were already twice the proportion of the Australian population as they were in England.

'Populate or Perish'

The history of Australia is bound tightly into two aspects—the economics of colonization and the story of immigration.

The first free immigrants came out on the Bellona, and were given small landgrants on Liberty Plains (the Strathfield-Homebush area). The first family to arrive included a millwright who had been on the hulks in Britain for a minor crime and been released. It was Major Grose, acting as the Administrator after the departure of Phillip, who observed ' from some dirty tricks he has already attempted, I fear he has not forgotten all he learned as a former prisoner. He is evidently one of those that his country could well do without'.

Governor King wrote in his report – The State of the Colony in 1801 – on the subject of free immigrants:

"Settlers are of two classes i.e. those who come free from England and those who were convicts and whose terms of transportation are expired, or who are emancipated. Of the first class, I am sorry their industry and exertions by no means answer the professions they made in England, several of whom are so useless to themselves and everyone about them that they were not only a burden to the public but a very bad example to the industrious. As they brought no other property than their large families, many have been and will continue an expensive burden on the public, or starve. The settlers are maintained by the crown for eighteen months and have two convicts assigned to each, which is very sufficient to provide against the time of doing for themselves, but that period too often discovers their idleness and incapacity to raise the least article from a fertile and favourable climate, after having occasioned an expense of upwards of 250 pound for each family, exclusive of their passage out The desirable people to be sent here are sober, industrious farmers, carpenters, wheel and mill wrights, who having been used to draw their food from the earth, secure sand manufacture it, would here find how bountifully their labour would be rewarded".

It appears that King did not have a very high opinion of the potential for free migration to the colony.

Phillip's successor – Governor Hunter—was instructed by the Colonial Office to 'encourage free settlers without subjecting the public to expense'. They were to be given larger land grants than the emancipists and as much convict labour as they wanted. Hunter observed in one of his submissions to the Secretary of the colonies that 'free immigrants would not come to the country whilst the needs of the colony were supplied from Government farms'.

The economic factors hit the immigration concept in 1801 when Governor King, as Hunters successor wrote to the Duke of Portland, as Colonial Secretary and suggested family immigration. It was turned down on the basis that transporting a family would cost 150 pound and annual maintenance until they were self-supporting would cost 250 pound (HRNSW)

In 1802, the HRNSW records that free settlers (28 in one group) arrived by the Perseus and Coromandel. More came in the Navy ship Glatton, including a person supposedly bearing 'perfect knowledge of Agriculture, having held a very considerable farm in his hands, but which through youthful indiscretion, he found it necessary to relinquish'. The governor was asked to place him 'above the common class of settlers'. The government, Governor King wrote 'was much imposed on' by these free settlers. The Glatton settlers were sent to the Nepean, where they were wrote King ' going on with great spirit and well applied industry'

King reported to Lord Hobart in 1804 that 'there were 543 free settlers supporting 351 wives and 589 children and utilising 463 convicts'. Further free settlers are recorded as being in the William Pitt in 1805, mainly because land and subsistence was being replaced by the lure of wealth coming from the fine wool being promoted by John Macarthur. This endeavour and attraction of wealth brought a different and probably better class of free settler – the Blaxland brothers arrived on a charter vessel with their families, servants and capital of over 6,000 pound. Again the governor received instructions. 'They are to be allowed 8,000 acres of land and the services of up to 80 convicts for 18 months at the commissary store's expense. Governor Bligh was given similar instructions in reference to a 'lady of quality' – a Mrs Chapman, a widow, Governess and teacher. Bligh was directed to 'afford her due encouragement and assistance'. The next governor, Lachlan Macquarie took a different stance – he discouraged free immigration, probably because the flow of convicts was almost overwhelming his administration. His position is not readily understandable. As a quasi social reformer and developer of free enterprise in the colony, one would have expected Macquarie to welcome free settlers for what social and economic values they could contribute. When the Bigge report was published in London, it raised the interest of men of wealth in the colony and a Lieutenant Vickers, an officer of the East India Company, volunteered to emigrate with 10,000 pound of capital, an unblemished reputation and a purity of private life ' hitherto known in any class of society', and in return demanded privileges by way of land grants, livestock and a regular seat at the governor's table. Brisbane, as governor, was directed by Lord Bathurst as Colonial secretary to give Vickers 2,000 acres of land and a house allotment near Newcastle. Brisbane investigated Vickers and found him to be little more than 'an adventurer, a bird of passage, and boycotted by his fellow officers'. Marjorie Barnard concluded, 'Only distance made his deception possible'. Opportunities followed good publicity, and the floating of the Australian Agricultural Company in London in 1823 did much to promote the colony in Britain, and brought another spate of free settlers to the colony.

This then is the early trend in the free settler movement – it had not been seen yet as a government opportunity. But that was about to change. Lord Bathurst came along with an idea, urged by the Wakefield supporters and the rash of economists waging war on the increasing unemployment, poverty and lack of investment opportunities in Britain.

A privately sponsored scheme was funded by a loan to Dr. J.D. Lang by the governor in the amount of 1,500 pound, which brought out 100 selected 'mechanics' (semi-skilled labourers) and their families. Land used a charter vessel to transport these immigrants, and the understanding was that the immigrants would repay their expenses from future wages. In 1831 this was an inspiring move to privatising a government policy.

Three factors were set to establish an on-going immigration policy. The three factors were bad times in England; shortages of skilled labour of both men and women in the colony; and the cessation of the assignment system.

A commission on Emigration was established in England to select and despatch suitable agricultural labourers. A plan to tax landowners of assigned convicts failed when the difficulty of collection was recognised. There were still 13,400 convicts on assignment in 1831.

The governor agreed that official funds would contribute 20 pound towards each immigrant family and try to recover it after the family settled. The collections were rarely made.

It was left to Governor Bourke to formulate a workable plan. The 'bounty system' relied on sponsored workers funded by government. The government paid 12 pound out of the 17 pound passage money. The Emigrants Friendly Society existed in Sydney to help and protect these sponsored migrants.

A more refined method was needed to select and sponsor these migrants. Glenelg reformed the financial side in 1837. He allocated the revenue from land sales in the colony as a means of affording immigration. The land as well as any revenue derived from its sale, lease or rental, had remained the property of the crown, not the colonial administration. Two-thirds of these funds were to be allocated to migrants by way of grants – 30 pound for a married couple, 15 for an unmarried daughter, 5 and10 pound for children depending on age.

The zenith of immigration success could be seen in the 1830s under Governor Gipps. Land revenue was high, the colony was prosperous and plenty of migrants were on offer and the colony could successfully absorb them. The severe drought at the end of decade (1838) cause land revenue to fall sharply. Gipps proposed a loan to the Land Fund in order to continue the immigration program. He requested of the British Treasury a loan of 1 million pound. The intention of floating the loan would ensure the repayment of the loan. English interest still dwelt on the export of her paupers and her unemployed. The response by Gipps to Lord John Russell's criticism of the Gipps approach to immigration was that the bounty system had caused the depression of the 1842-44 periods and not the reverse.

The Report of the 1837 'Committee on Immigration' opened up for opposition to the traditional White Australia policy.

"This committee was appointed to consider and report their opinion made to the government of New South Wales, for introducing into the colony certain of the Hill Labourers of India; and to consider the terms under which Mechanics and Labourers are now brought from Europe".

EXPLAINING THE COLONIAL ECONOMIC DRIVERS 1788-1856

In order to understand the growth of the colonial economy, we must understand the economic drivers that underpinned, sustained and supported the colonial economy. There are at least six, if not seven, such economic drivers. They include the factors of (a) population growth, the (b) economic development within the colony, the (c) funding sources such as British Treasury appropriations and the (d) revenues raised from within the local economy (for example, taxes and duties on imports) and (e) foreign investment (both public and private). The traditional concept of growth within the colonial economy comes from (f) the rise of the pastoral industry. A seventh driver would be the all-important Land Board, which played such an important role within the colonial economy The Land Board played an important role in co-ordinating crown land policy, controlling land sales, squatting licenses and speculators, re-setting boundaries of location, establishing set aside lands for future townships and for church and school estates, carrying out the survey of millions of acres of land transferred by grant and sale, and offering terms sales for crown lands and being responsible for the collection of repayments, rents, license fees, quit-rents and depasturing fees. In addition the land board was vested with road reserves for hundreds of miles of unmade roads but important rights-of-way that would well into the future protect access to remote pastoral and farming properties. The main thrust of published material about the Land Board is in conjunction with crown land sales policy, but the Board had a much larger role and the overall Board policies sand performances are what are to be reviewed here.

Although an important factor it is no more important that our other five motivators of the colonial economy between 1802 and 1856. Why have

I selected these two specific dates? 1802 was when Governor King first imposed an illegal, but justified and well-intentioned impost on the local free community to build a local gaol to replace one burnt to the ground through a lightening strike but which the British would not replace. The local residents thought a more solid and durable prison was a worthwhile community investment. At the other end, the year of 1856 signalled the first real representative and responsible government in the colony, and although it was not the end of the colonial era, it was certainly the end of Britain's financial support of sand for the colony and as such the colony was expected to stand on its own two feet.

These six factors will be discussed as mechanisms for 'growing the colonial economy between 1802 and 1856'

One consideration that must not be forgotten is the externally enforced pace of colonial expansion, particularly through the organised rather than the market-induced inflow of both convicts and assisted migrants. What this means is that instead of market forces requiring additional labour and human resources, extra labour and resources were imposed on the colony and there was an obligatory process of putting these people to work, in many cases by creating a public works program and pushing development ahead at an artificial pace rather than at a time and rate suited to the local economy. In much the same way, the 'assignment' system in the 1810-1830 period forced landowners to create clearing and development programs in order to utilise the labour available rather than only develop land as demand required.

1. Population growth including immigration of convicts & free settlers

The reason the colonial society did not change very much in the 1820s is that relatively few immigrants arrived. During 1823, Lord Bathurst, Colonial Secretary, sent instructions to Governor Brisbane (Macquarie's successor) altering the administration of the colony of NSW in most of the ways Commissioner Bigge had recommended in his reports.[64] One

---

[64] Commissioner J.T. Bigge had been sent by Bathurst to Enquire into the State and Operations of the colony of NSW in 1819; the House of Commons had demanded an inquiry into the colony and had threatened to hold one of its own; Bathurst pre-empted a difficult government situation by appointing

result of the Bigge Reports was that Macquarie was officially recalled to Britain even though he had canvassed his retirement before Bigge's arrival in 1819. Macquarie was distressed by the Bigge Reports and took very personally the recommendations made for change. Although there were many implied criticisms Macquarie considered that the public perception was that he had not acted properly in his role as Governor. Macquarie set to and compared the circumstances of the colony at the time of his arrival in 1810, with the great achievements he had made through 1821. In hindsight, Macquarie had accomplished much, mostly by means of arrogantly pursuing a series of policies without the pre-approval of the Secretary or the Government in London.

The arrival of only a few immigrants was because Bigge and the Colonial Office believed that only men of capital would emigrate. Labourers and the poor of England should not be encouraged and, as these people rarely had money to pay for the long passage to Sydney, few of them arrived.[65] Although the numbers were small, few of them came unassisted. In 1821 320 free immigrants arrived and this increased each year; 903 in 1826; 1005 in 1829, but slipping to 772 in 1830. Mostly they were family groups with some financial security.

In 1828, the first census (as opposed to musters) of white persons in NSW was taken. 20,930 persons were classified as free and 15,668 were classified as convicts. However, of the free persons, many had arrived as convicts or were born of convicts. In fact, 70% of the population in 1828 had convict associations. However, by 1828, one quarter of the NSW population was native born; 3,500 were over 12 years of age

There was another side to this migration of unregulated souls. Shaw writes" The cost of assistance, the unsuitability of many emigrants, their ill-health, and the numbers of children and paupers that were sent – all these gave the colonists a source of grievance".[66] A large part of the problem was that the English wanted emigration – but those they wished to see emigrate were

---

Bigge with a very broad and wide-ranging terms of Enquiry. Bigge held two years of investigations in the colony and reported to the Commons in 1823 with the printing of three Reports.

[65] Australian History – The occupation of a Continent *Bessant* (Ed)
[66] Shaw, A.G.L. *The economic development of Australia* p.44

not welcomed in the colony. A growing opinion in the colony was that free migrants could not work with convicts; the convicts by themselves were too few and with growing expense; therefore transportation must stop and immigration be encouraged. However, immigrants of a good quality were not those the English wanted to send; its preference was for the paupers and the disruptive in the society. To stop transportation would be "attended with the most serious consequences unless there be previous means taken too ensure the introduction of a full supply of free labour". [67] In the next five years, the number of free immigrants increased so much that transportation could be stopped with little political backlash. Between 1835 and 1840, the colony was quite prosperous (it was a case of boom and bust—the great depression came in 1841); sales of crown land were large, and consequently the funds available for assisting immigrants were plentiful.[68]

In 1838, land revenue was over £150,000 and assisted migrants numbered 7,400; in 1839, land revenue was £200,000 and assisted migrants 10,000; in 1840 revenue was over £500,000 and assisted migrants 22,500.

Between 1832 and 1842, over 50,000 assisted and 15,000 unassisted migrants arrived in NSW; or they might have arrived as convicts, and over 3,000 arrived that way each year. Thus between 1830 and 1840 the population of the whole of Australia increased from 70,000 to 190,000, with 130,000 of those in 1840 being in NSW. Of these 87000 were men and 43000 were women; 30,000 had been born in the colony; 50,000 were free settlers, 20,000 were emancipists and 30,000 were convicts.[69]

---

[67] HRA Bourke to Colonial Secretary *Governor's despatches* 1835

[68] The British Treasury had agreed to put 50% of land sale proceeds into assisting immigrants with shipping costs; a further 15% into assisting Aborigines' and the balance was for discretionary use by the crown. These percentages changed in 1840 when all sale proceeds were spent on immigration but the land fund still ran out of funds in 1842 and no further assistance was made to immigrants other than by the colonial government borrowing funds in the London market through its own credit.

[69] Shaw *ibid*

2. Foreign Private Investment

We need to make the distinction between foreign public investment, and foreign private investment. The British Treasury appropriated specific funds for infrastructure programs in the colony, such as public buildings, churches, gaols, roads etc.

One reason that local colonial taxes and duties were imposed on the colony was to give the governor the funding source for discretionary expenditures in order to improve his administration. There were many instances of expenditures which could not be covered by the British funds, such as a bounty to recapture runaway convicts, building fences around the cemeteries and whitewashing the walls of public buildings (for instance barracks) in the settlement. The British Treasury would have considered such items of expense as being unnecessary. Road repair and maintenance was intended to be covered from toll receipts but they were never sufficient to make necessary repairs. Governors Hunter and Bligh did little to improve public and community buildings, roads and bridges and by the time Macquarie arrived in the colony in 1810, there was a major backlog of building work and maintenance to be undertaken. Macquarie expanded the local revenue tax base in order to give himself more flexibility in pursuing improved conditions for the settlers and the population at large.

Although Macquarie did not specifically seek new free immigrants for the colony, word of mouth circulated that the colony was in a growth stage and worthy of being considered for either immigration or investment. Usually one accompanied the other. The first private investment came with the immigrants. Free settlers would either cash up in England or transfer their possessions to the colony, and this small level of private investment was the start of a major item of capital transfers to the colony.

However, private capital formation took many forms; the early settlers, bought or built houses, they built or bought furnishings; they had carriages and often employed water conservation.

As the system of land grants was expanded and farming was encouraged the spread of settlement required a combination of public and private investment.

The government had to provide roads and townships, and the settlers had to provide pastoral investment. This pastoral capital formation consisted of five main types of assets:

Buildings – residence, outbuildings, wool shed or grain storage
Fences – stockyards, posts and rails
Water conservation – dams, tanks, wells
Plant – cultivators, tools
Stocks – food, clothing, household items, materials for animal care and general repairs—livestock

Stephen Roberts offers an interesting insight into the colony of 1835.[70]

"It did not need much prescience to foresee the whole of the country united by settlement – so much had it outgrown the coastal stage of Sydney town. It was a new Australia – a land of free settlement and progressive occupation – that was there, and the old convict days were ending.

Both human and monetary capital were pouring into the various colonies and transforming the nature of their population and problems. Convicts no longer set the tone; even autocratic governors belonged to a day that was passing, and instead, the country was in the grip of a strangely buoyant, and equally optimistic, race of free men".

As part of our private capital formation, we must remember the growth of human capital and the needs for specific labour. Capital requires labour with a specific role. The establishment and expansion of farming meant more than shepherding and ploughing. There was a considerable demand for building skills, for construction and maintenance of equipment such as drays and carts, harness making and repair, tool-making etc. It became important, in order to support and sustain capital growth and economic development to be able to employ labour with multi-skills. This was a new

---

[70]   Roberts, S.H *The Squatting Age in Australia 1835-1847 (published 1935)*

phenomenon for the colony, especially since Britain did not develop these types of broad skills and self-motivation in its criminal class. The Rev. J.D. Lang sought a temporary answer by specifically recruiting 'mechanics' in Scotland as immigrant for the colony.

3. British Public Funding transfers

Public Capital formation is obviously different to private capital formation. I have given an example of rural-based private capital formation elsewhere in this study and will do so again here, in order to demonstrate both types of capital investment.

Private capital formation took many forms; the early settlers, bought or built houses, they built or bought furnishings; they had carriages and often employed water conservation techniques, which included tanks or earthen dams.

As the system of land grants was expanded and farming was encouraged the spread of settlement required a combination of public and private investment.

The government had to provide roads and townships, and the settlers had to provide pastoral investment. This pastoral (rural-based) capital formation usually consisted of five main types of assets:

Buildings – residence, outbuildings, wool shed or grain storage
Fences – stockyards, posts and rails
Water conservation – dams, tanks, wells
Plant – cultivators, tools
Stocks – food, clothing, household items, materials for animal care
and general repairs—livestock

Public capital on the other hand was a socio-economic based government asset, and included:

Roads, bridges, crossings, drainage, excavation and embanking, retaining walls

Hospital, storehouses, military barracks, convict barracks, Court-house,
police posts, government office buildings
Market house, burial ground, Church, tollhouse, military magazines.
Obviously the list can go on and on.

Major Public Works in NSW 1817-1821

Roads
Sydney to Botany Bay
Sydney to South Head
Parramatta to Richmond
Liverpool to Bringelly, the Nepean and Appin
Buildings
Sydney
A military hospital; military barracks; convict barracks; carters barracks; Hyde Park
Toll-house; residences for the Supreme Court Judge, the Chaplain and the
Superintendent of Police; an asylum; a fort and powder magazines; stables for
Government House; a market house; a market wharf; a burial ground; St. James
Church
Parramatta
All Saint's church spire; a hospital; a parsonage; military and convict barracks; a
Factory; stables and coach-house at Government House; a reservoir
Windsor
St. Matthew's Church; military barracks; convict barracks
Liverpool
St. Luke's church; a gaol; a wharf; convict barracks

4. Economic Development

K. Dallas in an article on *Transportation and Colonial Income* writes,
"The history of economic development in Australia is concerned with
the transplanting of British economic life into a unique and novel
environment. All colonial societies resemble each other in the problems of

transplanting, but only in Australia was there no indigenous communal life vigorous enough to influence the course of future development"[71]

Dallas in the same article declares, "The economic effects of the transportation system are usually misunderstood. The real development of Australia begins with the pastoral industry and the export of wool in the 1820s. Until then, penal settlements were a base fore whalers, and made the pastoral possibilities known to English capitalist sheep farmers earlier than they would otherwise have known."[72]

Since this is such a major point on which much disagreement exists, an analysis of its merits is required. No less authority than N.G. Butlin, J.Ginswick and Pamela Statham disagree and they record in their introduction to 'The economy before 1850 "the history books are preoccupied with the pastoral expansion in NSW. It is reasonably certain from the musters that a great many complex activities developed and Sydney soon became not merely a port town but a community providing many craft products and services to the expanding settlement".[73]

The next section of this study outlines the remarkable contribution of Governor Macquarie between 1810 and 1821, most of the physical development taking place before the arrival of Commissioner J.T. Bigge in 1819. The table of infrastructure and public building development below confirms that the greatest period of economic development in the colonial economy took place under the Macquarie Administration and did not wait until the spread of settlement and the rise in the pastoral industry (which brought with it so many economic problems) in the late 1820s and 1830s.

IMPACT OF THE COLONIAL ISOLATION DURING THE 1800S

The question of isolation was of positive benefit to the British authorities because the concept of creating a *'dumping ground for human garbage'* was

---

[71]   Dallas, Keith *Transportation & Colonial Income* Historical Studies ANZ Vol 3 October 1944-February 1949

[72]   Dallas *ibid*

[73]   The Australians: Statistics Chapter 7 'The economy before 1850'

synonymous with finding a *'penal wasteland that was out of sight and out of mind'*.

However the disadvantages to the Colonial authorities were numerous

There was the tyranny of distance—the huge risks, of frightening transportation by sailing ship to a land hitherto unknown, uncharted and unexplored, promising huge risks and great loss of life.

Food preservation during the voyage and in the Colony was a challenge with no refrigeration or ice. The only preservatives being salt and pickling.

Communications between Sydney and London made exchange of correspondence, obtaining decisions and permission tiresomely long. It often occurred that the Colonial Governor wrote to a Colonial Secretary, who during the twelve months of round trip, had been replaced with another person.

Laws and justice, in the Colony, were to be based on British law, but in reality, local laws became a mix of common sense and personal philosophies eg Lt Governor Collins, as Advocate-General in the Colony desperately needed law books to practice, but they were never sent. Bligh, as Governor, ruled virtually as a despot and tyrannical dictator, knowing that a sea trip of seven months was between him and any admonishment or complaints being heard.

Factors Affecting British Investment in the Colony

A number of factors affected the level of capital investment into the colony – many were ill informed and relied on delayed newspaper reports on activity in the various settlements.

a. The offer of assisted migration
b. The failing economic conditions in Britain
c. Economic expansion for the pastoral industry due to successful exploration in the colony

d. The settlement at Port Phillip and the eventual separation of Victoria from New South Wales would promote great investment opportunities

e. The rise of the squattocracy

f. The crash of 1827-28 in the colony shakes British Investors

g. The Bigge's' Report of 1823 breathed new life into capital formation especially with Macarthur sponsoring the float of the Australian Agricultural Company

h. Further along, the good credit rating of the colonies (and there being no defaults on loans) encouraged larger investments and loans into the colonies

i. Shortage of Labour in the colony and the offer of land grants to new settlers became a useful carrot to attract small settlers bringing their own capital by way of cash or goods or livestock with them.

j. Two other steps had important consequences, one in the colony and the other in Britain. In 1827 Governor Darling began to issue grazing licenses to pastoralists, and the terms were set at 2/6d per hundred acres, with liability to quit on one month's notice. From this movement grew, writes Madgwick in Immigration into Eastern Australia, the squatting movement and the great pastoral expansion, and the idea of the earlier Governors that the colony of New South Wales should be a colony of farmers was thus abandoned. The concurrent event was the floating of the Australian Agricultural Company in London. Development by the AAC and by the free settlers brought increasing prosperity. Exports tripled between 1826 and 1831.

k. There is a connection between availability of factors of production and the level of investment. In the early days of the colony, labour was present—bad labour, convict labour, but still labour. The governors had demanded settlers with capital to employ that labour and develop the land. They proposed to limit land grants in proportion to the means of the settler. Governor Darling declared (HRA ser 1, vol 8) that 'when I am satisfied of the character, respectability and means of the applicant settler in a rural area, he will receive the necessary authority to select a grant of land, proportionate in extent to the means he possesses.

Under Macquarie the colony had boomed with new buildings, new settlements, new investment and lots of convicts. Under Brisbane the needs for economic consolidation and new infrastructure would be addressed, together with an appeal for free settlers.

Some significant events took place during the Brisbane guardianship

The British were intent on accessing every available trading opportunity with the colony, and formed in Scotland *The Australia Company*

A road was built to connect the Windsor settlement to the new settlement at Maitland. This decision opened up the Hunter River district to new farming opportunities

The responsibility for convicts was transferred from the Superintendent of Convicts to the Colonial Secretary, although this move was to be reversed within the next decade

The first documented discovery of gold was made. It was hushed in the colony lest convicts run off to find their fortunes

In Bigge's third and final report, he recommended extra colonial import duties and less British duty on imported timber and tanning bark

The most significant event of all was the confidence placed in Bigge's favourable opinion of the potential of the colonial economy by the London Investment community and the resulting subscription of one million pound for the Australian Agricultural Company. The subscription was accompanied by a grant of one million acres of land around Port Stephens and the allocation of 5,000 convicts, but also brought inflation to livestock prices and availability throughout the colony.

J.F. Campbell wrote about the first decade of the Australian Agricultural Company 1824-1834 in the proceedings of the 1923 RAHS.

"Soon after Commissioner Bigge's report of 1823 became available for public information, several enterprising men concerted with a view to acquire sheep-runs in the interior of this colony, for the production of fine wool.

The success which attended the efforts of John Macarthur and a few other New South Wales pastoralists, in the breeding and rearing of fine wool sheep and stock generally, as verified by Bigge, gave the incentive and led to the inauguration of proceedings which resulted in the formation of the Australian Agricultural Company.

The first formal meeting of the promoters took place at Lincoln's Inn, London, (at the offices of John Macarthur, junior).

Earl Bathurst, advised Governor Brisbane in 1824 that . . . .

His Majesty has been pleased to approve the formation of the Company, from the impression that it affords every reasonable prospect of securing to that part of His Majesty's dominions the essential advantage of the immediate introduction of large capital, and of agricultural skill, as well as the ultimate benefit of the increase of fine wool as a valuable commodity for export.

The chief proposals of the company are:

> The company was to be incorporated by Act of Parliament or Letters Patent.
> The capital of the company was to be 1 million pound sterling divided into 10,000 shares of 100 pound each
> A grant of land of one million acres to be made to the company
> That no rival joint stock company to be established in the colony for the next twenty years
> That agents of the company would select the situation or the land grants.
> The shepherds and labourers would consist of 1,400 convicts, thereby lessening the maintenance of such convicts by an estimated 30,800 pound or 22 pound/per head/ per annum.

The Royal Charter of 1824 forming the company provided for payment of quit-rents over a period of twenty years, or the redemption of the same by paying the capital sum of 20 times the amount of the rent so to be redeemed. These quit-rents were to be waived if the full number of convicts were maintained for a period of five years. No land was to be sold during the five-year period from the date of the grant".

Being important that the investment be seen to have the support of strong leaders in Britain, and democratic governance, the company operated with· One Governor; · 25 directors; and 365 stockholders (proprietors). The old English structure was retained, that of, Governor and his Court, with the directors being the members of the Court whilst the Governor was the Chairman of the Board or Court

Leading stockholders included

- · Robert Campbell
- · Chief Justice Forbes
- · Son of Governor King
- · Rev'd Samuel Marsden
- · John MacArthur
- · Each Macarthur son, John Jr, Hannibal, James, Charles, Scott & William John Oxley. The Colonial-Surveyor (Oxley) had recommended the area of Port Stephens as an eligible spot for the land grant. The local directors inspected and approved the site but John Macarthur was extremely critical of the selection, the management plan and the extravagance of the first buildings.

This venture was the first major investment into the colony and set the scene for later developments. In 1825 the Van Diemen's Land Company was chartered by the British Parliament and granted land on the northwest corner of the territory.

Both the A.A. Coy and the VDL Coy still operate today after nearly 180 years of continuous operation, a record beaten only by the operation of the Hudson Bay Company in Canada.

Sir Timothy Coghlan was the colonial statistician whilst he was involved in preparing the series 'The Wealth and Progress of New South Wales

1900-01'. He was later appointed as Agent-General in London before compiling the 4-volume set of 'Labour and Industry in Australia'.

Circumstances in Britain contributed greatly to the climate of 'greener pastures' over the seas.

Conditions were never more favourable for emigration than they were during the 1830s. The decade had opened with rioting in the agricultural districts in the south of England. This was followed by the upheavals of the Reform Bill of 1832, the Factory Act of 1833 and the Corn Laws, which kept wages low and unemployment high. The Poor Law of 1834 withdrew assistance from the poor and re-introduced the workhouse. The Irish rebellion was creating both upheaval and poverty

These conditions were met by the enthusiastic reports coming from Australia of the progress being made in agriculture, commerce and the pastoral industry. The assistance granted to emigrants as a result of Edward Gibbon Wakefield's reforms made possible the emigration of people who had previously been prevented by the expense. It is almost certain that free passage would not have been a sufficient enticement if conditions in Britain had not been unfavourable. It is significant that years of small migration coincided with good conditions in England accompanied by unfavourable reports from the colony.

4. Creating Opportunities in the Colony

Availability of land and labour to yield profit on invested capital is the constant decisive condition and test of material prosperity in any community, and becomes the keystone of an economy as well as defining its national identity.

British Government policy for the Australian colonies was formulated and modified from time to time. Policies for the export of British capital and the supply of labour (both convict and free) were adjusted according to British industrial and demographic and other social situations, as well as the capability and capacity of the various colonial settlements top contribute to solving British problems.

By the 1820s there was official encouragement of British Investment in Australia by adopting policies for large land grants to persons of capital and for the sale of land and assignment of convict labour to those investors. Then followed the reversal of the policy of setting up ex-convicts on small 30 acre plots as small proprietors. The hardship demanded by this policy usually meant these convicts and families remained on the commissary list for support (food and clothing) at a continuing cost to the government. It was much cheaper to assign these convicts to men of property and capital who would support them fully – clothe, house and feed them.

We can ask, what led directly to the crash of 1827?

a. Firstly, the float of the Australian Agricultural Company raised a large amount of capital, mostly from the City of London investment community, and this contributed to speculation and 'sheep and cattle mania instantly seized on all ranks and classes of the inhabitants' (written by Rev'd John Dunmore Lang) 'and brought many families to poverty and ruin'.

b. When capital imports cease, the wherewithal to speculate vanished; speculation perforce stopped; inflated prices fell to a more normal level, and wrote E.O. Shann in Economic History of Australia 'because those formerly too optimistic were now too despairing, and people had to sell goods at any price in order to get money; men who had bought at high prices were ruined, and perforce their creditors fell with them'.

c. In 1842, it was the same. The influx of capital from oversees, pastoral extension, and large-scale immigration, caused much speculation. The banks, competing for business, advanced too much credit. Loans were made on the security of land and livestock, which later became almost worthless; too much discounting was done for merchants. (Gipps, HRA Vol 23) In the huge central district on the western slopes, along the Murrumbidgee and the Riverina, the squatters triumphed, as was inevitable. He had the financial resources to buy his run – especially after the long period of drought. Four million acres of crown land was sold for nearly 2.5 million pound. The confidence of British investors was waning. A crisis in the Argentine and the near failure of the large clearinghouse of Baring's made them cautious. Stories of rural and industrial strife in the colony were not inducements to invest: and wood and metal prices were still falling Loan applications being raised in London were under-subscribed, at the same time, the banks were increasingly reluctant to lend money for land development, which was so often unsound.

5. Assisted Migration

The dual policy of selling land to people with sufficient capital to cultivate it, and keeping a careful check on the number of free grants was adopted after 1825. 'Yet the Colonial Office', says Madgwick, 'failed to administer land policy with any certainty (R.B. Madgwick 'Immigration into Eastern Australia'). There was no uniform policy adopted to encourage economic development in a systematic and rational way. The Wakefield system found new supporters. The principle had been established that the sale of land was preferred to the old system of grants. The dual system of sales and grants had failed to encourage local (colonial) purchases. They were willing to accept grants or even 'squat' rather than purchase land. Sales to absentee landlords and investors stepped up, and as can be seen from the following table, provided extensive revenue to the British Government to promote free and sponsored migration.

6. Successful exploration promotes new interest in the Colony

A period of rapid expansion followed the change in economic policy. Wool exports by 1831 were 15 times as great as they had been only 10 years earlier (in 1821). The increase in the number of sheep led to a rapid opening of new territories for grazing. It was the search for new land with economic value that underpinned most of the explorations. Settlers and sheep-men quickly followed exploration, and growth fanned out in all directions from Sydney town.

However, exploration was not the only catalyst for growth. a. The growing determination to exclude other powers from the continent stimulated official interest in long-distance exploration by sea and by land and in the opening of new settlements. For instance, J.M. Ward in his work ' The Triumph of the Pastoral Economy 1821-1851' writes that Melville and Bathurst Islands, were annexed and settled between 1824 and 1827, whilst Westernport and Albany were settled in order to clinch British claims to the whole of Australia b. When Governor Brisbane opened the settlement at Moreton Bay in 1824, it was to establish a place for punishment of unruly convicts and a step towards further economic development, and of extending the settlements for the sake of attracting new investment

7. Colonial Failures fuel loss of Confidence

The collapse of British Investment can be traced to one or two causes, or indeed both.

I. The British crisis of 1839 reflected the availability of capital for expansion by the Australian banks of that day – The Bank of Australasia and the Union Bank. These banks, three mortgage companies and the Royal Bank went into a slump due to shortage of available funds and deferred the raising of new funds until after the crisis. Stringency in the English Capital market had a serious impact on the capital raising opportunities in the colonies.

II. The second possibility is that the sharp decline was initiated by bad news of returns in the colonies, and that its role accentuated a slump with the dire consequences experienced in 1842-43. Recovery was delayed and made more difficult as there was 'no surplus labour in the colony'

It would be dangerous to imply or decide that every slump in Australia could be explained as being caused by economic events. British investment was independent then, as it is now, and so the more valid explanation of the downturn in British investment in this period is that negative reports from the colonies disappointed and discouraged investors with capital to place.

Most facts about public finance in New South Wales lead to the conclusion that it was disappointed expectations that caused the turn down in the transfer of funds. At this same time Governor Gipps (Sir George Gipps) was being pushed by bankers and merchants to withdraw government deposits from the banks and thus this action caused a contraction in lending by the banks which in turn caused a slow down of colonial economic activity. The attached statistics of land sales, registered mortgages and liens on wool and livestock reflects the strong downturn in the agricultural economy, which naturally flowed on to the economy as a whole.

CHAPTER 12

GOVERNMENT BUSINESS ENTERPRISES AND THEIR IMPACT ON THE COLONIAL ECONOMY 1788-1830

The purpose of this study

The purpose of the thesis project is to analysis, interpret, define and detail the operations of the government—or state-owned enterprises between 1802 and 1835

Such an evaluation has not previously been undertaken on this topic, although its importance is generally recognised by economic historians. The impact of the operations of state-owned enterprises were numerous, Firstly they supported the transportation program by having skill-making, ready work upon the convicts entering the colony; secondly they put convicts in the colony to productive if unpaid work, which made them at least theoretically 'earn their keep'; and it created economic development to a level previously unanticipated. The supporting arguments for these Government Business Enterprises (GBEs) will centre on detailing how the enterprises operated; the range of products manufactured; the sourcing of the raw materials for production; the number of convicts utilised, their training, supervision and productivity. Thus the detailed explanation of the GBEs will develop the argument, whilst annualised values of production will assist any reflection on the amount the GBEs added to the GDP for the period.

There is no special understanding required. The explanation of the operations will suffice to instil the reader with the amazing value of the GBEs to the economic development of the economy, the benefits to the convicts within the assignment and transportation program and the value added (not previously assessed) to the GDP. The context of the argument and its development will be that of colonial Australia economic history, and the provision of government services as an alternative to private sector initiative, whilst overall the story of the GBEs can be woven into the story of a transition from penal to free market economy; the development of a secular form of Australian capitalism and the creation of a peculiar breed of Australian entrepreneurs. What dates will be covered? The overall aspects mentioned above really relate to the dates between 1788 and 1856; i.e. from first settlement to self-government! However, for practical purposes the GBEs were in business for the shorter period of between 1802 and 1835, and these narrower dates serve the nature and understanding of the story quite well.

The overall purpose of this thesis is to argue the merits of the results of a detailed study of the (GBEs) – their origins, development, operations and benefits-,whilst also being a treatise on the philosophy and outcome of the state owned operations in the Colony of NSW between 1788 and 1835.

There are two levels of understanding for this study:

A. The first is to establish a hypothesis on the importance and relevance of the GBEs exists which needs verification or disproving
B. The second is to examine each of the theories of operating convict labour in state owned enterprises and their contribution to GDP

There are many aspects to this story

1. The hunt for staples as an export product
2. The creation of entrepreneurial influences
3. Establishing a manufacturing sector

4. The Transportation program as a service for convict labour utilisation
5. Assessing the skills and experience of the convicts and their relevance to the labour market
6. Should landowners and employers pay for the use of convict labour?
7. Should the government bear any of the direct or indirect expense of maintaining the convicts?
8. Should the government financial support from Britain or the colonists have included an accounting of outputs from convict work?
9. Measuring the economic benefits of the state-owned enterprises which employed government labour and how did government enterprise output add to the recognised GDP
10. How to assert and test this hypothesis

Each paragraph above will be supported in outline terms, such as to enable a fleshing out of purpose and intent more fully in any advanced study.

The initial challenge was to authenticate the relevance, importance and benefits of the GBEs.

An introduction to the GBEs

The original goal of this study was to establish the credentials of the government business enterprises as essential economic drivers. This was to involve a description of their operations, their output and manpower. This done, it was intended to outline the role of these public enterprises as part of the transportation program, convict management initiatives and an essential instrument of utilising convict labour(chapter 1).

The enterprises performed numerous roles – from food production to supplement the production under the 30-acre farmlets system of Phillip, Hunter and King, to a manufacturing unit, to provide items on a timely basis. This was followed by the use of the main enterprises as import replacement mechanisms. On the other hand, there was always the role of certain public enterprises to provide building items that could not be imported. And because they were readily available locally, they became an essential service of the enterprises e.g. bricks, tiles, timber framing etc. Upon the transfer of certain production from the public to the private sector, the catalyst was created for creating the role of entrepreneur for the growing secondary industry (chapter 2)

Thus public enterprises became an important mainstay of the colonial and filled the role as an economic driver by employing over 4,000 convicts in a variety of productive jobs. These ranged from clerical work for the government to road making gangs. However the biggest concentration of workers were in the lumber yard and the associated enterprises of public farming and the timber yard (chapter 3)

Obviously understanding the mechanism and vagaries of the colonial economy, at least before 1830 is a relevant task. The economic policies and highlights of the Phillip, Hunter and King administrations are provided, before turning to details of convict management in the colony (chapter 3).

The commissariat operations were a constant theme through this study and its role in underpinning, supporting and encouraging the growth of a manufacturing industry in the colony was pursued in chapter 6. The detailed examination of the government farms became necessary when research in the NSW State Records failed to provided information relating to the size, location, or output of the various farms. From the traditional understanding of their being 5 or 6 locations producing grain vegetables and livestock management, the current list sets at 23 the number of active sites, which includes a shell collection depot for the making of lime and mortar (chapter 4).

How the commissariat accounted for all this production and labour is the subject of chapter 7? The bottom line is moot because the British Treasury gave no value to convict labour or convict production, even though the revenue from the resale of their labour or output was recorded in the correct way,

A novel approach is taken in attempting to measure the economic impact of the enterprises on the colonial economy. In previous computations to establish a GDP for the period, no assessment was made [e.g. by N.G.Butlin *Forming a Colonial Economy*] of the output of the enterprises, thus perpetuating the falsity of giving no value to the convict output. By including the convict output into the manufacturing sector, another long-term myth has been exploded – the manufacturing sector between 1810 and 1820 far outperformed the primary industry or agricultural sector. This revelation contradicts the traditional views of all economic historians and certainly the thinking of traditional, mainstream historians, who all decided that the agricultural economy drove the way forward.

Thus this study finishes on a positive note. The economic impact of the government business enterprises can be measured and they demonstrate a new understanding of the colonial economy.

This was the story of government business enterprises (GBEs) and the colonial economy. Of what made the GBEs so important to the growth and development of the colonial economy and such an important aspect of Australian history, and why this importance not been recognised sufficiently before this time?

The main identification of value and importance comes via the estimates of sector GDP in this period. Butlin notates[74] that there were only two aspects of GDP before 1835,—the agricultural sector and the secondary industry sector. These two sections, Butlin concludes, generated 100% of GDP. However, if the sub-components of GDP are studied, then private enterprise (in Butlin's opinion), even in its limited format, prior to 1835, outperforms public enterprise. And yet, we know that the GBEs employed by 1819 over 5,000 workers in public farming, construction material manufacture, gang work (roads, construction, land clearing, and public services) and other light component manufacturing. These belong then to the agricultural or secondary industry sectors of GDP, or better still they belong to a ***public enterprise*** sector of Butlin's GDP, where they outperform the private enterprise sector by a factor of 3. Thus their importance lies firstly in their contribution to GDP; then in the concept of employing transportees within the government services (a policy which was not planned or even considered in London). Instructions to successive governors contemplated the assignment of convicts to private service, in particular the military officers inclined to farming. With the small

---

[74] Butlin *Forming a Colonial Economy*

numbers of military officers so inclined, the idea of land grants spread to expirees, emancipists and even enterprising convicts [e.g. James Ruse] A third contribution to the importance of GBEs lay in the concept of government enterprise—not a usual practice within traditional British political thinking, especially within the settlement planning process. Then the introduction of the Macquarie taint of adding transfer arrangements to the government enterprises back to the private sector, along with trained workers, market position and even equipment, was like adding fuel to a fire. However, Macquarie was merely ahead (like in so many aspects of his policy development) of his time, and the overall policy of encouraging a private secondary sector was eminently beneficial and valuable. So for these three reasons, and probably for a number of others, the GBEs were important, beneficial, relevant and of significant contribution to the colonial economy before 1835.

A.G.L. Shaw offers a set of circumstances and events which support the role and importance of the GBEs. These opinions are taken from Shaw [752]pages 16-29

1 Shaw states that by 1792 over 7,000 acres were granted to 177 farmers. About 120 were time-expired convicts and the balance was military officers. He further opines that it was one thing to establish small farmers, but another to keep them. Many of the expirees only wished to raise money to return to England. (16)

2 The poor quality of the free settlers and their lack of farming knowledge and equipment made the governor's task of increasing the food supply a hard one (18)

3 Hunter (1795-1800) tried to revive public farming, but without success—too few convicts available, too little knowledge amongst officials, a growing private farming sector competing for the commissariat purchasing regime. By 1800 there were 8,000 acres under cultivation within the settlement, compared with only 3,000 in 1795 – the increase was mainly due to military officers cultivating their farms along with assigned convict workers. (18)

[75] Shaw, A. G. L. *The Economic Development of Australia* (Longmans, Victoria 1944)

4   Governor King faced a similarly serious condition upon reaching Sydney in September 1800. He also set out to revive public farming, whilst sensing a potential weakness in the private farming sector He increased the acreage of public farming to over 1,000 and the total number of acres of wheat in 1802 yielded 68,000 bushels for the government store, which was sufficient in that year for colonial needs. At that time, 32 officers owned 10,000 acres and from these the majority of wheat was yielded. In addition 5450 peasant farmers owned an average of 40 acres each. Macarthur and Forbes at this same time owned a further 5,000 acres of land grants. (19)

5   By 1820 324,000 acres had been granted – three-quarters by Macquarie. Of this 55000 acres were held by 'time-expirees' and 29000 acres by those who had been pardoned; and over 240000 acres was held by free settlers. Meanwhile Macquarie was fostering the development of the colony as best he could. **If the government did much itself, it was because as yet there was no-one else to do it. The time for free enterprise had not yet come; the conditions which make freedom possible had still to be created**

6   Not only town buildings, but roads and bridges were constructed by this energetic governor. Exploration was funded and supported and new lands had to be opened up. Permanent roads could not be constructed at the entire expense of the inhabitants and they imagined that they had a right to expect that at least part of the colonial revenue should be laid out and appropriated to the construction of permanent roads and bridges, streets and wharves. The British government still considered the settlement as a 'receptacle for offenders which indirectly meant keeping down expenditures whilst Britain balanced its post-war budgets and the Government took the position for the colony that 'So long as they continue destined for the purpose of being a receptacle, their growth as a colony must be a secondary consideration and the leading duty of those to whom their administration is entrusted will be to keep up in them such a system of just discipline as may

render transportation an object of serious apprehension [Bathurst to Bigge][76]

7   This was what Macquarie was ***not*** doing. His efforts were mainly directed to developing the colony, and making it more attractive to free men. At the moment these were mainly emancipists; as the time for free immigration was still in the future. The British government was objecting to this Macquarie policy and the associated expense. Bigge was despatched to investigate the conditions of the colony. Before Bigge's arrival two other achievements had helped to make the colony more suitable for the normal development of a free economy. NSW moved from barter to a currency economy with the Bank of NSW being established in 1817. Macquarie also encouraged the pastoral industry by building roads, stabilising currency, granting lands, promoting exploration and having licences approved for free export of wool to England.

8   However, there was a chasm between the Macquarie thinking and the Macarthur thinking. Macquarie wanted the settlers to have freedom to make money, and by so doing would help the colony. In the Macarthur thinking, transportees would be assigned to the free settlers whilst emancipists would be considered as landless labourers for a sheep aristocracy yet to be established. Macquarie, on the other hand felt that *guiding* the economy and using the power and persuasion of government and indeed, *patronage,* would benefit the economic growth that immigration and development depended upon.

Another sequence would be that rather than await free enterprise, mainly because the penal settlement was considered a long term receptacle for transportees; government enterprise was an alternative for self-preservation, such as public farming, putting convicts to gainful employment, and engaging in light manufacturing in order to support the gang system. A modified policy was required when into the early 1830s the colony became a *pastoral economy* and the secondary sector added farming equipment to its activities. Before Macquarie left the colony, a public light manufacturing sector had developed for import replacement purposes,

---

[76]   [Bathurst to Bigge HRA 1:10:4-5]

for usage of convict labour and development of useful skills, and as an essential support mechanism for the public works and building program underway in the colony.

In summary, therefore, the GBEs provided productive work for up to 5,000 transportees. The public farming component of the GBEs contributed an important and valuable food source at least for the transportees. The concept of public service and government service developed with convict clerical assistants, and the growth of service industries, such as grass cutting, harbour water taxis and a hauling system for goods to reach remote areas. If analysis were made for the period 1800-1830, the result would be that the annual contribution of the public enterprise sector would be a £ million annually growing in 1820 to over £2 million, before falling away as deployment of resources for public works was cut.

Concluding the argument

Many economic historians have written about the work practices of convicts[77], and many others have described their impressions of the development of the colonial economy[78]; others concentrate on entrepreneurs in the early colony[79]. What do these economic historians have in common? Their studies omit to explore the role, function and operations of the Government Business Enterprises, which structure put a large number of convicts into gainful employment at a time when the private sector could not have practically absorbed the higher volume of incoming convicts. The resulting contribution to GDP has not been measured, can be measured and is measured in this study. The relevant and important point to be made here is that recently revised thinking suggests that the colony was selected by Britain not only as a dumping ground for prisoners, but as a strategic port for pursuing trading interests with India and China and as a source of commercial natural resources for British industry[80] These circumstances then raise the further question as to why, with the trade and commerce potential, there was not more encouragement and a more formal approach to establishing early primary and secondary

---

[77] Nicholas, S *Convict Workers*

[78] Abbott & Nairn *Economic Growth of Australia 1788-1821*

[79] Hainsworth, D.R *The Sydney Traders*

[80] Blainey and Frost [AEHR]

industries in the private sector of the settlement. Wool was an accidental resource discovery, whilst boat-building and the pursuit of sealing and whaling was a deliberate pursuit of a staple export commodity for trade purposes. There were obvious needs for repair and maintenance services in the settlement. From little services bigger industries grew, but in the case of NSW the industries grew under the sponsorship of the government as part of a network of import replacement manufacturing. The concept of government farms and government manufacturing enterprises was anathema to the government in London, where free enterprise prevailed, but, in the colony, a new factor made this scheme not only essential but the only way to proceed. A steady stream of prisoners arrived in the colony and needed to be put to gainful employment gainful in the sense that a 6 day a week job would keep them off the streets and away from the temptation to re-offend. In the early days, some could be placed under the supervision of military officers who had received grants of land, but the better result was to use them in the Lumber Yard for repairs and maintenance, road gangs, land clearing gangs and other outside work such as whitewashing fences, grass cutting and building bridges and culverts.

In a rare understatement, N. G. Butlin writes about the GBEs in the following way[81]

> *'In the first settlement years, unfree labour, working under direction, was under pressure to provide a range of immediately needed goods and services. These included the catching, collection and ultimately the production of foods, the assembly of local materials for buildings and other structures, the clearing of land and the distribution of goods supplied by Britain. To support these activities, official ration allowances of food and clothing were organised through the commissariat as recipient of British supplies and local output.*

A concise understanding of the 'convict workhouse' is offered by Commissioner J. T. Bigge in his third report[82] [p 20-21]

---

81   Butlin, N. G. *Forming A Colonial Economy* p. 71 CUP 1994
82   Bigge, J. T. Third report on the Colony of NSW

The principal place of convict labour in Sydney is the Lumber Yard . . . The trades carried on in this place, are those of blacksmiths, nailers ,iron and brass founders, bellows makers, coopers, sawyers, painters, lead casters, harness and collar makers, tailors and shoemakers, carpenters, joiners and cabinet makers. All the different sheds in which the workmen are employed front towards the yard that they enclosed, and in the centre is deposited the wood that is brought from Pennant Hills and Newcastle. The dockyard likewise furnishes employment to a considerable number of workmen, either in construction of the quays or in the building and naval equipment of boats and vessels. The gaol gang are generally employed at this place, in unloading the cargoes of the colonial vessels and in delivering them on the quays of the dockyard and they are made to work in chains . . . The office of the principal superintendent of convicts is in the lumber yard and two convict clerks are constantly employed in keeping the books and making entries , copying returns of labour, writing orders for the signature of the superintendent, numerical and nominal lists of the gangs of workmen and labourers and in receiving the applications of individuals for convicts.

The *enterprising* colonial economy

A significant omission in packing for the First Fleet was any real equipment, other than four forges, for manufacturing small items in the new settlement. The type of items required to be made locally, if Captain Phillip had put his mind to it, were axe heads and handles, adzes, picks, shovels, hand-hoes, and mattocks. All these items had been brought out with the general supplies, food and rations, but the quantity and quality were inadequate and inappropriate.

It took 14 years or so for the foundation of the colony to become settled; with land clearing for barracks, basic housing, a church, and cart tracks, bridges a brick-making facility to be completed, and then a second settlement commenced at Parramatta; before government minds turned to a 'manufacturing' centre. The concept of government ownership of any means of production was unacceptable to the British government, but rather essential for a penal settlement. Obviously there were precedents for public ownership in the settlement prior to Macquarie's arrival in 1809 – government-owned and regulated farms had been in existence since 1788 as there were no free settlers available to carry on the work of farming, raising of grain, livestock, vegetables and even fresh fruit. The plans for settlement had not hit their stride much before 1800 and there were insufficient numbers of prisoners to create specialisation of labour and so prisoners were on rotation to any task assigned on a daily basis. Building was in great demand as was the supply of timber. Phillip had already created the basic tenets of government sponsored enterprises by establishing public farming, directing public labour for timber harvesting and the directing of construction, land clearing and road-making gangs. These gangs [for land-clearing, road making and building construction] were a central theme of the colonial economy and government enterprises until well into the 1830s. So government business enterprises were an early theme of economic growth and development. Government business enterprises (GBEs) were a necessity in the colony and played an increasingly important role in the economic development of the colony and in the daily life of the settlement.

The GBEs were a government instrument to control the farming, manufacturing and communication sectors of the public economy. If organised and operated successfully, the public operation could throw doubt on the expected expansion of the settlement into a private sector. Butlin in *Forming* terms it a bridgehead economy, but as a public sector economy it was essentially closed: Why then encourage settlers for agricultural pursuits?; Why encourage free mechanics and labourers for a private sector—why not just train the government workers for these tasks?; Why encourage entrepreneurs, traders and even speculators?; Why worry about a transition from penal to directed economy, the denial of which would remove the need for a bridgehead? Could a public sector economy with access to almost unlimited numbers of government assigned labourers and access to the almost limitless supplies of natural resources be able to sustain itself and survive without free enterprise planning and capital? Was a private sector essential to economic growth and a successful economy?

This then is the story of the evolvement of fully-fledged government enterprises and their operation. They were the back-bone of the colonial economy between 1802 and 1830. They were the planning arm of the commissariat operation of the settlement which had begun in 1776 with the assembly by Captain Phillip in England of the supplies and provisions of the First Fleet in readiness for the initial settlement. Being a relatively low level officer in the Royal Navy, Phillip's association with the settling of the new colony set the scene for a relatively low-key planning and operational exercise. It was outside the competency, training experience and general expertise of Phillip to undertake such an assignment (although in retrospect, he was a superb selection as an administrator), and so oversight by the Naval Board in the procurement process further undermined the quality of the provisioning side of the expedition. The Naval Board was being challenged to keep the costs of the expedition to a minimum and to Phillip's later regret the quality of the tools and supplies were of a lesser quality {and in many instances, also of quantity) than the exercise deserved.

This level of second-rate provisioning long pervaded commissariat operations in the settlement. Plates and mugs, as well as tools, were inadequate, sub-standard and not of sufficient quantity for the 1000 + personnel in the settlement. The tools supplied to convict workers for land clearing were unsuitable and inadequate in the field and most failed in service. In the same vein, food supplies had been underestimated and there was great pressure on Phillip to replenish the victuals in stock with fresh supplies produced locally. By 1800 much of the initially planning for land utilisation had been completed. At this time Hunter felt comfortable in thinking that some form of local revenue would be useful in supplementing British Treasury appropriations for the colony. In order to remain within the law of England and follow his own instructions, his approach was not to generate revenue as such, but rather he planned to seek reimbursement for providing government services. His plan was to rebuild, as a community activity, the original wooden gaol. Hunter's successor, P G. King, was not as reluctant in his revenue generating plans. He selected another project which the Treasury would not support with funding—the socialising of the settlement's orphans and abandoned children. For this he planned a governor's discretionary fund – one for the orphans, which he called the Orphan Fund, and a second for rebuilding the gaol, which he called the

Gaol Fund. The obvious point here is the colony had no treasury; it was considered under-funded in terms of establishing a new settlement and creating a wide-range of infrastructure and there was the beginning of a move to transfer certain treasury responsibilities to the colonial governor.

This funding shortage and transfer of fiscal requirements to the colony were to be a trademark of the colony for the first 502 years and during much of this time these two aspects of colonial administration were to be a standard of policy and practice. The two underlying main-stay aspects of policy were, firstly, the raising of local revenues and of using convicts for much of the public labour requirements. Thus building and construction of public buildings (barracks, civil service housing, government office buildings, hospitals and churches) and all public works (roads, bridges, wharves, stores, water delivery) were carried out by convicts assigned to government service.

The same policy planning that created local revenue for official purposes, and created the usage of a declining percentage of convicts for government service, also planned to find a staple export commodity to create foreign exchange. The generation of foreign exchange was needed to offset the growing importation of consumption and capital goods in an increasingly trade-oriented economy. Foreign exchange can be effectively generated in two ways—firstly, by the sale of goods and services outside the economic frontiers, and secondly by reducing the importation of goods and services by making them within the local economy. Both policies were actively pursued by successive governors from Phillip to Macquarie. The encouragement of exports was necessarily limited because of the unavailability of goods, other than basic, unprocessed natural resources and then primary agricultural goods. Coal and timber were the first such export commodities, followed closely by staples such as sealing and whaling products. Transfers between Van Diemen's Land, Norfolk Island and NSW were considered inter-governmental, but over time became quite substantial and important to each settlement.

Obviously the first need in a fledgling economy was to support its victualling requirements as much as practicable. The concept of public farming must have been anathema to the Colonial Secretary's office in London. Britain had built its international economic prowess on private enterprise and thus public farming was a novel if an unwelcome necessity. Equally, resentment would grow in London towards a government manufacturing operation. But then the London authorities did not have to manage a settlement with instant demands, and remoteness from the real world of about 18 months.

However the necessity for both forms of business enterprise sponsored by government became inevitable once the colony became established. The circumstances became that labour, in the form of a large (and growing) number of convicts, was available for work; there was a definite and often dramatic need for fresh rations for this growing population; and this enormous turn-around time was equally cumbersome to manage and accept. An immediate need developed for local skills and local repair/replacement capability if these circumstances and strictures were to be satisfied. In his initial store inventory on the First Fleet, Phillip had brought 6 forges, brick moulds, and a variety of axes, hoes, picks, adzes, and other tools, as well as various grinding wheels. They were the makings of basic industries. It was the poor quality of these tools that became a limiting factor in moving ahead with the development of the infrastructure required in the settlement. Thus the first workshop for repairing, sharpening, renewing and replacement of tools and equipment took shape quite early in the timeframe of the settlement. This move also coincided with the establishment of timber camps, the timber yard with its saw pits and kiln, brick-making and the public farms. What a multi-faceted economy Phillip was trying to operate. This repair and maintenance facility was only an adjunct to the main 'store' which provided the rations, issued the initial tools and spare parts, in addition to the receiving, storing, inventorying, issuing and collecting all the normal items required by government and kept by the commissariat. Without the skills and machinery available in Britain, only basic repairs and replacements could be carried out by the commissariat before Macquarie's arrival in 1810, at which point the whole structure and philosophy of government business enterprises, in particular government manufacturing, changed.

Even the concept of public farming changed. After 1814, the government not only participated in vegetable growing and small livestock management within the County of Cumberland, but it commenced broad-acre grain growing and large livestock herds outside the county. The colony depended very heavily on government grain supplies, both for price management and regularity of supplies, and Macquarie set the purchase price of grain from the private sector at the beginning of a planting season and in an effort to keep his convict maintenance costs low. Often he underbid for grain with the result that less than necessary supplies were available. Private growers often complained that a price of only 8/—per bushel did not cover their costs. Yields on small acreages were insufficient to make any price less than 10/—attractive. The Commissariat officials in conjunction with other senior planning officials in the Macquarie Administration gave a great deal of thought to the location of the 22 identified government farm facilities. Usually the locations were adjacent to, or in the vicinity of flowing rivers, and the multiplicity of locations balanced the almost annual management challenges of droughts, floods, insect pests and other vagaries of nature, so that all public farm crops did not fail in the one season. A well-designed practice that took hold from the early days was that of running livestock on farming areas alongside vegetables and grain. In this way the livestock waste was used as fertiliser for the cropping areas. Such farming practices were learnt from local experience for few convicts or free settlers with British farming experience came the way of either the Principal Superintendents of Works or Convicts. The next step in progressive public farming came about when crop rotation practices and basic equipment were put to use. To supplement a rather slow beginning in public farming, Phillip commenced a system of land grants to interested emancipists, military personnel and, in the case of James Ruse, of convicts who showed interest in working for themselves. Naturally the intent was to take these people 'off the store' and make them subsistence farmers on a 30, 50 or, in the case of the military, 100-acre farmlets. Phillip acknowledged that any output from these ventures would hardly cover the needs of the farmer himself, let alone offer a surplus for the government store, but he pressed ahead so that every possible person could be taken 'off the store', and save that amount of rations for another day. The system also opened the way for a limited number of convicts to be allocated to these minimalist farmers and, with such allocation, came the hope that these extra workers could be supported 'off the store'. Lack of skills and experience, small acreages, underperforming land and lack of commissariat credit for seed, made such a hope almost pointless. The policy of convict assignment to private masters with full support was not to become official policy until Macquarie's arrival in 1810. Although not as successful as first thought, public farming made a significant contribution to the settlement's economy. Government farms kept growing in every other respect—more locations were opened both within the County of Cumberland as well as the nine counties within the approved limit of locations and more convicts were utilised in working on the public farms. A number of the farms (but not all) provided barrack accommodation for onsite convicts. Without a treasury in the colony, any farm output such as grain, meat etc, had to be bartered for a sale to be consummated. In the absence of a currency, settlers were willing to accept 'store receipts' which in turn could be bartered for face value either with the government store or with most merchants. Obviously output from the government farms had priority of acceptance with the stores, although few surviving records identify transfer from a specific farm to a store location.

The needs of a rapidly expanding economy and its demanding population set the scope of operations for the government business operations. The various farms provided the settlers with fresh grains, vegetables fruit and dairy products. The demand for housing and public buildings created a continuous need for stone blocks, bricks, tiles and timber framing for floors, walls and roofing. With interior fit-out essential the need for doors, hinges, windows and even furniture was also met by a government business enterprise – the Lumber Yard. So a pattern of operations emerged. The enterprises commenced in the new settlement with brick and tile facilities—on Brickfield Hill and then on the south bank of the Parramatta River at Rosehill, followed by the timber camps, timber yard, lumber yard and the stone quarries. The rather attractive local sandstone was used for construction of the more grandiose government office buildings and the most elegant of private houses. In time, the majestic colonial buildings still standing today were built of the historic Sydney sandstone – for example The Lands Department building, the colonial secretary's office, the Sydney Hospital, the King Street church and Law Courts and Hyde Park barracks.

So the public enterprises evolved from humble, but essential beginnings, born of necessity, and grew into an integrated series of government service centres. They were mostly output oriented although spreading the enterprise productive work over the work gangs—road-making, construction land-clearing, grass-cutting and ferrying services took the enterprises squarely into the realm of both goods and services. Then followed the adjunct services, such as boat building, ship loading and provisioning, watering and repair work. A multitude of products services and outcome resulted, with surprisingly little criticism or official questioning for even the most hard headed free enterprise proponent would have recognised that there would not have been private entrepreneurs with sufficient capital to start most of these businesses on a timely basis. It took the genius of Macquarie to underpin the future secondary industries of the new colony by planning for a transition and hand-over of methodology, equipment and skilled labour between the public sector and the private sector.

The value of government enterprise output continued to increase as a growing number of convicts became available for government assignment and expanded demand for the broad range of products produced by the various enterprises—the lumber timber, brick, dock and stone yards, the naval yard, the government farms, and the various gangs used for construction, land-clearing and road-making. Towering over these subsidiary operations was a complex organisation and planning operation. Consider the planning involved here. There were over 5,000 labourers available, so the potential output was considerable. To achieve such output, raw materials had to be available on site. The labourers needed to be trained, fed, and ready to work, and proper and adequate supervisors were required, as well as roofed facilities and access to plenty of equipment. There needs to be storage facilities for finished products and an inventory system based on clerical recording of production. The most important aspect of the planning work was knowing what public works were in the pipeline, and the materials quantities will be assembled. For instance, Greenway had the designs ready for the Hyde Park barracks and we know that Governor Macquarie intended to inspect and approve the working plans himself. Once approved the production planners assembled a materials list setting down the number, dimension and finish of sandstone for the Quarry supervisor. Quantities of bricks, roofing tiles, timber framing and flooring, the wall sections, the roof-trusses were also listed and circulated to the other supervisors. Once received by the supervisors and depending on the lead-time involved work would commence. The principal enterprise supervisor would inform the sub-supervisors of the production schedule and an area would be set aside for finished output. The more demanding work of loading carts and pulling laden carts full of materials to the worksite would also be completed to a schedule so that construction workers were not delayed by any shortage or unavailability of materials. Such planning was a massive exercise under the control of the commissariat and such work was a credit to the stewardship of the senior commissariat officials.

Earlier, I speculated on the success or otherwise of a closed public sector economy. However, without the growth provided by free settlers, and therefore from a private sector, such an economy would fail. It could not generate growth, for consumption could only match the rate of growth, or else an internal tangible surplus would result and the asset would be wasted. However, if certain circumstances had been somewhat different, the colonial economy could well have surged forward both financially and structurally.

So what were the limiting circumstances?

1. There was no treasury in the colony before 1824
2. The British treasury was starting to limit its appropriation to the colony placing more responsibility on the colonial revenues for the funding of local needs, rightly the duty of the conquering power.
3. A growing number of convicts were being transported to NSW from Britain.
4. The best turn around time for orders to NSW from British suppliers was still 12-18 months
5. However, the most negative and therefore limiting factor facing the colonial administration was the British treasury placing 'nil value' on convict labour or on their output

Following the non-existent Money Trail

That convict workers and their output had no value was, in fact, a two-edged sword. On one hand, there were the great negative factors which will be discussed later On the other hand; Macquarie made excellent use of this inane policy requirement using it to successfully hide much of the real and 'opportunity' cost of his public works program from his London supervisors. The Colonial Office never seemed to understand the financial processes behind the transportation program. They seemed to assume that costs associated with convict management in the colony were fixed rather than variable. The Colonial Secretary wrote memorandum after memorandum to the governor urging that costs be cut, trimmed, deferred and even eliminated all based on faulty, mindless comparisons of expenditures on convict maintenance between previous administrations and the current one. The Colonial Office's main charge against Macquarie was that by comparison with Hunter, King and Bligh, the Macquarie administration was overspending-not on 'per head' terms, but in absolute terms. No allowance was made for the growing number of new convict arrivals or any inflationary impact on prices – just the constant need to cut, cut, and cut! The reality was that in 'per head' terms, Macquarie had brought costs down substantially, but the numbers of convicts arriving in the colony was increasing annually and the number emancipated or released was slowing. The real problem was that Macquarie's total convict numbers were growing exponentially and he was keeping a growing percentage 'on the store'. The instructions had been to assign a majority to private masters, and keep for only the essential few for construction and maintenance work, grass cutting etc. in government service However, Macquarie kept over 5,000 almost 50% of all convicts for government service and used them in his enterprise and gangs program. Of course they were all well employed and in fact earning their keep, but the system did not recognise their contribution – only their cost. To counter this frustration Macquarie devised a devilish plan, one that used the circumstances and the system rather brilliantly. The criteria confronting him were quite simple with an equally simple solution. The Colonial Secretary of the day, Lord Bathurst required that no building costing £200 or more be constructed without first submitting the plans, specifications and justification papers for approval by the colonial office. He was also aware that, contrary to any logical explanation, the value of convict labour and their output was 'nil'. Now he put these two factors together, but obviously no building could cost more than £200. In fact no building should have any cost! Macquarie sought approval from the colonial office only once, and for his troubles, he was refused. His new government house in Sydney was the project declined, but by then his administrative fortunes had waned so much that he was under recall and would never have lived in his new house in any case.

This subterfuge was the other edge of the sword. On one side there were numerous burdens imposed on the colony because of the growing maintenance cost at first borne by the British Treasury, then shared with the colonial revenue, before finally being passed on fully to the colonial revenue. As Butlin points out in, *what a way to run a colony, fiscally*[83]?: 'From Britain's viewpoint, it could not have been better—a colony as dumping ground for the unwanted from Britain; full and exclusive access to natural resources and then a wool clip, all for a little up front investment – a fraction of what it would have cost to build penitentiaries in Britain, if these prisoners were to be housed and maintained at home'.

As pointed out above, the colonial office was blinkered in its ambivalent pursuit of cost control. This lack of logic and common sense applied to the British treasury that colonial convict labour and convict output had no value, and impacted on colonial development for many years. The hypocrisy of this policy had ramifications through all layers of colonial governance: As their work had no value, the cost of convict maintenance had to be kept under strict control. The corollary to this policy was that, if convict labour or convict output had been assigned a real value, this negative, damaging bureaucratic approach to cost control could have been replaced by a very positive approach to productivity development. What better way could there be for developing the public face of the colony than by putting the government assigned convicts to constructive work?

The treasury endeavours towards cost control encouraged, in fact, demanded a majority of convicts be assigned to masters within the private sector – mainly the agricultural or farming sector. Treasury assumed that masters could fiscally justify the cost of convict maintenance – victualling, clothing and housing, and be able to conclude that the costs of this assigned labour was still a better value than employing free labourers. Of course, one of the challenges in this regard was that there were virtually no free labourers available to employ. However the Treasury rationale applied only to the private sector, for they could not see that those convicts retained in government service were in effect supporting themselves by producing outcomes of value.

---

[83] Butlin, N. G. *What a way to run an Empire, Fiscally WPEH*

So in a perfect world, Treasury would have based convict maintenance funding not on absolute amounts, or even on a per head formula, but rather on outcomes. Even on a 10p.in the £ basis, with treasury offering a reimbursement to the colonial government of 10p for every £1 of valued production, the colonial revenues would have covered the full cost of convict maintenance of government-assigned convicts and would have swept aside the ludicrous efforts by treasury to compare maintenance costs under Governor King with those under Macquarie. 10p in the £ is really a most conservative estimate and places a minimal value on production (the labour rate for convicts in 1820 being used is only 4/6 per day) with Coghlan approved adjustments for productivity difference between free labour and convict labour.

Thus the main impact of this demented policy to not value convict labour or output was a failure to meet the fairness test. What incentive was there for governors other than those with a Macquarie-style ego drive, to put government-assigned convicts to tasks or projects of great value rather than mundane beautification? Shaw claims that a simple practice like land-clearing by convict gangs was of value and valuable, more valuable than the public works programs but without the longevity of results.

A. G. L. Shaw, in his excellent study *Convicts and Colonies*[84] makes an interesting argument in support of questionable economising:

> *Gradually it began to appear that transportation would never be as cheap as some hoped. Colonial governors were as repeatedly ordered to economise as they were told to be rigorous, and the British government looked forward to expenditures falling as more settlers became ready to take prisoners of their hands, that is, to act as private gaolers for nothing. But when they did so, they were accused of being too lenient and when governors kept men in penal gangs for punishment and discipline, they were told that they were retaining too many at public expense. The convict that would cost little or nothing was the well-behaved convict. Those not well behaved could be employed on public works; but*

---

[84]   Shaw, A.G. L *Colonies and Convicts*

those benefited the colony and not the British government;
to the latter they seemed only a useless drain on the Treasury.
[p.18]

Shaw goes on to remind his reader that there was an alternative.

But if transportation was not cheap would it not be simpler
for Britain to pay for the punishment of her criminals at
home. [p.19]

Submissions to the House of Commons Committee of Inquiry on Transportation in 1812 show that the prisoners housed on the Thames hulks had a much lower earning capacity than did the convicts in the colony. Shaw's argument in favour of the British government was predicated on Britain building a series of large penitentiaries. The opportunity cost of this building program would have been many millions of pounds, and, unless convict labour and output were valued, capital expenditure would not have a return. There would be an opportunity cost based on the cost of the transportation program to NSW, but that would not justify the capital expenditure program required in Britain.

The operating divisions within the GBEs

As background information, the SRO records in its *concise guide*[85] that the Principal Superintendent of Convicts was involved with the assignment of convicts from 1790 onwards, whilst the day to day management of the working convicts, at least until 1826, was the responsibility of the Chief Engineer. At this point (1826-28) responsibility for assignment was placed in the charge of a Board appointed to report on Applications for Convict Servants and Labourers, with the Principal Superintendent of Convicts handling the administrative correspondence. This Board was replaced by a Board for the Assignment of Convict Servants from December 1831 and then by the Commissioner for the Assignment of Convict Servants in June 1836. The Office of Commissioner was abolished in February 1842. The Office of Chief Engineer included well-known and capable men including Gill, Druitt, Ovens, Kinghorne and Dumaresq and reported directly to the

---

[85]   State Records NSW *Concise Guide to the State Archives of NSW*

governor of the day. In January 1836, this system changed and the position of Colonial Engineer was installed with the first occupant being Captain George Barney of the Royal Engineers. This change came about as a result of the inefficient way in which public works were being carried out by contractors. His services were required for several major works, including the reforming of the Circular Quay area and other major infrastructure works which were the responsibility of government. Then in 1836, the Colonial Engineer took over from the Surveyor-General responsibility for construction and maintenance of roads and bridges throughout the colony. His duties as Commanding Royal Engineer included the construction of buildings for the convict establishment. (*Concise Guide to the State Archives* – State Records NSW).Governor Darling in structuring his public service included numerous stand alone positions—all responsible to the Colonial Secretary—including Surveyor of Roads and Bridges, the Government (Colonial) Architect and the Chief Engineer. Due to staff shortages of skilled workers, these personnel and others were merged into the Public Works Department in October 1856, but until that point and under the British administration, such subordinate positions were important to the assessment and reporting structure within the colony. The new department was in three operating sections – the Engineering section, the Harbours and Rivers section and the Roads and Bridges section.

Economic circumstances in Britain contributed in large part to the incentive for creation of the government business entities. The end of the European wars in 1815 left Britain in political and economic turmoil and interest on the national debt rose to 60% of national income. Departmental budgets including, those for the colonies, were pruned and colonial administrators (and governors) were constantly advised 'no expense was to be incurred on public buildings, except for the preservation of those necessary for defence or accommodation.' The British Treasury viewed the fiscal circumstances in the colony of NSW with dismay and attributed the burgeoning costs of the commissariat and public works to Macquarie's mismanagement. Even an alarmed Bathurst warned Macquarie to curb his expenditures, but, Macquarie rightly pointed out that since 1810 his expenditure per year per convict had been substantially reduced.

Before leaving the concepts of public works in the colony, Lenore Coltheart offers us two opinions in her essay 'The Landscape of Public Works' in 'Significant Sites'[86]

> 'The idea of changing wilderness to civilisation was fundamental to the colonising experience in NSW and it was explicit in the ways colonists and colonisers recorded and imagined that experience. Public works had a special place in this process as the material evidence of transformed bush landscapes. These public works were understood as the products and the symbols of the 'galvanising' effect of English colonialism'. [p160]

> 'The first great era of public works in the colony was during Lachlan Macquarie's governorship from 1810 to 1821, during which the incoming population grew from less than 12,000 to more than 30,000. Despite the obstruction to spending on public works as a result of the reports of one of the most trenchant opponents of the idea that the penal colony could change into a civilised city, Commissioner Bigge, Macquarie made his mark on town and country. Among the official reprimands to Macquarie's public works program was the injunction of the Secretary of State that splendid public works were the offspring of and not the parents of internal prosperity'. [p.164]

The story of the government enterprises is based on needs. A need to put the convicts to productive work, a need to trim the costs to the colony on account of convict maintenance, and the need to generate economic development and other public works. The umbrella framework of these public enterprises was a mix that achieved each of these outcomes. So, for building and construction work, there were the lumber, timber, brick and stone yards; for progressing the colony economically and making trade opportunities, we have the dock and naval yards. The female factory

---

[86] Lenore Coltheart 'The Landscape of Public Works' in 'Significant Sites – History of Public Works in NSW' [Hale & Ironmonger 1989]

served the dual purpose of separating the women prisoners from the rest of society and of producing woven and fabric products.

Over 22 government-owned and operated farms in the County of Cumberland and the Bathurst area have been identified, covering grain, vegetable production and livestock management. A 23rd operation on the foreshore of Sydney Harbour was charged with gathering sea shells for lime production. The gang system provided the bulk of the manual labour and controlled the more unruly prisoners. The gangs usually consisted of 8 convicts with a working convict overseer. The land-clearing gangs, the road-making gangs, the construction gangs and the in-town gangs for grass cutting, wood cutting, ship loading and unloading were all part of this outdoor group of convict labourers. Other out-of-town labour groups included farm workers sent into special areas to assist with coffee and tea production as well as those responsible for livestock slaughtering and the hauling of goods from camp to store or from store to store. The more trusted convicts were assigned to the remote timber-felling camps of Pennant Hills and Lane Cove. In all over 5,000 convicts were assigned to government service in this way, contributing a substantial output for their labours. Naturally there was a cost involved – the convicts had to be maintained and depending on their labours, the rations had to be adjusted, but even computing the value of their output at 4/6 per day, the cost of their victualling, slops, and accommodation was estimated at between £13 and £15 per annum or about 5/—per week compared with an output of over £25 per week

The Public Works program supported by the GBEs.

In the *Sydney Gazette*[87] of October 1810 Macquarie described his concept plan for Sydney town. It was to be developed on a plan 'for the ornament and regularity of the streets of Sydney, to secure the peace and tranquillity of the town.' The early timber structures had decayed rapidly, and Macquarie was busy establishing civic institutions: schools, churches, public buildings of various kinds including asylums and barracks. This extensive public works activity required the full support of the GBEs in providing extracted materials, stone, timber, bricks and gang labour.

---

[87]   *Sydney Gazette* of 6 October 1810

The Commissariat's involvement in the GBEs

Peter Bridges in *Foundations of Identity*[88] records

> *England had no tradition of planting Crown colonies and the sending of the First Fleet was the rare example of a venture which was not primarily motivated by commercial enterprise. Nor did England have a centralised organisation for carrying out public projects – works of national benefit were for the most part the products of the private commercial initiatives taken by entrepreneurs such as the Duke of Bridgewater, the canal builder. [p.1]*

This section is intending to describe the hierarchy of government enterprises, their locations, production role, and the demarcation lines of supervision of the enterprises and how they operated. There were eleven main enterprises as well as the gang system which was adjunct to and supported the enterprise system.

The most common dissent from the concept that the commissariat was the umbrella component of the GBEs is that it did not oversee all aspects of the enterprise operations. This observation and commentary is certainly true but it tells only part of the story. The commissariat was the government store, not a policy-making body or a government department. It was the arm of government that filled an essential role, storing the necessary tools, parts and finished inventory for supply to the various branches of government.

Is there a modern equivalent in government today? There is in the military services, but it is divided into stores and ordnance. The store is the food and equipment supply chain; whilst the ordnance section supplies armaments and ammunition. In the civilian arena, the government printing and supplies office keeps all levels of the public service in stationary and supplies and maintains all assets with on hand supplies, parts and skilled labour, whilst the Public Works Department also maintains tangible supplies of equipment and parts for roads, bridges, wharves, public buildings and

---

88   Bridges, Peter *Foundations of Identity*

public hospitals. Local needs have been devolved to the current government enterprises, such as ferry services, train and tram transport services and postal services. Each current enterprise is responsible for carrying out its own repairs, maintenance, capital acquisitions and placement, although one matter than complicates the pattern today is that much of this work is contracted out with little if any work being completed is kept 'in-house'.

Not so the early commissariat. If the store did not have a part, or could not repair an item, there were no suppliers or merchants nearby to supply that missing item. Supplies from Britain involved a turnaround time of 12 – 18 months and it was the convergence of need, urgency and commercial isolation that led to the store stocking policy and encouraged the governor's enterprise policy. In the context of the GBEs, the role of the commissariat was not to allocate convicts to tasks, select convicts for government service, supervise them or punish them. Its role was on the business side, limited to production planning, raw materials provisioning and finished goods inventorying. The hierarchy of the GBEs was simplistic but workable.

The **Superintendent of Works** determined the jobs to be worked on.

The **Superintendent of Convicts** selected convicts for government service and allocated them to the most appropriate enterprise for work.

The **Superintendent of the Enterprise** coordinated all aspects of the operation other than punishment.

There was a **supervisor** of each section within the enterprise. Most commonly there was one supervisor for each eight working convicts. Their responsibility was to ensure raw materials and tools were available, allot tasks, supervise training and quality and quantity of output, account for finished goods and inform the Superintendent of the enterprise of work completed.

So these four levels of hierarchy were accompanied by the overall **production planning** and raw materials supply. In addition the commissariat directed the hauling gangs, so that materials and supplies were available at each building or construction site (or to another enterprise) as needed. This production planning exercise was almost the core focus of enterprise management. In 1820 there were over 5,000 convicts in government service; this production planning was accompanied by manpower planning which allocated convicts in government service to the necessary tasks. There was a core manning structure so that the routine work and output was completed each day, but the real planning was for special or large jobs, such as major public buildings or major public works construction.

To analyse each of the enterprises requires an understanding of the geographic location of each facility, its role, output, worker numbers and its relationship to other enterprises.

Enterprises Locations in Operation 1822

1. Commissariat Main Building
2. Commissariat Stores [5 locations]
3. Lumber Yard
4. Timber Yard
5. Stone Yard
6. Dockyard
7. Brick Yard
8. Naval Yard
9. Government Farms [22 in total]
10. Female Factory
11. Slaughter-house
12. Extractive industries such as coal, lime,

Gangs

1 Construction
2 Haulage
3 Roads
4 Land clearing

Initially all enterprises were located within the County of Cumberland. Once Macquarie encouraged exploration, and the limits of location expanded, then so did the working base of many enterprises, especially those of the broad-acre farming and grazing entities used in government farming.

The enterprises can be grouped in many different ways, but essentially there were the natural resources and public farming side of government enterprises and the manufacturing and value-adding side. It is important to recall that as with the establishment of a penal colony, the British government had little experience in establishing or operating public enterprises. This whole approach was abhorrent to the British Treasury. Free enterprise and private sector enterprise was the tradition, and these small colonial oriented operations were not understood by the Colonial Office.

It is obvious that the very nature of an enterprise would determine its location. It may be assumed, for instance, that all farms would be outside the boundaries of Sydney town. However, this is not so. Grose Farm which held the few government-owned horses and bullocks and grew hay and fodder for these animals and other livestock was located at the site of the present Sydney University campus. . Longbottom farm and Liberty Plains farm were also in the Field of Mars area. Castle Hill, Pennant Hill and Lane Cove farms were north of the Harbour and opened up new timber country. Emu Plains, Dundas and the Cow Pastures opened up the area to the west of Sydney and supported the township of Parramatta. *Green Hills* farm utilised the fine alluvial soils of the Hawkesbury area for grain and crops. Records of the Parramatta Lumber Yard[89] in 1803 show that over 73,000 nails were sent to the Castle Hill government facility for construction purposes, in addition to 36 felling axes, 56 axe wedges, 74 hoes and 30 sickles. Further equipment arrived before September 1803 consisting of anvils, forges and bellows. The records also show that in 1802 Governor King used 300 convicts to clear 700 acres of the Castle Hill government farm and to build a number of stone barracks.

Almost as important as the need for fresh food, was the need for construction of houses, barracks, storerooms and a hospital. Governor Phillip located suitable clay reserves in the vicinity of the settlement and named the area Brickfield Hill. It was here he commenced making bricks, using the moulds he had brought on the First Fleet, and built a kiln for finishing the clay products. Susanna De Vries-Evans writes in *Historic*

---

[89]   State Records NSW *Concise Guide*

Sydney as seen by its early artists [A & R 1983] writes about the Brickfield Hill facility.

Although brick-making clay was abundant, nothing could be found for a long time to hold these bricks permanently together. Lime, essential in making mortar, was in such a short supply that most brick buildings collapsed in a heap of rubble as soon as the walls were leant on, and Governor Phillip constantly appealed for limestone to be sent out as ballast in the ships from home. Shell middens left by the aborigines on the shores of the Cooks River and Botany Bay proved to be a vital source of lime, and many colonists managed to make a living gathering the remnants from thousands of years of aboriginal meals to supply their kilns. The central collecting point was the Iron Cove –Fivedock area, with lime kilns located off Kent Street, down froim Bunkers Hill Another lime kiln was located on Bennelong Point just north of the Domain. The second clay-field was found by Phillip on the south bank of the Parramatta River at Rosehill, near the site of the present Rosehill Gardens Racecourse. Between the two over 30,000 bricks were produced by hand each week, enough to carry out construction requirements in the towns of Sydney and Parramatta. At Brickfield Hill 22 men were set the task of digging clay, cutting firewood, moulding and burning the clay to make 30,000 bricks initially each month. As efficiency improved and Rosehill facility came into production total production from both brick-making facilities grew to 30,000 each week. Although good stone was plentiful, but because the quarrying, shaping, carting and building of stone was all so slow and the needs for buildings so great, brick construction was in common use and after the governor's house was completed, the storehouses were given priority for security and safety reasons. Roof coverings were a problem for early buildings. Thatched roofs of reeds or grass were neither durable, weatherproof or safe from fire. Thatching was replaced by shingles split from the wood of she-oak. However these were also not fireproof, but remained the most commonly used roofing material in the colony until iron sheets and slates were introduced. Clay tiles were suitable in use but proved difficult to manufacture – moulding was slow and burning requirements were different to bricks, although there was only one kiln. Breakage was common duriung carriage and large losses occurred during burnin—up to 20% of production was lost in the kiln process. An Oxley compilation in 1821 [Surveyor-General John Oxley] of buildings in Sydney gives a useful insight into the type of construction used. There were 1084 in all, mostly around George, Castlereagh and Pitt Streets, of which 31 were public buildings, and the balance being modest houses and small single-story commercial premises – 725 percent were timberframed and weatherboard 22 pe cent were brick and 6percent were stone.

Although the haulers will be discussed further under the sub-heading of work gangs which included construction, road-making and land-clearing, the haulers were initially associated with brick-making. 12 men would haul 350 bricks on a large hand-cart, the men being 'yoked' to the cart, making five round trips from Brickfield Hill to Sydney town each day. Susanna De Vries-Evans[90] writes in *Historic Sydney as seen by its early artists* [A & R 1983] writes about the Carters Barracks

'Carters barracks [as well as Hyde Park Barracks] merely provided overnight accommodation for the convicts constructing Sydney's first roads and public buildings. In 1839, James Maclehose wrote in Strangers Guide to NSW for 1839 [Government Printer 1839] that 'the Belmore or Carters Barracks were erected in Governor Macquarie's time for the accommodation of the convict carters of bricks and food'. In those days all goods had to be hauled into Sydney either by bullock carts or by convicts, yoked to heavy wooden carts. Food from the farms in Parramatta was also brought to Sydney the same way. Governor Darling issued regulations in 1829 that 'no oxen shall be employed in operations which

---

90   De Vries-Evans, Susanna *Historic Sydney as seen by its early artists* [A & R 1983]

can be effected by men and carts' and so heavy wooden carts,
to which a team of 8 and 12 convicts were chained and
harnessed continued to be kept overnight at Carters Barracks
where the men also lodged. In 1788, the settlement had 'three
brick carts, each drawn by twelve men. Seven hundred tiles
or 350 bricks were loaded onto each cart and each day every
cart had to bring in five loads of bricks or four of tiles'. These
items [bricks and tiles] were made at the kilns on Brickfield
Hill, near Hay Street [the current site of UTS and Paddy's
market]' p. 35.

The Lumber Yard and other manufacturing facilities

Susanna De Vries-Evans in *Historic Sydney as seen by its early artists* [A & R 1983] writes about another of the enterprise activities.

At the corner of George and Bridge Street stood the Lumber
Yard. These lumber yards or storage yards were a standard
feature of British colonial penal settlements. They were
in fact convict work camps and the Bridge Street Lumber
Yard contained workshops for blacksmiths, carpenters,
wheelwrights, tailors and shoemakers. There was also a
tannery where the convicts made their own leather hats and
shoes. Nails, locks and bolts, bellows, barrels and simple items
of furniture for the officer's quarters and the barracks were
also made here. [p.93]

One way of understanding the Lumber yard is to consider its location and internal layout.

It stood on the corner of George and Bridge Streets, opposite the Male Orphan School. An 8 foot high wall surrounded the yard itself with two huge swing gates facing George Street, adjacent to which stood the gatehouse, housing the security personnel and a clerical assistant. Inside the compound were located at least five large sheds and a supervisor/clerical office. There were services under cover situated along the wall adjacent to the Tank Stream [the east boundary of the facility] including shoe-making, slops and hat making; the forges for making nails, bolts etc; the area for coopering [barrel-making]; and furniture making area. Centrally located in the yard were the two saw-pits and a central shed for log storage and debarking. Along the Bridge Street wall was the storage area for reserves of bricks, tiles, lime and coal. Near to the front gate facing High [George] Street, was a tool shed for storing the various tools required in the field for land-clearing, road-making etc. Most tools required for daily work in internal lumber yard operations were kept in that section, in smaller storage bins. Convicts were searched going out of the yard each evening, since petty theft was such a serious problem. A brief list of production items coming out of the Lumber yard offers an interesting insight into the yard layout and operation. These items included slops[clothing], straw hats, bonnets, shirts, trousers, shoes, boots, caps, cloth, and the manufactured items included iron bolts, nails, general building materials , pit-sawn timbers, timber framing, furniture and tools.

The Lumber yard stored, dried and cut timber logs into usable sizes. The Timber yard, its associated facility, then received the rough-sawn and/or dressed timber and proceeded to make timber products [other than furniture]. The timber yard was located in the three story commissariat premises on George Street North, and used the rough sawn lumber to make window frames, door frames and doors. Timber for flooring [joists, stumps, and floor boards] and for roofing [trusses, and ceiling fixtures] were also made and kept in inventory.

The Stone Quarries were initially in Sydney town, but as new sources were found and proved, they too became operational. The first stone quarries were on Kent Street, next to the military hospital, and the second in George Street, opposite the main commissariat store. A third quarry was located on Bennelong point. The stone quarries became important to public building construction in Sydney and Parramatta towns.

The main three-story commissariat store was located on the western side of Sydney Cove adjacent to Hospital Wharf. With a public wharf and the governor's wharf being other landing spots for shipping, the commissariat wharf was restricted to unloading cargo carried on both passenger/convict ships and freight ships. The first dockyard and naval yard was on the north side of the commissariat building and between the store and John Cadman's cottage. Cadman was an assistant coxswain before he was appointed superintendent of government boats and given an official pardon. This main store was used to inventory all items not of a perishable nature. A perishables store was built on the western side of the Macquarie Place triangle. It was in the row of better class housing occupied by Simeon Lord, William Chapman and Mary Reiby. The Reiby house was later converted into the site of the first Bank of New South Wales. Work in the naval yard was restricted to His Majesty's vessels, for refitting, repairing, provisioning and taking on water. Work in the adjacent dockyard was for civilian ships or visiting ships which needed repairs, spars, sails, and provisioning; when the need for new vessels arose, the dockyard designed and constructed rowing boats, whaling boats, produce carriers for servicing the Hawkesbury and Parramatta areas and small ferrying craft. The authorities in London refused permission for the construction of larger vessels, claiming they could be commandeered by convicts trying to escape.

Economic benefits of the GBEs

In addition to the value of output from the GBEs set down in the summary, one enormous tangible contribution came from the public works program. Macquarie's rather peevish last letter to Earl Bathurst in July 1822[91] offers a list of 266 items of construction in a ten year public works program during his administration. This list can be costed in terms of 'valuing' the items. Greenway's arch rival. Henry Kitchen, informed Commissioner Bigge that the labour 'value' alone was valued at over £950,000, so by adding the estimated value of the materials used, the total project cost of all items would be more than £2 million. In this way, it can be seen that the convict and transportation program paid its way many times over, if the Colonial office and British Treasury had been sufficiently creative to analyse that putting the convicts to work would produce an outcome of public value.

The government business enterprises played an important, essential and pivotal role in colonial economic development. In much the same way as the commissariat filled the role of a quasi-treasury for the first 35 years of the settlement the enterprises filled a need for timely production of tools,

---

[91]   Macquarie to Bathurst HRA 1:10:671

goods and services, during the same period. The government farming enterprise kept the settlers alive and in food for several early years and, without this public commitment it is doubtful if the construction work or the communications or the delivery of rations would have succeeded. The convicts were beneficiaries as well. The opportunity existed for convicts to be assigned to private masters or to government service; those convicts accepting government service usually learnt important skills for when they were emancipated.

The only way we can assess the contribution of the GBEs is in terms of output achieved, services performed, and the use made of that output. As referred to earlier, output can be measured in two ways. The first is to assign a daily rate to the convict working population, in government service, and from there value the amount of labour performed. From previous computations labour represents approx. one-third of the total value of production. The alternate method is to value the individual items produced within the GBE system. Both methods have been tested at this point and the results are extraordinarily proximate to each other, thus verifying the results.

The results are as follows:

1. In 1817, there were 4747 convicts in government service with an estimated annual production value of £916,408
2. During the Macquarie administration, the value of labour used in construction gangs, was over £950,000, with a value assigned to the public works program of over £2 million.
3. The GBEs as part of the commissariat system were an important economic driver of the colonial economy.
4. A 'valuation' of the secondary industry items confirms that the manufacturing economy, between 1810 and 1830 outperformed the agricultural economy, even after the government farm output is considered.
5. The GDP figures for the period 1810 to 1830 are actually much higher than previously estimated by N. G. Butlin[92], because he did not include the value of convict output. Butlin followed

---

[92]   Butlin, N. G. *Forming*

the British Treasury methodology and made no allowance for 'valuation' of convict labour or convict output.

6. So the tangible benefits of the GBEs included not only an extraordinary value that can be placed on production, but on the whole value of the public works program, because most of the materials used in the Public Works program were produced by the GBEs and therefore paid for from the convict maintenance allowance rather than any direct appropriation from the British Treasury.

Then followed a most important transition – the gradual transfer of manufactures from the public sector [the GBEs] to the private sector, which in turn underpinned the future growth and prosperity of this secondary industry component of the colonial economy. Pressure for items to fit into the daily work pattern often resulted in fresh thinking and a novel approach to entrepreneurship. Innovation in the small settlement was important and contributed to the rise of a new type of entrepreneur – innovation without huge capital investment. Progressively a range of new local manufacturing industries evolved, including the manufacture of farm equipment suitable to local conditions. The manufacture of boats was the result of the need to service the new industry of sealing and whaling. The intangible benefits from the GBEs were just as numerous although not quantifiable in direct value terms including the development of a broad skills base and government services such as hospitals, schools, churches, outlying villages, ferry services etc. These socio economic benefits would not have arrived until much later if innovation, local revenues and the development of convict jobs had not evolved as they did. Other Macquarie innovations such as a more formal town planning system and a systemised system of trade and commerce assisted in the development process and can be attributed to the growing business approach to components of the colonial economy.

Convicts with skills

Douglass Baglin and Yvonne Austin in their work *Historic Sandstone Sydney*[93] (Rigby Press 1976) offer some interesting views of the selection and utilisation of stone in the Sydney area. '

> *All implements and materials used by these first settlers were of the poorest quality, and there were few skilled men available. The Expedition had been so poorly planned that even the cooking utensils were inadequate. As there was no architect, and only twelve carpenters, building projects were conducted largely by trial and error. The men felled many trees – of much harder wood than the woods found in Britain – and hastily put together the much needed shelters. Reeds for roofing were gathered at Rushcutters Bay, and shingles were cut from the she-oak. The building program was so intense that within three months not a single cabbage patch palm was left standing within 12 miles of the settlement. The natural beauty of this virgin country was quickly being desecrated. [p.30]*

> *'Once the need for shelters had been satisfied, the need for growing food took prime importance. Water was collected in 'tanks' cut into the sandstone bed of the 'tank' stream, but food rations diminished quickly as more convicts arrived. It was difficult to grow crops on the barren sandstone tableland, and disease, intensified by malnutrition, was rife. Phillip kept requesting tools, architects, farmers and tradesmen, but still not enough arrived. Four years later he was still asking for such basic needs as saws and axes'. Prior to 1810, all property was Crown land and leased on a short-term basis. Under this system, the lessee had no incentive other than to put up anything but shoddy buildings and as result there was little civic pride. Macquarie was determined to change all this. He gave grants of town land on the condition buildings erected would be of a certain standard. [p.31]*

---

[93]   Baglin & Austin *Historic Sydney Sandstone* Rigby Press 1976

The commissariat also established work centres for convicts over which the commissariat assumed the production planning roles: The main areas of forced convict work came from The Lumber, the Timber and Dockyards, whilst the Stone Quarries, timber cutting camps, land clearing and road-making activities were more 'gang' oriented and remained the preserve of the more difficult convicts and re-offenders. Until 1820, these centres employed over 50% of the convict population. Their output was directed at agricultural products, livestock supply, import replacement manufactures, materials required for the construction and building industries, materials required in the public works and infrastructure construction program, and the transport and storage requirements of the government. Colin White[94] has concluded that the colonial government controlled the local economic mechanism.

> *There were three main elements to the mechanism: first, the provision by the government of social infrastructure and of the public goods necessary to help individual decision-makers to manage or mitigate risk; second, the guarantee of a market, at fixed prices, for the output of the private sector; and third, the granting of free land, the giving of inexpensive credit and the assignment of cheap labour, and incidentally the return of redundant labour to public employment when necessary. The task in this high-risk environment was to reduce risk sufficiently to encourage investment in productive activities. [p.52]*

Whilst the role of government and the commissariat in this instance was to control internal price levels and to regulate purchases in order to provide a continuing market to the local agriculturalist, one way of minimising risk suggests Colin White was to offer a guaranteed market at a fixed price through the government store. [p.52]

To do this, our first question must be –'what brought about the introduction of state-owned enterprise'? Although not a novel idea to Britain, it was certainly not the operational philosophy that was to be actively encouraged

---

[94]   White, Colin *Mastering Risk – Environment, Markets and Politics in Australian Economic History* Page 52

in the fledgling colony of NSW. The preferred idea was for the settlement to be a 'distant' penal community. Its goals were self-sufficiency in food, resources, manpower and governance. However, there was a role for a central government. A military detachment was assigned, which cost was appropriated to the colony. Foreign representation of the settlement would also be left to Britain as was the civil administration whose cost was also appropriated to the settlement. It was hoped, if not expected that Britain would benefit economically from the establishment by having favourable trade, and having a commercial stepping stone to far eastern and Chinese trade. Always the optimist, Britain foresaw national shipping interests utilised in delivering these trading opportunities, as well as transferring merchants, insurance, manufacturing but mainly investment. The needs of Britain following its emergence from the industrial revolution was to locate quality outlets for expanded home production, especially investment in pastoral expansion, the demand for which products was paramount to British industry. Naturally the Parliament saw a possible net revenue raising from the settlement rather than a drain on the British purse which was already overwhelmed with demands from uneconomic but 'strategically essential' colonies.

Thus the setting was a commercial one for the Transportation program to replace the one lost in the Americas. However, what were not clear were the commercial aspects of financing the convicts. The former practice was to sell the convicts to landowners, for sufficient to cover their holding and maintenance costs whilst in the charge of the British authorities. Alternatives were to be considered as the distance from London to Botany Bay was very different to the London – Virginia distances and whereas white farmers were already established in the Americas, Botany Bay was 'terra nullius', or so it was claimed. Alternatives considered included putting convicts to work on establishing a colonial infrastructure, but how long would that take? The expected food production was not considered to be unachievable from putting some convicts to work. However, the only mould that Governor Phillip considered was that of putting the convicts to work on public infrastructure. The instruction to minimise the number of convicts supported by the government was in direct contradiction to using convicts for public works or even food pro\duction. The policy of 'valuing' convict output never saw the light of day, although such policy would have benefited the governor greatly.

Could it be possible to run a settlement along the lines of using public revenue by it being equated to 'output and benefit'?

Is it possible to think in terms of convicts being assigned to the private sector for work on a 'maintained' basis or preferably a 'fee for service' basis, OR a governor being given a 'public allowance for maintaining a convict (say, 1/3d per day) but being allowed to buy from a convict management board, the output of the convict labour, such that the public purse bought the output but the revenue so produced was used for convict maintenance? What a far reaching concept? Convicts working to pay for their own maintenance – food, clothing, living costs, and lodging. It could have worked even in the confinement of public practice in the settlement between 1788 and 1835

The second question to be considered must be 'just what type and how many were the GBEs and what did they produce

Type of Activity	Name of GBE	Main Products
Manufacturing & prefab	Lumber Yard	Timber, clay & metal pdts
Timber products	Timber Yard	Timber processing
Stone construction	Stone Yard	Cut stone and gravel
Spinning Weaving& sewing	Female Factory	Cloth & woollen products
Public farming	Government Farms	Meat, grain, vegetable & dairy products
Meat dressing/distribution	Government Abattoirs	Meat processing
Construction	Boat Yard	Boat construction
Maintenance	Naval Yard	Boat repair
Gang unskilled workers	Road, Land Clg & garden maintenance Gangs	Road construction and land clearing
Alternatives to horses or bullocks	Haulage Services & Ferry	Moving materials from the LY to construction sites

A third question then leads to the statement of general hypotheses and analysis of the core theorem of this study.

    i.   Government enterprises were an important stepping stone towards putting convicts to productive work, to carry out convict work training, security of subsistence and safety for a future existence.

    ii.   Government enterprises offered a range of important production centres and output which propelled the colonial development and underpinned the public works program.

    iii. Government enterprises created a valuable output which contributed directly to economic growth, and GDP and as such should have been valued as part of the GDP for the colony for those years.

    iv. Government enterprise output was a valuable import replacement activity and in the temporary absence of staples , it was a strong earner of export income

Some of the theories which accompany these hypotheses are rather underdeveloped but verifiable and add a strong economic flavour to the analysis

    a.   The British government had incorrectly assessed the amount of establishment capital associated with the colony. It spent over 5 (five) million pound in 25 years supporting the colony's economic growth.

    b.   It failed to correct for 17 years the unconstitutional collection of taxes and revenue from the free citizens of Botany Bay and then made this illegal public revenue part of its appropriation for the support of the colony. This resulted in a dramatic slowdown in direct 'British' spending on the colony

    c.   Although claiming to be altruistic in its approach to colonial policy and the maintenance of its protectorates, it can be proven that British 'tax' and import tariff collections on goods Imported from or arriving from the Colony of NSW before 1825, was far more than the direct parliamentary appropriation to the colony of NSW for the same period.

    d.   A philosophical argument could be made as to the right of the state to force its prisoners to face additional punishment, over and beyond imprisonment and incarceration, in the format of working on either private or public works, especially without more than subsistence food, lodging and living essentials.

e. A further argument could be made, in response and explanation of why convict 'output' was not measured – an explanation in addition to understanding how difficult the practice would have been—'should a government be allowed to profit from the labour of its prison population or would this, in effect, constitute slave labour, or worse, forced labour camps?

f. The hypotheses that need testing are

   i. Was the Transportation program and its integral policy of forcing convicts into labouring, analogous to slavery

   ii. Did enslavement of prisoners lead to their rehabilitation?

   iii. Did forced labour lead to preparedness for work after release from confinement?

   iv. Should prisoners be responsible for supporting themselves by working, and from the resale of the output of their labours?

   v. Should the output of GBEs constitute a measurable component of GDP for the colony?

   vi. Should the coloniser (Britain) be responsible for preparing and creating public work infrastructure in its own colony?

   vii. Should the output of GBEs add to government revenue or be an offset to government expenditure?

   viii. How did prisoner productivity compare with free worker productivity?

   ix. What level of training did convict workers receive in the workplace?

   x. Did convict workers encourage or distract from free worker involvement in a manufacturing sector?

   xi. Were the GBEs the precursor or forerunner to a manufacturing sector?

   xii. What overall contribution in economic and financial terms did the GBEs make to the Colonial Economy?

Here follows a brief supporting statement explaining each introductory aspect of the research project and the thesis

The hunt for staples

The importance of this specific enquiry is for the researcher to focus on the contribution of the GBEs to the balancing of imports and exports and its participation in economic growth. Successive governors, commencing with Arthur Phillip, actively pursued a staple for the export market. Timber, coal, sandalwood and fishery products came and went but there was never a basic commodity (until wool) that was a regular in the export trade from the colony. In economic terms and in opportunity cost concept, the import replacement activities of the GBEs brought enormous trade balance of payment benefits to the colony.

The creation of entrepreneurs

Sir Joseph Banks in testimony to the House of Commons stated "if the people [*of the proposed settlement*] formed among themselves a civil government they would necessarily increase and find occasion for many new European commodities; and it is not to be doubted that New Holland would furnish matter of advantageous return". The environment for the development of entrepreneurs was ripe for those with gumption and not least a few worthy ideas to take advantage of the numerous natural resources, the surplus of labour and the myriad of opportunities in a small vibrant settlement. The period 1802-1830 produced at least 28 settlers and emancipists that could be termed entrepreneurs. Commissioner Bigge identified 12 merchant traders (in his 1823 report on the Colony), 3 of whom were operated by emancipists. Each of these people made a mark on the secondary industry of the settlement and most benefited either directly or indirectly from the GBEs being in operation.

Establishing a manufacturing sector

It was to be expected that survival for the colony would be dependent on food production, but there was a wide range of work for convicts to complete in first establishing the settlement. Their work included building cart tracks, barracks for the military and civilian people and their families, hospitals, stores, wharves, and not least of all cutting and removing trees and cultivating the soil. The main challenge was to repair and maintain tools assembled by the commissariat store to enable the convict works to carry out their assigned tasks. Thus the 'lumber yard' came about. Initially it was a repair and maintenance shop for axes, saws, spikes, but also spades, shovels, picks, and mattocks. These tools were not of the best quality when purchased in England and were definitely not best suited to the early landscape of the settlement, thus the need for maintenance services to cater for breakages; sharpening and handle replacement were in daily demand. The lumber yard was manned by two convicts supposedly suited to the work and with some experience. From small and definitely humble beginnings, the largest manufacturing operation ever witnessed in the colony developed – the Sydney Lumber Yard was the first, largest and most important GBE. It was the forerunner of the manufacturing sector for the colony. This occurred in two ways. As the governor wanted to hive off routine productive jobs to the private sector, simple tasks were transferred to private operators. Trained convicts, upon their release, took the opportunity to set up cottage industries in the areas that their skills and experience supported, because the commissariat maintained them from the store for at least twelve months from their release. Upon the demise of the Lumber Yard, its former operations devolved into the private sector which also absorbed the skilled workforce that came with the production and materials.

The transportation program and convict workers

I have already outlined the way ahead for convict workers and questioned the validity of forced labouring. Why were the convicts, safely ensconced in Botany Bay in isolation and protected from external harm not given the option of being 'paid' to work for a living. Their environment was in reality, a free range goal, which offered the opportunity of private masters and the government both bidding for their services. Is it possible that the GBEs would not have evolved as they did in a freer environment? Were the GBEs a product of n circumstances based on forced labour for convicts? The transportation program was the catalyst for the GBEs and over time more than 60,000 convicts worked in and benefited from and contributed to government labour practices. I submit there was a better way!

Selecting workers for the GBEs

Were the selection practices for working at the GBEs sound and practical? It was much like fitting a round peg into a square hole. Rumours were rife from the time the prisoners left England that the selection process depended on certain answers from the prisoners to the interviewers on the wharf at Sydney town. Do you tell the truth about age, literacy and experience and risk getting a hard job, or did one plead ignorance to try and receive an unskilled task? Every prisoner made his own judgement but I doubt that many notations on the convict records were made objectively and thus assessment was made extra difficult

Supervising & Organising Convict Workers

Due to a shortage of free workers in the colony and a dearth of skilled civilian/government workers, it became a matter of convict supervising convicts. A rigorous management structure was put into place whereby foreman, trainers, pre-assembly and prefabrication personnel were all selected from the convict ranks whilst managers and some group supervisors were free civil employees. Although the above structure permeated the Lumber Yard, there is evidence that a gang structure also existed, and upon the closing of the GBEs under Governor Darling, only the work gang arrangement s survived but were restricted to 'special' government selected convicts.

Accounting for output

If we consider the raw numbers, then the 10 GBEs operating in and around Sydney between 1802 and 1825, employed over 60,000 convict workers. They would have cut millions of cubic feet of timber, made thousands of timber roofing, flooring and wall frames, forged thousands and thousands of nails, mould many hundreds of thousand bricks and tiles, windows, doors not to mention furnishings for hundreds of barrack room. The craftsmen in their ranks erected hundreds of buildings, houses, stores, churches, government offices. They made millions of shoes, and thousands of slops, hats, caps and blankets. They managed thousands of sheep and cattle, cut thousands of bales of hay, grew millions of vegetables, and many, many bushels of grain. Fruit, dairy products and chicken were well produced and they also tried their hand at growing such diverse items as hops, tobacco, tea and coffee. But not one attempt was ever made to value this output and try to explain and justify the British appropriations to the colony. Why, instead of complaining at various levels of insensitivity that there was too much expenditure on convict management, did the authorities not say we are contributing over £300,000 annually to maintenance of convicts in the colony, and this expenditure is being saved by replacing expenditure on imports, so the net cost of £170,000 per annum for convict maintenance is cheap

Should GBE output be valued for GDP purposes?

N.G. Butlin in his extensive study of GDP from 1802 to 1900 noted that his figures excluded the value of convict output. He questions whether it could have been measured, but in fact, measurement can be done in one of two ways. However firstly, inclusion of GBE output in to the GDP is essential, valid and important. Annual value of GBE output represented upwards of £500,000 and represented between 33 and 50% of other GDP. Thus the non-inclusive GBE figures are skewed and misrepresentative and Butlin recognised this fact, but didn't ever include the amended figures in his published research.

Summary of Research Plans

The core focus of the research is the operation, philosophy and benefits of the GBEs

Side focuses involve the convict labour utilised – how many, and to what economic effect? A further by-product is identifying the emergence and development of the manufacturing sector and the colonial economy overall. Economic development in the settlement took on many guises, not the least of which was the dual benefits of having local industry manufacture and build so many components of the public works and infrastructure whilst saving the balance of payments untold millions in savings.

Not least of all the benefits was the contribution made by the colony to import revenue generation in Britain, which exceeded the government appropriations to the colony.

Measuring the value of output from the GBEs is a major challenge for the research project as is the identification of production items and the respective quantities produced through the GBE system.

Introduction to Chapter One

From its commencement in 1788, the aim of the Colony of New South Wales was self-sufficiency even though it had been set up to solve the problem of Britain's overcrowded prisons. By 1823, the British Government had decided that it would limit its direct expenditure to the transportation of the convicts and their supplies while in transit; the Colonial Administrators would be responsible for the convicts' security, food, clothing and accommodation in the Colony. Furthermore, proceeds from the sale of Crown land were to be the exclusive reserve of the British authorities rather than the colonists. The Governors were therefore forced to look for ways in which the Colony could help to support itself through working the convicts to create food, minerals (e.g. coal production), roads, housing and public buildings. Other convicts were assigned to landowners on a fully-maintained basis, thus saving the British Treasury a great deal of money.

This policy of maintenance of convicts by the Government created the need for an accounting by the Colony to the British Parliament. This led to the appointment in 1824 of a Financial Controller/Colonial Accountant to prepare monthly and annual despatches to the British Colonial Secretary. Following self-government in 1856, the procedures changed as the Colony became fully responsible for its own economic planning and fiscal management.

A Brief Overview of the Government Store

The first storekeeper arrived with Governor Phillip and the First Fleet. Andrew Miller had been appointed whilst the Fleet was preparing to sail, initially to take responsibility for the loading and recording of requisitioned stores. Upon arrival in Sydney Cove, Miller's first task was to erect a stores tent, secure it as far as possible, and commence unloading from the ships the stores that would be required during the first few weeks. These stores and provisions included such items as tents, pots and cooking utensils, blankets, hospital equipment and supplies and tools for clearing the land and erecting tents. Little was known about local conditions and Phillip's plan to have a wooden storehouse built within a few weeks could not be accomplished. He had tried to anticipate a wide range of obstacles and challenges, but encountering a difficult landscape and understanding characteristics of the local forestry proved the most difficult of all. In their various reports, Cook, Banks and Matra all praised the local timbers after only a cursory evaluation but, with no expertise amongst his crew or the convict population, Phillip's task of clearing timber and using it for construction was almost impossible.[95]

Upon their arrival, Phillip relied on Miller to operate the most basic of stores and without burdening him with limiting rations as he anticipated that the second Fleet store ships would be carrying provisions for the next full year. Miller's biggest task was the security of the provisions; the remaining items were then to be unloaded so that the ships could return to naval service. Phillip later prepared a rationing program for Miller so that the provisions would last six months, the time Phillip thought the Second Fleet was behind his own.

The stress of establishing the commissary for the new settlement and acting as private secretary to the governor eventually broke Miller's health and he wanted to return home. However, he was not to see his home again; he died during the sea voyage back to England.

Miller's successor, John Palmer, had sailed as purser aboard Phillip's flagship, *Sirius*. He had joined the Navy at the age of nine and participated in a series of voyages to many parts of the world, including North America where he married into a wealthy colonial family. After the founding of the colony, and with the expectation that he would soon return to England, Palmer sailed with the *Sirius* to the Cape Colony and Batavia on a mission

---

[95] Cook & Banks had written positively (and subsequently amended by Beaglehole) about the lush landscape to be found at Botany Bay, and James Matra (another Cook crewman) extended this interest in local timber to its use as a trade item between the colony & Britain, when Matra submitted his recommendation of the use of the new land as a penal settlement. Refer also Beckett: 'Reasons for the Colony' in *British Colonial Investment in the Colony 1788-1856*.

to purchase food for the struggling, and hungry, colony of NSW. Whilst shipping provisions from Sydney to Norfolk Island, the ship struck an uncharted submerged rock just southeast of the Island and sunk. Palmer was saved, but the *Sirius* and its cargo was lost and Phillip found a new posting for Palmer in Sydney, replacing Miller as chief store-keeper. It was a further seven years before Palmer sailed for England, but he soon returned to the colony with his wife and sister, Sophia. The Palmer family became financially secure with a magnificent walled estate, carved from the rocky terrain of Woolloomooloo Bay, just east of Farm Cove. Sophia was to shortly marry Robert Campbell thus forming a most strategic alliance between the colony's first successful trading house (Campbell & Co, the chief supplier of stores to the colony) and the chief procurer of provisions for the colonial store (John Palmer).[96]

Governor Phillip was active in most facets of the initial colonial administration, especially the planning for the new settlement and the difficult challenge of feeding the people. He found the soil conditions around Sydney Cove were unsuitable for vegetables, grain and fruit. The vegetable patches located in the Governor's Domain failed to provide the produce desired, and Phillip was constantly looking for new, more fertile, locations. Travelling up what was to become known as the Parramatta River; he located more fertile soil, and what appeared to be a suitable clay reserve, on the south bank of the River; he named the area Rose Hill. Phillip planned a new settlement at the head of the river which he named Parramatta. Phillip recorded that, 'the soil is more suitable for cultivation than the hungry sand covering the hills near Sydney'[97.] It was imperative to grow food as quickly as possible and Parramatta offered the additional advantages of a constant supply of fresh water and a means of transporting food by boat rather than having to build building a road.

During the Palmer administration of the stores, new settlements had to be served in addition to Norfolk Island established in 1789. Settlements were developed and serviced by branch stores in areas such as Hobart (1802), Port Dalrymple (later Launceston, 1802), Liverpool (1803),

[96] Refer: Margaret Steven '*Merchant Campbell 1769-1846*' and Beckett '*John Palmer – Commissary*'
[97] HRNSW Vol 1, Part 2 p469 (Despatch by Governor Phillip to Hon W. Grenville)

Hawkesbury (Windsor, 1802) and Bathurst (1814). The role of the main store in Sydney was constantly changing as was its location. All the stores required personnel and organisation as well as a good supply of clerical assistance and many of these roles were set-aside for trusted convicts and ticket-of-leave men. The reason for the use of convicts in a sensitive and secure area of government was straightforward. As Butlin has established, the cost of convict labour was a charge against the English Treasury and not included in the appropriation to the colony, so the use of convicts as workers for the government kept government civil salaries understated and artificially low. It was Commissioner Bigge who reviewed the workforce and, observing the number of convicts employed within government and thus civil service ranks, became aware of the understatement of costs in the colony. Butlin adds, 'as public employees, a great deal of convict labour was engaged on farming and public infrastructure construction and thus avoided being charged as a direct cost to the colony. It was more convenient, however, to transfer them into the labour market.

The use of convicts as public Servants, in the sense of filling positions in the normal operations of government, has a special interest!'[98]

A list of some of the main provisions and supplies that arrived with the First Fleet indicated the role and difficulties facing the storekeeper. In addition to foodstuffs, supposedly sufficient for the first six months, some of the provisions and supplies which were shipped with the First Fleet in 1787, were:

---

[98] Butlin, N.G., 'What a way to run an Empire, fiscally!' *Working Paper in Economic History*, No. 55

(Australian National University, 1985) p.32. Butlin (p34) also questions the judgement of McMartin *Public Servants & Patronage* on this same point and states, "Colonial Officials chose to use convicts (in the public service context) because they were cheap and their charge loaded on Britain. Had the offer price for clerks been raised, one might expect more free or freed persons to seek the positions. Virtually none of the convict appointees appears as a charge in the Colonial Fund; they were supported by the Commissariat'. Butlin could also have pointed out that a subsequent head of the public service, and its main supporter (William Lithgow) found that there were virtually no trained or skilled clerical assistants in the colony and Lithgow took the time and opportunity to 'train' young men with potential for these roles, but then had great difficulty in retaining their services

TABLE 1.1 Supplies sent with the First Fleet

700 steel spades	63 coal buckets	700 clasp knives
30 grindstones	100 pairs of hinges	60 butcher's knives
700 iron shovels	80 carpenter's axes	500 tin-plates
330 iron pots	10 sets cooper's tools	100 pairs –scissors
700 garden hoes	20 shipwright's adzes	60 padlocks
6 hand-carts	40 corn-mills	30 box rulers
700 West India hoes	175 claw hammers	50 hayforks
4 timber carriages	12 ploughs	30 pincers
700 grubbing hoes	175 handsaws	42 splitting wedges
14 chains	50 pickaxes	100 plain measures
700 felling axes	140 angers	8000 fishhooks
14 fishing nets	700 wooden bowls	12 brick moulds
700 hatchets	700 gimlets	48 dozen fishing lines
5448 squares of glass	700 wooden platters	6 harpoons
700 axe handles	504 saw files	10000 bricks
200 canvas beds	10 forges	12 lances
747,000 nail of various sizes	300 chisels	

The complete list[99] of articles sent with the First Fleet was much longer and represented a storeman's nightmare if records of issues and returns were to be maintained. For instance, the unloading of stores and provisions for immediate use commenced on 7 February but; since the settlement held over 1,000 people, there was obviously not sufficient bedding, blankets, cooking utensils, or eating utensils for everyone[100]. The allowance of clothing for a male convict for a year was equally inadequate; although raw cloth, needles and cotton had arrived with the Fleet and female convicts could be encouraged to hand sew clothing if necessary. The records show that the total costs of all male and female convict clothing was only £4,144.

In 'Botany Bay Mirages', Alan Frost has raised the question of whether the inadequate quantity of tools and supplies was deliberate, or merely poor planning. A case can be made for improper planning rather than deliberate mismanagement. Phillip was left in sole charge of the voyage and received

[99] HRNSW Vol 1, Part 2 p.16
[100] The list of 'stores' and 'provisions' is found in both the HRNSW and in John Cobley 'Sydney Cove 1788' Vol 1

very little guidance, support or interest from the Secretary of State's office, the Naval Board or the commissariat division of the British Treasury.[101] It is unlikely that, after a fairly ordinary career as a naval officer, Phillip would suddenly have reverted to poor leadership. Indeed, he had commented to the Naval Board that the vessels allotted to the Fleet were not adequate in size or number. He also questioned the short amount of time allowed for the planning process, but received no worthwhile response. Clearly, this was not regarded as a voyage of high importance compared with British naval activities in other parts of the world. So, the fact that Phillip used a great deal of judgment and commonsense, speaks volumes for his quiet confidence and determination that he was the most suitable choice as the head of this mission.

For the first storekeeper, local circumstances were such that the supplies brought from England needed to be carefully protected against theft and loss. The tools, in particular, were to be issued daily and returned each evening; however according to Marjorie Barnard, within 14 days of arriving in the colony, over one-third of the tools loaned out for chopping trees and clearing land had been lost, stolen or deliberately concealed from the storekeeper.[102] The chief cause was the unwillingness of convicts to work; removing the tools meant they were unable to chop firewood or cut timber framing for the new camp. As a way of keeping the tools in repair, Miller had set up forges on the banks of Sydney Cove and used iron and steel pieces brought out as ballast to forge new tools and replace lost items. Watkins Tench in his '*Narrative of the Expedition to Botany Bay*' provides some useful insights into the conditions faced by Phillip and Miller. In November 1788 he noted: 'Temporary, wooden stores, covered with thatch or shingles into which the cargoes of all the ships have been lodged, are completed, and a hospital erected'.[103] However, the stores were not to remain as such for long as the end of one such building was converted into a temporary church for Sunday services. These frail structures were neither fire-proof nor rat-proof and the summer of 1789 saw the end to these temporary structures when Phillip designed a new, sturdier and more permanent store in a location closer to the settlement's

---

[101]   Alan Frost raises this possibility in '*Botany Bay Mirages*' Chapter 8 'No Cheaper Mode…' as does Barnard in '*Phillip of Australia*'.

[102]   Barnard '*A History of Australia*' *Chapter 3* 'Taking Shape' *p60*.

[103]   Flannery quotes Tench in '*1788 Watkins Tench*' p81

military camp. Later in 1789, Tench recorded that 'the storehouse was finished at Rose Hill (by then renamed Parramatta). It was 100 feet by 24 feet and was built of local brick, deep red in colour, but not as durable as the Sydney product'.[104]

Displaying rare frustration, Phillip wrote to Assistant Secretary of State, Phillip Stephens, in August 1790 'Leather is needed for soles for men's shoes and materials for mending them. Shoes here last but a very short time, and the want of these materials and thread to mend the clothing will render it impossible to make them serve more than half the time for which they were intended'. The following month Phillip wrote to Nepean, the Under-Secretary of State for the Colonies, and made two observations: 'I cannot help repeating that most of the tools sent out were as bad as ever' and, 'the wooden ware sent out were too small; they are called bowls and platters, but are not larger than pint basins. There was not one that would hold a quart'.[105]

Tench also described the development of the new town of Rose Hill and the buildings adjacent to the store: 'the new stone barracks is within 150 yards of the wharf, where all boats from Sydney unload. In addition there is an excellent barn, a granary, an enclosed yard to rear livestock, a commodious blacksmith's shop and a most wretched hospital, totally destitute of every convenience'.[106]

In 1790 Phillip told Nepean that the colony badly needed 'honest and intelligent settlers, and free men to act as superintendents of convicts'. Phillip also requested a new, more appropriate style of clothing for the convicts, even suggesting a form of mark to protect them from being sold. He badly needed a windmill, and requested axes, saws, combs, iron pots and 'two or three hundred iron frying pans which will be a saving of the spades'.[107] Unlike Macquarie some twenty years later, Phillip was of two minds about free enterprise in the colony. He did approve an open

---

[104]   Flannery *ibid* p127
[105]   Governor Phillip to Under- Secretary Nepean HRNSW Vol 1, Part 2 p481. In terms of the departmental hierarchy, the Colonial Office had a Secretary, an Under-Secretary and then a number of Assistant-Secretaries
[106]   Flannery *ibid* p 145
[107]   Governor Phillip to the Rt. Hon Henry Dundas HRNSW Vol 1 Part 2 p595

market, but then reverted to government importing 'specialty' items into the colony. According to Barnard, "in April 1792, Phillip established a regular market in Parramatta". It was for fish, grain, livestock, clothing and anything else that might legitimately be bought or sold. It was open to convicts. In October 1790, Phillip reported to Secretary Dundas in London: "The commissary was obliged to purchase various articles brought out by the sailing officers of the *Pitt*, where the private property sold in this settlement amounted to upwards of £4,000, which may serve in some measure to point out what might be bought by a ship loaded wholly on account of government".[108]

During 1792, Phillip was faced with a minor mutiny. The military under the leadership of Major Grose advised Phillip that they (the military) had chartered *The Britannia* to sail to the Cape for supplies. In spite of strong protests from Phillip, the ship sailed on 24 October and thus was born the 'pernicious system of private trading by the military'.[109] Phillip wrote movingly to the Right Hon. Henry Dundas, the Secretary of State in London, of this continuous struggle to get necessities: 'The period at which the colony will supply its inhabitants with animal foods is nearly as distant at present as it was when I first landed'. He added:

> *'I beg leave to observe that all those wants which have been pointed out in my different letters still exist: for iron pots, we have been nearly as distressed as for provisions: cross cut saws, axes and the various tools for husbandry are also much wanted; many of the articles are now made here, but the demand is greater than can be supplied because of the shortage of materials; many bales of clothing have been received, but arrive rotten and so injured from the damp that they have scarcely borne washing a second time'.*[110]

Butlin described the functions of the Commissariat in the following terms.

---

[108] Governor Phillip to the Rt. Hon Henry Dundas HRNSW Vol 1 Part 2 p.613
[109] Barnard, *Phillip of Australia*, p. 126
[110] Governor Phillip to the Rt. Hon Henry Dundas HRNSW Vol 1 Part 2 p.643

> *'The (British) Treasury described the commissary as one that 'keeps in the stores and issues provisions, fuel and light for the use of the service abroad'. Such a formal description fails to capture many of the crucial features of the Australian Commissariats and their subsidiaries. In addition the commissary in NSW became a source of foreign exchange and of local instruments of exchange. They were, at once, banks and credit agencies, and a springboard for banking enterprises. They were also the instruments for encouraging and reallocating productive activity for regulating staple prices and subsidies to such an extent that they have been perceived as 'staple markets'. The commissary also became the means for making supplementary allowances to officials, for compensating persons for performing public services for which no British appropriation existed or for totally funding some other public services. Through rations distribution, they effectively paid workers engaged in convict gangs on public infrastructure.'[111]*

That the commissariat operations reflected the changing needs within the colony is evidenced by its regular reorganisation. Until Macquarie's arrival, there had been stability in the organisation structure and only two commissaries had been appointed: the basic operations of victualling convicts and selected settlers had remained constant, as had the provision of tools and equipment to convict work parties. Under Macquarie, the expansion of services provided by the commissariat had grown disproportionately and into relatively uncharted areas. He recognised the need for banking and financial services in the colony but, when his proposal for a chartered bank was rejected, he imposed that role on the commissariat. Likewise, the growing intake of convicts into the colony led to vast organisational strictures on government, and these imposts were assigned to the commissariat.

The demand on the commissariat was always significant and varied according to the number of convicts arriving in the colony, which in turn depended on the military and economic circumstances prevailing in Britain

---

[111] Butlin, N.G.' *What a way to run an Empire, Fiscally'* p52

and Europe. On 1 February 1793, only five years after the First Fleet arrived in Botany Bay, Britain was at war with France, the Napoleonic Wars that dragged on until 1815. There were several important consequences: the attention of the British Government was distracted [18] away from the affairs of an insignificant and distant colony (Botany Bay); transportation of convicts more difficult and less necessary; the flow of free immigrants to the colony was reduced even further; and it enabled a small group of elite military officers stationed in the colony to create a monopoly position. In spite of the *Navigation Acts,* the war in Europe provided an excuse to develop trade between the British colony and the American colonies, although it was one-sided in favour of the American shippers.

Heavy economic commitments to the war in Europe and a downturn in the British economy from 1810-1815 led to constant pressure from the British Government to reduce expenditure in the colony. The Colonial Office in London thought this could be partly accomplished by moving people 'off the store' and reducing expenditures on public works. Both of these alternatives affected commissary operations. Apart from foodstuffs, the commissary mainly bought timber for building, leather for boots and shoes, wool (hair) for blankets and supplies such as barley for brewing beer.

The commissariat received supplies from four general sources: imports, government farms and workshops, civil and military officers and private individuals. In some matters, the commissary strongly supported private enterprise—for instance the area under grain on government farms never rose above 10% of the total farmed land in the settlement and by 1808 this was insignificant[19]. Similarly, government cattle numbers, notwithstanding the lost herd later found in the Cow Pastures at Camden, represented a decreasing proportion of total cattle numbers in the colony, falling from 70% in 1800 to 12% in 1814, whilst government sheep numbers fell from 10% to 2% of those in the colony in the same period.

The third Bigge Report provides an important insight into Commissariat activities. Commissioner John Thomas Bigge, a former Chief Justice of the West Indies colony of Jamaica, was appointed by Lord Bathurst to visit the Colony and assess progress and to evaluate the growing expenditures of Governor Macquarie. The instruction to Commissioner Bigge read in part:

> You will inquire into the courts of justice, the judicial establishments and the police regulations of the colony[5]. You will also turn your attention to the question of education and religious instruction. The agricultural and commercial interests of the colony will further require your attentive consideration. With respect to them you will report to me their actual state and the means by which they can be promoted.'

Bathurst added:

> I would more particularly refer to the authority, which the governor has hitherto exercised, of fixing the prices of staple commodities in the market, and of selecting the individuals, which shall be permitted to supply meat to the government stores. With respect to these regulations, you will investigate how far their repeal is likely to lead to any general inconvenience, or to any public loss. I am aware that when the colony was first established the necessity of husbanding the scanty means of supply and of regulating its issue, might justify an interference on behalf of the government; but now that the quantity of land in cultivation is so much increased, and the number of cultivators enlarged, I confess I have great reason to doubt the expediency of these regulations; at the same time I feel unwilling to recommend so material an alteration without some examination on the spot as to its probable effects.

A second letter of the same date and also from Earl Bathurst directed J.T. Bigge to consider the suitability of Sydney town as the main recipient of convicts and the opportunity of:

---

[5]   The first two paragraphs of Earl Bathurst's letter of 6th January 1819 to J.T. Bigge have been summarised for purposes of expediency

*'forming on other parts of the coasts, or in the interior of the
country, distinct establishments exclusively for the reception
and proper employment of the convicts, who may hereafter
be sent out. From such a measure, it is obvious that many
advantages must result. It would effectively separate the
convict from the free population, and the labour of forming a
new settlement would afford constant means of employment,
including that of a severe description. By forming more
than one of such separate establishments, the means of
classifying the offenders, according to the degree of crime,
could be facilitated. But on the other hand, you will have to
consider, what would in the first instance, be the expense of
the measures, and what may be the probable annual charge
which may result from their adoption.'*

Earl Bathurst, in a separate note113[6] to Viscount Sidmouth dated April
1817, set out his concerns of the mixing of convicts with free settlers and
the problems resulting from ever increasing numbers of convicts being
transported114[7]. He wrote:

*'Another evil resulting from the increased number (of convicts
transported), is the great difficulty of subjecting any of the
convicts to constant superintendence, either during the
hours of work or relaxation, and the necessity of leaving a
large proportion of them to the care of providing their own
lodgings during the night, from the inadequacy of public
buildings allotted to their reception, forms one of the most
formidable objections to the current system. I intend to
place the settlement on a footing that shall render it possible
to enforce strict discipline, regular labour and constant
superintendence, or the system of unlimited transportation
to New South Wales must be abandoned. I propose the
appointment of commissioners with full powers to investigate
all the complaints which have been made, both with respect to*

[6] *The full instructions from Bathurst to Bigge and the correspondence from
Bathurst to Sidmouth are printed with the third report by Bigge to Westminster,
as presented to the House of Commons in February 1823*

[7] Ritchie, John *Punishment and Profit*

*the treatment of the convicts and the general administration
of the government'.*

In his instructions to Commissioner Bigge, Bathurst had recognised
the impact of over-regulation and enforced pricing of goods sold to the
government stores. However, the commissariat (or Government store)
relied on imports for its grain and meat supplies and, until 1800, to a lesser
extent on the private sector. From 1804, grain was in reasonable supply,
except in periods of drought, floods and disease, and was grown mainly
by the small settlers. Cattle and sheep raising tended to be in the hands of
the military and civil officers and other settlers with larger holdings. The
government set basic prices for commodity purchases by the Stores, but
these were often exceeded because of the general shortage of labour115[7].
The governor set fixed prices for the commissariat for grain but the settlers
found they had to sell at lower rates to influential middlemen, who then
obtained the fixed price. This group had influence over what supplies
the stores would buy and from whom. According to Linge116[9,] a similar
clique 'was able to buy up ships' cargoes and resell them at ten times the
price and more' After 1800 Governor King tried to break the monopoly
position of these groups (mainly officers) but his efforts brought only
temporary relief to small settlers, many of whom were in debt.

The difficulty of changing the role and activities of small farmers was that
the vast majority was ex-convicts with little literacy and certainly neither
the knowledge nor capital to improve their farming techniques or buy
stock and equipment. In Van Diemen's Land, Lt-Governor Sorrell lent
small operators a bull or ram from the government herds and flocks for
breeding purposes in an endeavour to improve the herd and provide some
small assistance so these operators could acquire breeding livestock. Such
arrangements was not extended to or followed in the colony of NSW
although Samuel Marsden, a leading practitioner of flock improvement
in the colony, did loan some special rams to neighbours and parishioners
around Parramatta. The record shows Governor Darling loaned 'cows' to

---

8   Fletcher, B.H 'The Development of Small-scale farming in NSW under
Governor Hunter' JPRAHS, 50 pp 1-8

9   G. J .R. Linge ' Industrial Awakening'

small farmers although this was a strange way of increasing the private herds rather than the public herds.

Commissioner Bigge117[10] reported:

> 'Clerks in the Commissariat department generally consist of persons who have been convicts, and also of persons who are still in that position, but who have received tickets of leave. They receive pay, differing in amounts from 1s 6d to 5s per day, and 'lodging' money; they likewise receive the full ration, and a weekly allowance of spirits. A system must be installed that reduces the perpetual temptation to plunder from the necessary exposure of public property. It is for this reason recommended that public rations of bread should be baked by contract (at a potential savings of $1/6^{th}$ of the flour used); Private contracts (let under the tender process) to supply the hospitals with bread, meat and vegetables have proven to be of advantage to those establishments; both changes result in considerable savings to government'.

The report confirms that in 1820, those victualled in NSW numbered 5,135 to whom 7,027 rations were issued daily (some convicts were on 1½ regular ration because they were considered to be in heavy manual labour). In total, the numbers victualled, including military and civil officers, rose from 8,716 in August 1820 to 9,326 in December 1820. Bigge reported 'I see no reason for not applying the former rule by which the rations of those officers whose salaries exceeded £90 per annum were taken away. I recommend that they be taken off the stores and a compensating amount be paid to them from the Colonial Police Fund.'118[9]

The British Government constantly reminded colonial governors of the growing cost of running the colony and the need to take people 'off the stores'. During 1800-1803 more than 2000 convicts were transported, adding to the number dependent on the store: there was also a significant increase in the number of small farms allotted, mainly to the growing

---

[10] Bigge, J.T. Report # 3 Agriculture & Trade in NSW (1823)- p.132
[9] Bigge, J.T. Report # 3 Agriculture & Trade in NSW (1823)- p.149

number of convicts whose sentences had expired. At that time, a small 30-acre land grant, achieved at least three benefits for the new owners: they generally improved his social status (and therefore their mindset towards crime and property ownership); they were taken off the stores and told to be self-sufficient; and they became eligible to sell produce to the store thus becoming an important cog in the colony's food chain.119[11]

In his 'Working Paper', Butlin offers some interesting numbers with respect to the growth in farming activity, for the period 1800-1810. 'Excluding the holdings of civil and military officers, the number of farms grew from 400 in 1800 to 600 in 1804 and 700 in 1807. Thus, even though grain production had reached a reasonably satisfactory level by 1804 and 40 new farms were coming into production each year; the number of mouths to feed was increasing by only a few hundred annually at this time. However, meat remained scarce. Cattle were preferred to sheep because they were less prone to attack by wild dogs, thrived better in the wet and humid climate and were more suitable for salting down; whereas in 1801 the ratio was 6 to 1 in favour of sheep, by 1809 the ration was reduced to only 3 to 1'[11] The 'Epitome of the Official History of NSW' suggests the numbers of livestock in 1800 was 1,044 cattle and 6,124 sheep; in 1810 the number had increased to 12,442 cattle and 25,888 sheep; by 1821 cattle numbers had grown to 102,939 and sheep to 290,158[1]120[2].

This series of events before 1810 set the foundation for the future direction of the pastoral industry in the colony. Although there were troubling but isolated incidences of military officer domination of trade and profiteering, the colonial economy was growing and settling into a pattern of life suitable for self-sufficiency and growing independence and local governance. From 1811 to 1815, the pattern changed and turned into a commercial depression in the colony, brought about by a number of internal and external factors. 'Sealing vessels were having to sail further to find grounds not already picked bare by Colonial, British and American gangs, and in 1810, news reached Sydney that the British Government had imposed a

---

[11]   Butlin, N.G 'What a way to run an Empire, fiscally' (Working Papers in Economic History (ANU)

[12]   'An Epitome of the Official History of NSW' compiled from the Official and Parliamentary Records of the Colony in 1883, under the direction of the Government Printer, Thomas Richards.

duty of £20 per ton on oil caught in the Colonial waters.'[121][4] Further, in England the price for sealskins fell from 30/—to between 3/—and 8/-. Between 1810 and 1812 the British economy suffered a downturn and the financial troubles, brought on by a long drawn-out war in Europe, were soon transmitted to NSW. Indian and English merchant houses called up debts and refused to underwrite further speculations and the British Government pressed the colonial administration to further reduce running costs[1122][5]. Locally, the Commissariat's venture into money operations helped intensify the shortage of money in the settlement and, to add to these distractions; in 1813 local duties were imposed on sandalwood, sperm oil, skins and timber, whether intended for home consumption or export. The English Government weighed in with another cost cutting exercise by reducing the military numbers in the colony from 1600 in 1813 to 900 in 1815. Steven concludes that by 1815, 'Sydney's commerce had almost totally collapsed'[1123][6.] She also suggests that one side benefit of the commercial downturn was that, because individuals and partnerships could no longer see easy openings in trade, commerce, land and livestock, they may have turned their attention to industrial activity, establishing a profitable base for further local production of manufactured items and import-replacement industries.[1124][7]

CHAPTER OUTLINES

Introduction and Outline

Government business enterprises commenced from close to day one of the settlement in 1788. We can define them as government operated, financially supported and for the direct benefit of the colony as opposed to an export facility. The very first public enterprise was that of farming to raise food, supervise the few head of livestock that had arrived alive in the colony. \Public farming kept the colony alive for the first few years before private farming based on selective land grants commenced.

---

[14] Linge 'Industrial Awakening' *op cit*

[15] To these circumstances, Briggs and Jordan, writing the 'Economic History of England' adds the Malthus observations on a rising population (8% between 1808 and 1812) and the effects of the industrial revolution.

[16] M. Steven 'Merchant Campbell 1869-1846' p.136

[17] Steven *ibid* p.142

The role of the commissariat in government economic planning

The commissariat had two key roles. It was an important economic driver and acted as a quasi-treasury to the colony for the first 30 years, until the B of NSW opened in 1817.

Detailing the Enterprises

The main enterprises commenced with the need for food production but shortly after moved onto the need for construction work, building materials and an export staple.

Introducing the Colonial Economy

The colonial economy was destined to grow in response to increasing population, the development of an infrastructure to underpin the colonial growth and living standards and the need for import replacing activities, in addition to the goal of creating an export market

Convict management

With few free settlers to fill the role of supervisors, and the military abdicating their duties in this respect, the job of convict supervision was left to the best behaved convicts. This was a generally unsatisfactory position. The most prominent principal convict managers were Majors Druitt and Ovens, who were the first the reform convict work practices and set goals and plan targets for the convict workers.

Manufacturing in the commissariat

From the public business enterprises and the necessity of finding export staples, a secondary industry grew in the colony. Invention really was the mother of necessity. A secondary industry commenced in export replacement areas and spread to those areas of continuing need, such as agricultural equipment as that primary industry got underway, then onto manufacturing on behalf of British industries wanting to have a presence in the colony.

Operating and managing the government farms and the public enterprises

There was continual growth in the public farming and manufacturing areas for two reasons. The number of convicts arriving in the colony increased each month, so there were more mouths to feed, and more men to put into productive work. So output increased naturally but then so did the public works program, that kept the business enterprises operating, and then diversity of manufacturing commenced which meant more technical production and output. Much of this flowed to the private sector having been first established in the Lumber Yard.

Accounting and Finance in the public enterprises

The commissariat system after 1822 attracted many convict clerical assistants, so the bookkeeping indulgences were endless. Sadly few of these records survive, but we know that orders from government departments for supplies and the public works department for materials were prepare, whilst the commissariat and lumber yard used issue dockets to account for supplies transferred. The main accounting was not the number of inventory items made or issued in the commissariat but the money it was spending. Bills drawn by the commissariat supposedly reflected the amount of value going through the commissariat as opposed to the raw materials used the convict output or the value of materials issued on account of public works.

Measuring the economic impact of the enterprises on the economy

This will be the most difficult chapter to prepare. We will have to assess the GDP annually for the colony from 1800, and try and indicate what part was generated by the business enterprises. This will have to be done on an industry by industry basis to estimate the items of output the number of convicts in use for each item of manufacture and compare it with the gross GDP. The problem with this methodology is that most items produced by the commissariat enterprises had no value due to the convicx6ts having no value as labourers and raw materials have no assigned value, thus convict output had no value.

An overview of the Literature

This topic is covered fully in Chapter 2 but for completeness an overview is covered at this point.

Links in Literature accepting that public enterprise is not covered in the Literature

i. Convict Management
ii. Economic Development
iii. Growth of Manufacturing
iv. Growth of the Public Service
v. Supervision and human skills in the public service
vi. Building the Public Infrastructure
vii. Development of Public Works
viii. Trade exports and imports (Import Replacement)
ix. Foreign Investment
x. Convict Work Skills
xi. Transportation Policy – Assignment policies
xii. Commissariat policy and management

These 'links' or topics closely associated with public enterprise operations leads to a wealth of literature but for some strange reason, the topic of public enterprise management, operation, development or transfer has never been undertaken, until now

Dr Bill Robbins undertook a study into the management of the Lumber Yard, as part of a labour management series, but largely omitted the task of learning of the layout, output or labour operations of the facility; however his study is an interesting and valuable contribution to colonial labour organisation and convict management. The operation of the GBEs was, of course, much more than just the labour aspect. In fact labour management and organisation is much more than just the convict organisation. It revolves around selection of suitable workers, their training and skills development

CHAPTER 13

BIBLIOGRAPHY

A. Australian Dictionary of Biography—*Pulsford, Edward*
B. McMinn, W.G.—*Essays in Australian Federation*
C. Pulsford, E.—*The Rise, Progress and Present Position of Trade and Commerce in New South Wales.*
D. Pulsford, E.—*The British Empire and the relations of Asia and Australasia*
E. Pulsford, E.—*Commerce and the Empire*
F. Hansard—*Senate Budget Debates 1905-6-7-9*
G. 'Our Country'—*'Our Country'*The Federal Freetrade Organisation Newspaper 1900-1901
H. 'Our Country' newspaper articles and speeches 1900-1901
I. 'Daily Telegraph'—Obituary September 1919
J. 'The Town & Country Journal'—Obituary September 1919